NEAL-SCHUMAN

DIRECTORY OF LIBRARY TECHNICAL SERVICES HOME PAGES

BARBARA STEWART

NEAL-SCHUMAN NETGUIDE SERIES

NEAL-SCHUMAN PUBLISHERS, INC.
NEW YORK   LONDON

Published by Neal-Schuman Publishers, Inc.
100 Varick Street
New York, NY 10013

Printed and bound in the United States of America.

Library of Congress Cataloging-In-Publication Data

Stewart, Barbara, 1953–

   Neal-Schuman directory of library technical services home pages /
Barbara Stewart.
        p.   cm.—(Neal-Schuman net guide series)
   Includes bibliographical references and index.
   ISBN 1–55570–286–4
   1. Processing (Libraries)—United States—Computer network
resources—Directories. 2. Web sites—Directories. I. Title.
II. Series.
Z688.5.S74   1997
025.04—DC21   97–25195

Contents

Acknowledgments

I would like to thank my colleagues in the Original Cataloging Department at the University of Massachusetts, for their encouragement and editorial assistance. In particular, thanks to Pat Banach, who encouraged me from the beginning, and to Mel Carlson and Janet Hughes for their editorial assistance. Thanks to Brian Julin and to Sharon Domier for help with the screen captures. Thanks also to Cindy Spell, Sarah Thomson, Nadia McIntosh, and Judy Schaeffer. On the Acquisitions side, I want to thank Leslie Horner Button. Finally, I would like to thank my husband, John, my strongest supporter, and my children—Jessica, Greg, and Andrew.

List of Figures

Preface

When I first saw the World Wide Web demonstrated in 1994, I did not immediately recognize either its potential for library services in general or its specific utility for library technical services. As I began searching the Web from my home, however, I came across many sites that saved me time. I asked my colleagues on the Autocat and PACS-L Listservs to tell me about how they used Web pages in their technical services work. Once I had leads to relevant Web sites, I realized that I was saving not only time—but money—because access to information on the Web reduced the need for many print tools normally consulted in technical services work.

This book represents the product of both my own searching and the leads I received from my virtual colleagues. However, the *Neal-Schuman Directory of Library Technical Services Home Pages* is much more than a mere printed and bound listing of useful Web pages for technical services work. It has been conceived and designed as a ready reference guide specifically for the working technical services librarian. It is meant to be a useful guide to be kept by your workstation and consulted whenever you have a need for information that might be found on the Internet. As such, it is divided into three broad parts, each designed with a particular technical service user in mind:

- Part I, "Web Pages of Special Use for Acquisitions Librarians," leads you to Web pages that various acquisitions departments have put together, a myriad of publisher and vendor home pages, pages geared to preservation and conservation, as well as some developed by gift and exchange departments. Discussion groups, Listservs, tables of contents from acquisitions and serials journals, and some general purpose home pages providing information such as addresses and currency rates needed daily by acquisitions librarians complete this section.
- Part II, "Web Pages of Special Use for Catalogers," opens with some pages of broad interest to catalogers before turning to specific areas of concern, including authority control, classification and indexing, cataloging of special formats like music and serials, and topics of timely concern to catalogers like workstations. This part closes with other useful Internet sources, such as cataloging organizations and Web-based research papers as well as Listservs, e-journals, and archives concerning cataloging.
- Part III, "Web Pages of Special Interest for All Technical Services Librarians," contains two major sections. The first describes technical services departmental home pages in detail. The second covers technical services associations (both here and abroad, as well as multinational ones), discussion lists, e-journals, and newsletters.

With the exception of the publishers' Web pages in Part I, the Web pages listed here are intended to be a comprehensive selection representing what was available when the book went to press. Because there were 40 to 50 times more publishers' pages than there were any other category, I selected publishers' pages for inclusion based on these criteria: 1) extensive original content; 2) an outstanding collection of links, preferably with logical explanatory remarks; and 3) colorful, clean graphic design and creativity.

The *Neal-Schuman Directory of Library Technical Services Home Pages* can make it much easier for you to envision a home page for your library, because it makes it convenient and easy for you to see what other libraries have done to set up their own departmental home pages. Whether you are looking for an out-of-print book, an obscure cataloging rule interpretation, a helping hand cataloging a French language serial, or a means for staying current on the latest changes in SGML standards, there's an Internet source listed in this directory to help you. As you will see as you browse through this book, having easy access to technical service information on the Web makes the working librarian's job easier.

Hints for Finding Pages That Have Moved

Anyone who has used the Web for even a day or two quickly discovers that Web pages have an annoying habit of moving. URLs change daily, links are broken, and frustration mounts. This section describes two reliable methods for tracking down Web pages that seem to be missing in action.

The first way to find missing pages is to use a search engine. My favorite two search engines are Alta Vista and HotBot, because they seem to be especially successful in leading me to relevant Web sites even if the specific one I'm looking for doesn't turn up. Some hints for successful use of search engines that I rely on are:

- read the help pages;
- formulate your search appropriately for the particular engine you're using;
- use all lowercase letters for your first search attempt; use capitalized first letters only if this search fails; and
- use the most relevant words (e.g., if you're searching for the United States Book Exchange, enter "Book Exchange").

The second method is a hierarchical search. For example, if you're looking for an acquisitions department's home page, first search for the parent institution (e.g., the university). Once you find the parent institution's home page, choose libraries, then acquisitions. This method is almost always successful since many Web pages are evolved from gopher menus.

If both of these methods fail, don't give up! Perhaps the Web server is down—give it a few days (or weeks) to come back. Technical problems are a reality and sometimes a server can be down for weeks at a time. Unfortunately, however, some Web sites do just disappear.

PART I

WEB PAGES OF SPECIAL USE FOR ACQUISITIONS LIBRARIANS

OVERVIEW

Acquisitions librarians are arguably the first group of professionals in the "library function." After all, if the material is not ordered, claimed, processed and received, then the cataloger cannot describe it and assign access points, the archivist cannot preserve it, the reference librarian cannot recommend it to patrons, and the circulation librarian cannot circulate it! Even though you and I see how invaluable acquisitions staff can be, there are still administrators, board chairpersons, and others who believe that just about anybody with any purchasing experience can acquire library materials, with no prior knowledge of the collection or the library involved. They believe this despite the increasing complexity of acquiring new formats (CD-ROMs, computer disks, multimedia, audios, videos, new databases, and new library OPACs)! Some of you are even involved with document delivery, ILL, and other areas in addition to traditional acquisitions processes. How can using World Wide Web home pages solve this dilemma?

The most important thing to remember about utilizing the World Wide Web is that you and your library do not exist in a vacuum. Most probably you do not work in one of the largest libraries in the world—but now, with access to those libraries' home pages, you can learn many things about acquisitions departments without having to experiment yourself (sometimes resulting in expensive ramifications!). Not only have other libraries already tried a particular vendor or automated their acquisitions functions years ago, but when they put their department manuals up on the Web, that implies a willingness to share their knowledge with you. Most home page designers, and librarians for that matter, provide a clickable e-mail address for comments, questions, etc. Through personal experience, I have found acquisitions librarians to be some of the most helpful people in cyberspace. So, what are you waiting for? Use the sources listed here and then put up your own acquisitions page!

1.1

Web Pages From Library Acquisitions Departments

Here you will discover a broad assortment of acquisitions department home pages. Some of them are quite small, listing briefly what they do, which staff person is responsible for what duty, and perhaps listing a few of their favorite, most helpful links.

Medium-size libraries might include their acquisitions policy, a budget document, and a form for patrons or book selectors to request that a title be ordered by the library. Larger libraries may include everything you need! You will locate extensive, subject-specific new acquisitions lists, lists of foreign vendors, very specific approval plan synopses, and in-house documents concerning library funding, relationships with collection development staff, and all the "how-to-do-it" documents concerning claiming, direct orders, cessations, and expenditures. Acquisitions departments worldwide share a common purpose—each wants to streamline the purchasing process, facilitate order requests, and maintain an easily accessible list of names and addresses of publishers and vendors used by their institution. I think you'll be fascinated (and grateful) to see what types of material are available.

1.1.1 ACQUISITIONS DEPARTMENTAL HOME PAGES

Acquisitions and Collection Management at Merriam Library
California State University, Chico, California
http://www.csuchico.edu/library/acq/acq.htm
> Materials budget information, gifts, and a large and detailed Yankee Book Peddler Approval File. Monthly new acquisitions lists for both books and periodicals.

Acquisitions Department Procedures
University of California, Santa Barbara
http://www.library.ucsb.edu/depts/acq/proctoc.html
> Documents on "Corcataloging" (cataloging upon receipt with little alteration and no authority work) and more.

Adquisiciones Bibliograficas
Biblioteca, Universidad de las Americas, Puebla, Mexico
http://www.udlap.mx/udla/biblioteca/servicios/servicios.html
> Beautifully organized page of annual statistics, recent acquisitions, lists for various departments, links to publishers, and information on cancellations.

Auburn University Libraries Acquisitions Department
Auburn, Alabama
http://www.lib.auburn.edu/acq/index.html
> Provides links to the libraries' goals and objectives, a book order request form, a roster of department personnel with job descriptions, and links to other Internet resources for acquisitions. See Policies and Procedures for NOTIS Holdings Screen, Macros, and O/P/R Screen (*http://www.lib.auburn.edu/acq/docs/staff/policy.html*)

Baylor University Libraries Acquisitions Department
Waco, Texas
http://ccis09.baylor.edu/Library/LibDepts/MMLandJones/Acquisitions/ACQ.html
> Nothing fancy, but it gets the job done. Essential links are listed on the Acquisitions Staff Resources Page, including links to the international edition of *Books Out of Print* and *British Books in Print*.

Brigham Young University, Harold B. Lee Library Acquisitions Department
Provo, Utah
http://www.lib.byu.edu/~hcb
> Check out the extensive *Bibliographic Record Inputting Guide*.

Clemens and Alcuin Joint Libraries
College of St. Benedict/St. John's University, St. Joseph—Collegeville, Minnesota

http://www.csbsju.edu/library/catalog/acqfile.html

> Provides Searching the PALS Acquisitions File, which clearly defines search commands, stop words, abbreviations for "status" line notes, and a sample record in the ACQ file.

Dartmouth College Baker Library Acquisitions Services
Hanover, New Hampshire

http://www.dartmouth.edu/acad-support/library/libacq

> Very useful and specific listings for those involved in acquisitions, as well as a chart of Bibliographer Assignment by LC Classification. Their listing of University Press Approvals is nicely done, and their Collection Development Policies are exceptional. Dartmouth has an incredible amount of subject-specific acquisitions lists on the Web. To put "incredible amount" into perspective, I counted 48 different lists on my last visit. These lists run the gamut from language-specific acquisitions (French, German, Islamic, Italian, Portuguese, and Spanish) to such lists as Physical Sciences Reference, Orient Acquisitions, and Math Library Acquisitions. For an example, see the Women's Studies Acquisitions List at *http://www.dartmouth.edu/~library/New_book_lists/womn.html*.

Duke University Libraries Current Acquisitions / Serial Department Home Page
Durham, North Carolina

http://www.lib.duke.edu/intop/acqser/AcqSer_Home_Page.html

> This colorful page is only a small portion of what's available at this team-approach library. See the Current Approval Plan Vendors and Brief Profiles/Bibliographic Searching Team Manual, Duke University Libraries (*http://www.lib.duke.edu/intop/casst/profiles.html*). This is a fantastically useful list. Every publisher contained in Duke's profile with Yankee Book Peddler Approval Plans is listed. Also available are profiles for the Divinity School, Karno Art, Trade Press, and University Press.

Emory University Libraries Acquisitions Department
Atlanta, Georgia

http://www.emory.edu/LIB/ACQ

> An excellent page, spiced up with a sense of humor. Their official motto? "We'll try to get it for you!" Their unofficial motto? "Ours is not to wonder why, ours is but to buy and buy!" And their VERY unofficial motto? "But don't bug us!" Emory's alphabetical format in the Acquisitions Process section is quite helpful, encompassing everything from accounting and antiquarian materials to vendor information. Also find here the Statement on Principles and Standards of Acquisitions Practice.

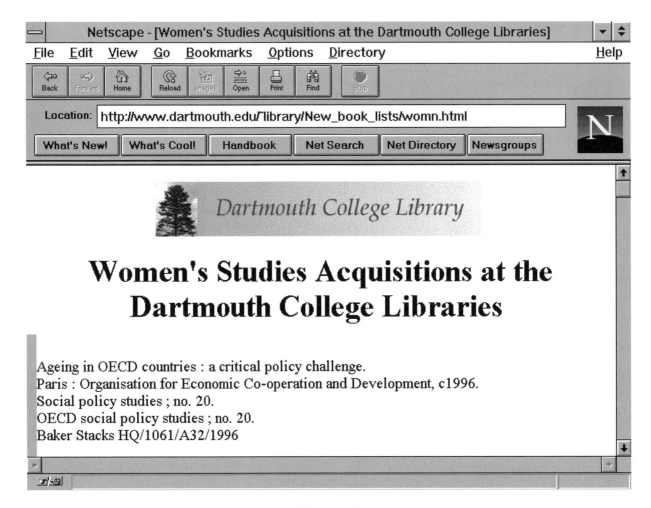

Figure 1.1
Dartmouth College Library—Women's Studies Acquisitions at the Dartmouth College Libraries

Forvarvsenheten
Acquisitions Department, Royal Library, National Library of Sweden,
Stockholm
http://www.kb.se/fs/fseng.htm
   See Guidelines for Acquisitions.

**Generaldirektion der Bayerischen Staatlichen Bibliotheken,
Kommission fur Erwerbung**
Universitat Bavaria, Augsburg, Bavaria, Germany
http://www.bibliothek.uni-augsburg.de/ke/erwerb.html

**Georgetown University Lauinger Library Acquisitions
Department**
http://gulib.lausun.georgetown.edu/dept/acq
   Of primary interest here is their purchase request form.

**Ina Dillard Russell Library Information Acquisition Georgia
College and State University**
Milledgeville, Georgia
http://peacock.gac.peachnet.edu/~techserv/acquisitions.html
   Includes a monthly updated section of subject-specific new additions to
   their collection.

**IUPUI (Indiana University–Purdue Indianapolis University
Library) Acquisitions Home Page**
Indianapolis, Indiana
http://www-lib.iupui.edu/libinfo/acqpage.html
   Informative home page. Check out their annual reports and Tips for Better Order Placement sections, which contain deadlines for encumbrances
   by fiscal year, as well as specific instructions for filling out approval slips
   and choice cards.

**Johns Hopkins University Milton S. Eisenhower Library
Acquisitions Department**
Baltimore, Maryland
http://milton.mse.jhu.edu:8001/library/acq/acqdept.html
   MSEL's Acquisition Department is divided into four units—Monographs,
   Serials, the Financial Unit, and the Preparations Unit. All units contribute to the MSEL Acquisitions Department Statistic Reports, which are
   so detailed that they even include a month-by-month listing of letters
   written and reference assistance given. Statistics are also available for
   ordering activity and maintenance, receipts, current periodicals area, etc.

Lehigh University Libraries Acquisitions Department
Bethlehem, Pennsylvania
http://www.lib.lehigh.edu/acq.dept.html
> A small acquisitions home page with a detailed gift policy page.

Library of Congress Acquisitions Division
Washington, D.C.
http://lcweb.loc.gov/acq/acquire.html
> Details how to contact the Library of Congress regarding the donation, purchase, or deposit of library materials. Explains the Document Expediting Project, a "centralized acquisition service for obtaining U.S. Government publications which are not designated as depository items and are not available by purchase at the Government Printing Office." Links to LC's Overseas Participant Program, its Surplus Books Program, and Collection Policy Statements.

Marriott Library Acquisitions
University of Utah, Salt Lake City, Utah
http://choengmon.lib.utah.edu/~amy/acqu/indacq.html
> For those libraries forced to trim journal titles, see Marriott Library Journal Cuts, Fiscal Year 1996/97 (*http://choengmon.lib.utah.edu/~amy/acqu/letter.html*).

MIT Libraries Serials and Acquisitions Services
Massachusetts Institute of Technology, Cambridge, Massachusetts
http://macfadden.mit.edu:9500/seracq.html
> One notes immediately the politeness in the staff listing in Serials Receipt: "Please call Buddy with non-standard serial problems, billing problems, payment questions, and other non-routine serial queries." Six gopher format databases about serials in MIT are available for searching. These include Government Documents, Monograph and Serials Receipts, as well as an Item Database, a Serials and Journals Commitments List, a Serials and Journals Vendor List, and the IEEE Database. The Monograph Acquisitions Policies Page links to local policies for cancelling an order when a gift copy is received and ordering back issues of journals and out-of-print and replacement copies. See *http://macfadden.mit.edu:9500/sercan/top.html* to review the 1995/1996 Serials Review and Cancellation Project. Statistics cancellations date back to 1983.

National Library of Australia Staff Presentations and Papers—Acquisitions
http://www.nla.gov.au/nla/staffpaper/acquire.html
> Of particular interest here is the article "Defining the National Library of Australia's Role in the Acquisition, Control, and Preservation of Australian Electronic Materials" by Lesley Bezear. See also "Acquisitions and Liaison Visit to Laos and Cambodia, April 1996" by Vacharin McFadden.

Northeastern State University Library (Tahlequah, Oklahoma) Acquisitions Team

http://www.nsuok.edu/jvl/ts/jvlts.html

> The Collection Development Page contains vendor reviews, best seller lists, and an excellent compilation of review sources on selected subjects.

Northern Territory University Library Who's What Where in Purchasing, Cataloguing, and Processing

Casuarina, Australia

http://www.ntu.edu.au/library/who_pcp.html

> See the Benchmarking Page, which focuses on "the acquisitions receipt and cataloguing process, i.e., the process from when an ordered item (monograph or audiovisual) is received into the University Library to its availability for client use." Lots of practical information here.

Northwestern University Library Serials and Acquisitions Services (SAS)

Evanston, Illinois

http://www.library.nwu.edu/sas

> Links to Monographic and Serials Acquisitions and to Gifts and Exchange pages. Each page contains statistics, lists of staff, and useful links.

Penn State University Libraries Acquisitions Services

State College, Pennsylvania

http://www.libraries.psu.edu/iasweb/acq/hpg_acq1.htm

> Team approach is used here, with one librarian and 31 staff members organized in self-directed workteams. Check out their page on the Innovacq Serials Control System.

Princeton University Library Order Division Home Page

Princeton, New Jersey

http://infoshare1.princeton.edu/order/ordhome.html

> Sections on the Order Unit, the Approvals and Continuations Unit, the Periodicals Receipts Unit, the Invoice Unit, and the Monograph Receipts and Hold Unit. Each unit provides appropriate links. For example, links to Blackwell North America, B. H. Blackwell's, and Yankee Book Peddler are found on the Approvals page.

QTECH Home Page Acquisitions Tools and Resources

Queen's University Libraries, Kingston, Ontario, Canada

http://130.15.161.74/techserv/qacq.html

> An array of good links to acquisitions discussion lists, serial acquisitions sites, and vendor and publishing tools. New icons are extremely useful for repeat users.

Sector de Aquisicoes Bibliograficas
Universidade do Minho, Braga e Guimaraes, Portugal
http://www.sdum.uminho.pt/vgaquis-pt.htm

Service des Acquisitions
Universite du Quebec a Montreal, Canada
http://www.unites.uqam.ca/Service/Services_techniques/ACQservice.html
   Small general overview. Check out Sites d'Interet pour les Acquisitions
   and Sites d'Interet des Acquisitions P.E.S. (Publications en Serie).

State University of New York at Buffalo Acquisitions Information
http://ublib.buffalo.edu/libraries/units/cts/acq
   The Library of Congress Resource File: Copy Cataloging, compiled by
   Sue Neumeister, was written to describe MARC fields, location codes,
   and size requirements for acquisitions staff, in particular for those working with CIP (cataloging-in-publication) copy. They provide a Foreign
   Vendor Codes List and a very clear, specific document concerning rush
   orders, with a sample of a faxed rush purchase order.

Syracuse University Library Bibliographic Services Department
Syracuse, New York
http://web.syr.edu/~libweb/aboutsul/depts/bibserv/template.htm
   A Bibliographic Services QuickSheet is available for Interpreting Monographic Order/Pay/Receipt Records, as well as links to primary vendors
   and to *Wessex Books and Records*—an author-searchable catalog of over
   5,000 out of print titles, updated monthly.

TPOT: Acquisitions
Technical Processing Online Tools, University of California, San Diego
http://oclcgate.ucsd.edu
   A truly exceptional site, containing just about everything you'd ever want
   to know about acquisitions at UCSD. Minutes of the Acquisitions Committee are thorough and informative, especially for other Innopac users.
   The Acquisitions Training Policy is a useful, in-house way to address training requests. The Acquisitions Tools List of Bibliographic Resources for
   Searching is a very useful guide, which could be tailored for other libraries' benefit. Their Government Documents Section is extensive and includes every possible procedure concerning GPO Depository processing, such as MARCIVE information, statistics, and even a Boolean search
   calendar. Innopac Record Number Ranges are available for authority,
   bibliographic, check-in, course, item, order, and patron numbers. The
   Ordering and Receiving Page discusses approval and blanket orders, added
   volumes and copies, claiming, cancellations and cessations, direct orders,
   invoice processing, and sample issues. Cumulative statistics are also available upon downloading the Adobe Acrobat Reader.

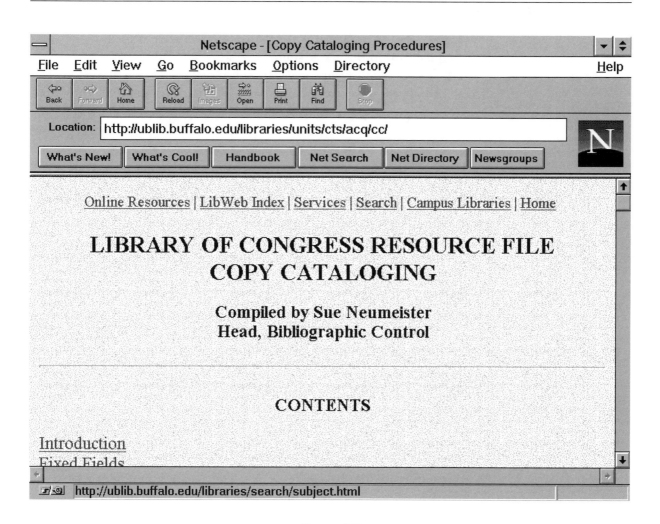

Figure 1.2
Library of Congress Resource File: Copy Cataloging
(State University of New York at Buffalo Acquisitions Information)

University of Ballarat Library, Australia—Services of the Acquisitions and Access Team
http://www.ballarat.edu.au/is/ej/index.htm
> Includes weekly listings of new items added to the library collection, book requests, and suggestions for filling out the purchase requisition form.

University of Haifa Library Acquisitions Services
Haifa, Israel
http://www-lib.haifa.ac.il/www/rekhesh/acquisitions.html
> Contains a list of tools and directories of e-mail addresses. *See* TRIP— Top Resources on the the Internet for Library Professionals.

University of Miami Libraries Acquisitions Department, Otto G. Richter Library
Miami, Florida
http://www.library.miami.edu/acqui/welcome.html
> A nicely structured page containing descriptions of all units (including the Fiscal Matters Unit), as well as an organizational chart of the Acquisitions Department, and specific information for patrons, bibliographers, faculty liaisons, and acquisitions department staff.

University of North Carolina at Chapel Hill Acquisitions Department Home Page
http://www.unc.edu/~acqdept/hmenubs.html
> Comes with a web page disclaimer. Their Acquisitions Department Accomplishments are most impressive, especially the compilation of a list of over 600 e-mail addresses of vendors/publishers—see *http://www.lib.unc.edu/acq/befr.html*. The UNC-CH Library Expedited Acquisitions Plan (LEAP) details the selection of a primary library domestic vendor (in this case, Yankee Book Peddler). The Acquisitions Department provides training sessions on a multitude of subjects, including searching WorldCat, Folio, LAN, Web, and Windows classes. Also available is "What To Do When Your Terminal/PC Talks Back To You." Finally, the Acquisitions Online Reading Room provides an extensive list of vendor, publisher, and other Web-related information.

University of Oregon Acquisitions Department
Eugene, Oregon
http://libweb.uoregon.edu/acq.dep/acqdept.html
> In addition to services offered, they also detail services NOT offered, such as book appraisal. An annual report entitled "Measure of Acquisitions Department Activity," complete with graphs detailing firm orders, firm receipts, and all other receipts, is also available.

University of Otago Library Acquisitions Services
Dunedin, New Zealand

http://librius.otago.ac.nz:800/Library_menus/Services/
Acquisitions_services.html

The *Library Liaison Officers Handbook* must be of great help to academic departments involved with selecting materials for the library. It includes guidelines for recommending material and explains library topics, such as funding, the collection development, selection, library guides, and how to contact library staff. Recommending Material for the Library includes an Online Book Recommendation Form and an interesting selection of publishers, reviews, exchange rates, and other library acquisitions home pages.

University of Prince Edward Island, Robertson Library Acquisitions Department
Charlottetown, PEI, Canada

http://www.upei.cd/~library/DEPARTMENTS/ACQ

Lists acquisitions personnel, gifts procedure, and provides an acquisitions department order form, as well as links to other sites.

University of Southern California Acquisitions Department Home Page
http://www-lib.usc.edu/Info/Acqui

Includes links to a very extensive collection development section and an interesting Acquisitions Procedures for Selectors page. Check out the Electronic Order Request Form for library selectors and bibliographers.

University of Sydney Library Acquisitions Department
Sydney, Australia

http://www.library.usyd.edu.au/Services/Acquisitions

Concise listing of the responsibilities of the acquisitions department. Different library funds are listed, including departmental research allocations and blanket order materials. See also Ordering Materials for the Library Collection.

University of Washington Libraries Acquisitions Division
Seattle, Washington

http://weber.u.washington.edu/~acqdiv

An incredible site that is divided into sections for book selectors, acquisitions staff, and vendors. The Acquisitions Division Description details the procedure for 70 selectors to follow. Listen to these statistics: "Each year, Acquisitions spends over $1,000 each hour for monographs, orders over 18,000 titles, acquires another 20,000 books via 12 approval programs, adds about 9,000 gift titles, plus another 3,000 books through cooperative foreign acquisitions programs and other methods." Add in 20,000 to 45,000 non-book items (mostly microfiche) and you have a good idea of what these folks are up to! The General Orientation Document for New Selectors is a work of art, and well worth reading by anyone involved with collection development. Gift and Grant Funds Used by Acquisitions is arranged both alphabetically by fund name and by fund code. Innovative-Related Information includes a very comprehensive document entitled Initial Articles to Ignore. A highlight of this site is their approval program information. Subprofile structures and parameters are listed for each program, which include approved author lists and specific lists of series to be excluded.

Peter Stevens, webmaster at this site, has set up a ratings system for acquisitions departments home pages that is both thoughtful and accurate. The new Vendor section is outstanding. Also, check out Vendor Assignments and Discounts, and the useful list of Electronic Order Vendors. Finally, take a look at Acquisitions Division Unit Costs.

University of Waterloo Electronic Library
Waterloo, Ontario, Canada
http://www.lib.uwaterloo.ca

A keyword search of acquisitions brings up numerous references. Of special interest is the Acquisitions and Budgets Information at *http://www.lib.uwaterloo.ca/staff/mis/acq.html.* New acquisitions lists are updated every Monday morning.

University of Wisconsin–Oshkosh Libraries and Learning Resources General Acquisitions Policy
http://www.uwosh.edu/departments/llr/depts/collect.html

Here's an example of a general acquisitions policy home page. For other policies, see *http://www.howardcc.edu/library/acqpol.html* (Howard Community College Library, Baltimore, Maryland) or the Acquisitions Policy Page of the Indiana University School of Dentistry—*http://www.iupui.edu/it/dentlib/acq.html.*

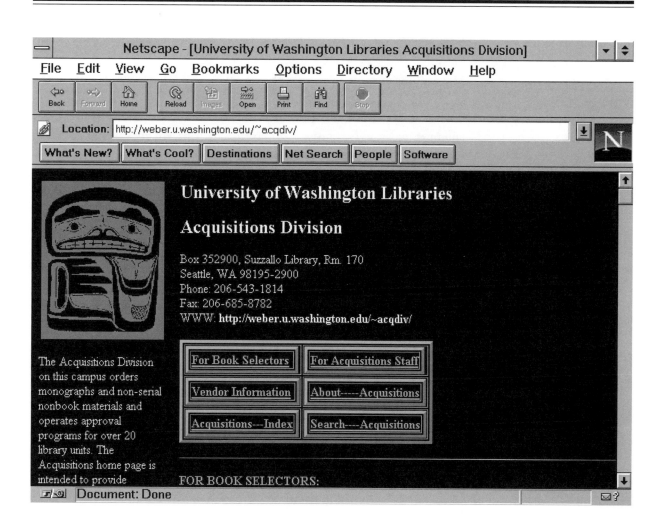

Figure 1.3
University of Washington Libraries Acquisitions Division

1.1.2 BINDERY AND PRESERVATION OPERATIONS

Many libraries include preservation and bindery departments within the acquisitions department. Yes, that's right—not only do you have to order it, process it, receive it, and pay for it, but you must also bind it if necessary and preserve it, so that present and future patrons can get some use from it. Never fear—there's a goodly section of home pages in the Bindery and Pres-ervations Operations section. Learn how to preserve old pulp paperbacks, marbling, and calligraphy, as well as see how some of the big guys (Library of Congress, Yale, OCLC) set up their departments and what kind of ser-vices they offer.

Bookbinder's Toolbox
http://www.redmark.co.nz/tool.htm
> Illustrated examples of adhesive, case, library style, fine binding and much more.

Bookbinding, a Tutorial by Douglas W. Jones
http://www.cs.uiowa.edu/~jones/book
> Primarily teaches how to preserve the contents of old pulp paperbacks "by photocopying them onto archival paper and then binding the results using an archival binding technique, the long-stitch."

Bookbinding and Bookbinders
http://www.xs4all.nl/~cremers/bbinding.html
> Wonderful annotated listing.

Book Doctor, Dr. Brian A. Roberts
http://www.stemnet.nf.ca~barobert/.bindery/doctor.html

Commission of Preservation and Access Newsletter
http://palimpsest.stanford.edu/cpa/newsletter/cpanl.html
> Complete text of newsletters from June 1988 to present. Newsletters are high quality, illustrated, and current on new developments in the field.

CoOL Conservation Online: Resources for Conservation Professionals
http://palimpsest.stanford.edu
> It doesn't get any better than this page. Walter Henry maintains this most comprehensive site. Find out about international training programs, vari-ous types of storage media (CD-ROMs, optical disks, videotape), and what ethical issues are involved with conservation. Ergonomics, library binding, pest management (of the insect variety), and reprographics are also included. Site has links to the USMARC 583 Field and Its Use in Preservation page and to a survey report of 96 libraries entitled "Book Repair Survey: Circulating Collections" by Clara Keyes. Also check out

the Newsletters of the European Confederation of Conservator-Restorers' Organizations. Finally, do not miss the excellent Online Conservation/Preservation Serials page.

Cornell University Library Department of Preservation and Conservation

http://preservation.library.cornell.edu

Learn about commercial binding, conservation treatment, and brittle books. Do not miss Preserve/Net and its list of conservation resources by subject.

EPIC—European Preservation Information Council

http://www.library.knaw.nl/epic/ecpatex/welcome.htm

Discusses preservation of all paper-based materials, sound, photographs, film, and digital archives.

Guide to the Book Arts and Book History on the WWW (World Wide Web)

http://www.cua.edu/www/mullen/bookarts.html

Guild of Book Workers

http://palimpsest.stanford.edu/byorg/gbw

"National non-profit organization for all book arts." Areas of special interest include bookbinding, printing, conservation, marbling, calligraphy, and papermaking.

Information Conservation Inc.–the Web Page

http://www.webmasters.net/bookbinding

Links to eight U.S. library binderies.

Library of Congress National Preservation Program Office

http://palimpsest.stanford.edu/bytopic/orgs/natprovw.html

General overview. For specific details on mass deacidification, magnetic media preservation, care, handling, and storage of photos and recorded sound preservation, see *gopher://marvel.loc.gov/11/services/preserv/bibs*. Also available is a National Policy on Permanent Papers, and a Primer on Disaster Preparedness, Management, and Response. See Preservation Directorate: Saving the Library's Legacy by John Sullivan and Jennifer Johnson—*http://palimpsest.stanford.edu/bytopic/orgs/legacy.html*

National Digital Library Federation

http://lcweb.loc.gov/loc/ndlf

National Institute for the Conservation of Cultural Property

http://www.nic.org

Their motto: "It is no small thing to outwit time."

National Library of Australia National Preservation Office Annual Conference
http://www.nla.gov.au/3/npo/conf/annual.html
> Read full-text conference presentations from 1994 (Preservation Microfilming: Does It Have a Future?) and 1995 (Multimedia Preservation: Capturing the Rainbow). Also see the Statement of Principles: Preservation of, and Long-Term Access to Australian Digital Objects—*http://www.nla.gov.au/3/npo/natco/princ.html*.

National Library of Australia Staff Presentations and Papers— Preservation Issues
http://www.nla.gov.au/nla/staffpaper/preserve.html

OCLC Preservation Resources Home Page
http://www.oclc.org/oclc/presres/preshome.htm
> "Provides customized preservation microfilming for unusual materials and unique formats." In 1995, they began to offer processes to scan and digitize micrographic images to electronic formats. Read Preservation Resources: Past, Present, and Future from the *OCLC Newsletter no. 217* at *http://www.oclc.org/oclc/n217/n217sr.htm#sr1*

Page Attachment Decision Tree for College and University Libraries
http://www.webmasters.net/bookbinding/09–b-3s.htm

Preservation at Yale
http://www.library.yale.edu/preservation/presyale.htm
> Outstanding Preservation Department contains five units: Collection Care, Conservation, Core, Preparations, and Reformatting. Project Open Book is "a research and development program that is exploring the feasibility and costs of large-scale conversion of preserved materials from microfilm to digital imagery." Currently, they are converting 3,000 microfilm volumes to digital imagery, and eventually hope to reach 10,000 volumes.

Preservation Department, Syracuse University Library
Syracuse, New York
http://web.syr.edu/~libweb/aboutsw/depts/preserve/index.htm
> Full-time preservation department in operation since 1990. Check out their various disaster plans (for print, nonprint, and audio recordings), as well as specific conservation treatments (wooden board binding, vellum rebacking, etc.).

Preserving the Whole: A Two-Track Approach to Rescuing Data and Metadata
http://palimpsest.stanford.edu/cpa/misc/preswhol.html.
> By Ann Gerken Green and JoAnn Dionne.

Preserving the Written Record: Evaluation of Preservation Programs at 5 Major European Libraries—*http://www.lib.berkeley.edu/Collections/Germanic/jsart.html.* By James H. Spohrer, University of California, Berkeley.

 Discusses France's Bibliotheque Nacional, the Netherlands' Koninklijke Bibliotheek, Germany's Herzog August Bibliothek, the Sachsische Landesbibliothek of Dresden, and the State Library of Saxony.

Robert C. Williams American Museum of Papermaking
http://www.ipst.edu/amp

 Take a colorful virtual tour.

Simple Book Repair Manual
http://www.dartmouth.edu/~preserve/tofc.html

 Excellent resource created by Preservation Services of Dartmouth College. Simple repairs include torn pages, erasing pencil marks, tipping in a single page, hinge repair, etc.

University of Vermont Historic Preservation Program
http://www.uvm.edu/~histpres

 Check out the full-text *Historic Preservation Web Journal*.

1.1.3 GIFT AND EXCHANGE PROGRAMS

Gifts and exchanges are usually handled through the acquisitions departments and can sometimes play a major role in augmenting a meager materials budget. Gifts can be solicited, or they can be unsolicited (and a major headache to boot). For an extremely positive viewpoint of gifts and exchanges, see the University of Florida Gifts & Exchange Home Page. I guarantee that your view of both of these activities will never be the same!

Advanced Book Exchange Inc.
http://www.abebooks.com
Buy anything. Sell anything. Free.

BackMed
http://www.readmore.com/electron/backserv/backmed.html
This list is "exclusively devoted to the information exchange of medical serial back issues and books among libraries." See **Backserv** for more details.

Backserv, the BACK Issues and Duplicate Exchange SERVice
http://www.readmore.com/electron/backserv/backlist.html
An informal, unmoderated forum for the exchange of back issues and duplicates among libraries. Dealers are welcome to monitor these lists but cannot post messages to them. The last eight weeks of archives are maintained online. Also available are several back issue dealers' catalogs.

Canadian Inventory of Resource Sharing: Collections
http://www.nlc-bnc.ca/resource/cirs95/eshract3.htm
Discusses the Canadian Book Exchange Centre, a "clearing-house service provided by the National Library of Canada, for the distribution and exchange of publications which are deemed surplus by some, but needed by others." Unfortunately, only Canadian libraries and organizations are eligible.

Canje de Publicaciones de la Biblioteca Nacional
http://www.bne.es/14acanje.html
Activities and exchange partners of the National Library of Spain.

Duplicates Exchange Union (Sam Houston State University)
http://www.shsu.edu/~lib_www/dev/deu.html
Submit exchange lists by anonymous FTP or by e-mail.

Euroback (Francopholistes)
http://www.cru.fr/listes/euroback@um1.ulg.ac.be/index.html
Periodical exchange list for European libraries.

Library of Congress Exchange and Gift Division Surplus Books
gopher://marvel.loc.gov/00/services/acqser/surplus
> Surplus books are available to "educational institutions, public bodies, and nonprofit, tax-exempt organizations in the United States." For a contact person regarding donations, deposit of library materials or purchase of materials, see *gopher://marvel.loc.gov/00/services/acqser/acq.cont*.

lis-medjournal-duplicates
http://www.mailbase.ac.uk/lists-k-o/lis-medjournal-duplicates
> Journal exchange between U.K. medical libraries.

National Agricultural Library's Acquisitions and Serials Branch
Beltsville, Maryland
http://www.nalusda.gov/acq
> Of interest here is NAL's Gift and Exchange Program, which involves over 2,700 exchange partners and accounts for 60 percent of the material currently received by the NAL. There's also a link to the Federal Depository Library Program Activities, and instructions on how to request surplus publications.

National Library of Australia International Gift and Exchange Activities
http://www.nla.gov.au/internat/gande.htm
> Thirty percent of the National Library's serial collection is obtained via gift, exchange, or deposit.

Teri's Web Palace
http://www.mercer.edu/swilley/dupmain.htm
> Exchange of duplicate serials sponsored by Mercer University, Atlanta, Georgia.

United States Book Exchange (USBE)
http://www.readmore.com/electron/backserv/usbeinfo.html
> Has a well-stocked shelflist of back issues, which members can choose from at a cost of $7.00/issue. Libraries are invited to contribute their duplicates to the stock. Great for replacement copies for lost or damaged items.

University of Florida Libraries Gifts and Exchanges Home Page
http://www.uflib.ufl.edu/ge/p1.html
> This library truly values gift additions to their collections. In 1993–94, gifts added 5,587 monographs to their holdings, or 7.6 percent of their total additions. Check out their spectacular Titles Offered on Exchange Page at *http://www.uflib.ufl.edu/ge/pagetwo.html*. Links to major exchange partners could also be of interest.

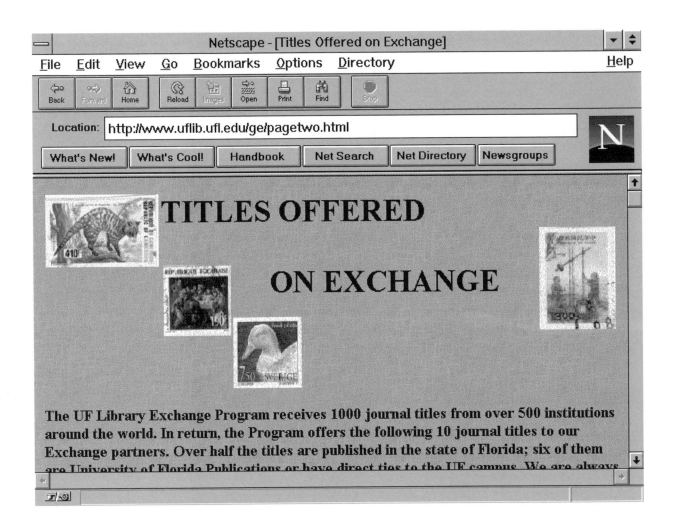

Figure 1.4
University of Florida Libraries Titles Offered on Exchange Page

1.1.4 OTHER GENERAL ACQUISITIONS HOME PAGES

Acquisitions librarians are involved on the cutting edge of library services, and they need to know what's new, who's doing what, and even who was bought out by whom, in a timely manner. In the Other General Acquisitions Home Pages section, you will find sites that will keep you occupied for hours. Check out some conference reports while you're here, and don't leave without a peek at the Principles and Standards of Acquisitions Practice home page!

AcqLink: Resources for Acquisitions Librarians
http://catriona.lib.strath.ac.uk/ISC88
   A gem of information for the European acquisitions community, edited by Catherine Nicholson, Glasgow Caledonian University, Scotland.

Acquisitions in an Electronic Age: Building the Foundations for Access
http://www.nlc-bnc.ca/ifla/IV/ifla61/61–vicj.htm
   Paper presented by Jim Vickery, British Library, at the 61st IFLA General Conference, August 20–25, 1995.

AcqWeb
http://www.library.vanderbilt.edu/law/acqs/acqs.html
   The time has come to talk about the Acquisitions Librarians Electronic Network , or AcqWeb, a sister publication of ACQNET, and by far the best, most all-inclusive site around. Originally developed by Ms. Acquisitions herself, Anna Belle Leiserson, AcqWeb contains a multitude of links and resources for pre-order verification, ordering, and collection development. Come here to find the largest lists of library vendor and publisher home pages and/or e-mail addresses. Publisher and vendor lists are divided into such sections as Rare and Antiquarian Books, Art, Business, and Economics, Literature and Fiction, and Government Publications. Outstanding directories of journals, newsletters, listserv archives, and usenet newsgroups can be found here. Don't miss Web News for Acquiring Minds, a humorous and facts-packed listing of what's new in the acquisitions world.

AllezCat: Our Initial Response to PromptCat Version 1.0
http://gort.ucsd.edu/jarcher/allezcat.html
   John F. Archer, University of California, San Diego, created this illustrated guide showing how one library uses bar-coded Library of Congress Card Numbers and Innopac order record numbers to reduce throughput time of processing electronically transmitted approval book shipments. Other goals are to eliminate the possibility of overlaying wrong bibliographic records and to expedite searching on OCLC.

Book Industry Study Group, Inc.
http://www.bookwire.com/bisg
> "Membership-supported, not-for-profit research organization, comprised of organizations from every section of the publishing industry." BISAC (the Book Industry Systems Advisory Council) has been instrumental in promoting ISBN usage and in creating an electronic purchase order format. Adopting ANSI standards in 1990, BISAC published the *X12 Purchase Order Subset* in 1991. They also have strongly encouraged international standardization of bar coding for book covers and jackets, and development of the Machine-Readable Coding Guidelines for the U.S. Book Industry. SISAC (the Serials Industry Systems Advisory Committee) "develops standardized formats for the electronic transmittal of serials information" (*http://bookwire.com/bisg/sisac.html*). They've developed the Serials Item and Content Identifier (SICI) and are now working on developing EDI (Electronic Data Interchange) transactions.

Feather River Institute Web Site
http://www.csuchico.edu/lbib/acq/conference/featrivr.htm
> Roster of participants and images from the 1996 conference "Death and Rebirth in Library Acquisitions."

IFLA (International Federation of Library Associations) Section on Acquisition and Collection Development
http://www.nlc-bnc.ca/ifla/VII/s14/sae.htm
> Read their objectives and goals from 1992 to 1997, as well as their annual report.

LibLicense (Licensing Digital Information: a Resource for Librarians
http://www.library.yale.edu/~Llicense/index.shtml
> As acquisitions librarians become more involved with acquiring digital information, this site is a must for current information, a Listserv, Liblicense-L, links to actual examples of publisher's licenses, and a license glossary.

National Diet Library's Approach to Digital Collections and the Economic Issues
http://www.nlc-bnc.ca/ifla/IV/ifla62/62–hurm.htm. By Meitetsu Haruyama.
> Discusses acquisition policies for electronic librarians in Japan.

Principles and Standards of Acquisitions Practice
http://www.cc.emory.edu/LIB/ACQ/Stand.html
> MUST reading for all acquisitions staff.

To Link or To Copy? Four Principles for Materials Acquisition in Internet Electronic Libraries

http://fas.sfu.ca/101projects/ElectronicLibrary/project/papers/e-lib-links.html/

By Robert D. Cameron, Simon Fraser University.

1.2

Web Pages from Vendors and Publishers

Now that we've looked at pages for library acquisitions departments, it's time to look at ones from the places where we spend all those acquisition dollars.

The pages listed in this section range from the simple to the elaborate . . . from text-only catalogs to animated sites, where you can place an order online. The specialty sites available can replace all those odd little catalogs that used to get misfiled as well as help you track down hard-to-locate titles. Enjoy and use these pages!

1.2.1 BOOK AND SERIAL JOBBERS FOR LIBRARIES

It has been estimated that 95 percent of libraries now use vendors for part, if not all of their acquisitions nowadays. The rationale is simple . . . why deal with 500 separate publishers when you can deal with one or two vendors? Approval plans, standing orders, firm orders, blanket orders—what to do when there's such a plethora of choices? Vendors describe their electronic ordering software, customized collection development programs, document delivery services, and much, much more. Most vendors are busily listing "value-added" services to their home pages to attract your patronage. Although most of them claim to be the "biggest" or the "best" in something or other, it's actually quite convenient to have all their information at your fingertips. As web purchasing becomes more secure, acquisitions librarians can order their material and also pay for it through the Web, saving up to two thirds of the original invoicing costs!

Baker and Taylor
http://www.baker-taylor.com

"Privately held information and entertainment services company," founded in 1828, that "supplies books, video, audio, software, and related services to more than 100,000 bookstores, schools, and public and university libraries internationally." Accesses more than 220,000 English-language titles from 35,000+ publishers. *Academia Online*, their monthly annotated bibliography for librarians, is now exclusively issued in electronic format. Continuations are addressed in the quarterly publication *Connections*. Automatically Yours is an approval program based on 300 popular authors, chosen by librarians. Baker and Taylor also offers approval programs for videocassettes, compact disks, audio cassettes, media, and software. The *Book Price Report* lists prices and variances for all approval books and for books sorted by Library of Congress classification number, all university press titles, by physical format, and even by country of publication. Read about Baker and Taylor's historic contract with the Hawaii State Public Library System in the "Cataloging Outsourcing" section of this book.

B.H. Blackwell Home Page
Oxford, England
http://www.blackwell.co.uk/libserv

Largest academic and scientific book stock in the world, with over 220,000 titles. The U.K. bibliographic database contains over 2.5 million records and over 100,000 publisher and distribution records, and promises to supply any book published or commercially distributed anywhere in the world. They offer firm orders and standing orders for all series titles. Together with Blackwell North America, they maintain a series database of over 80,000 active titles with a further 36,000 records of completed or discontinued series. They also offer approval plans, with bibliographic data available in MARC format for downloading to NOTIS, INNOVACQ, and Geac systems. Detailed interest profiles based on an extensive subject thesaurus may be matched weekly against records of newly published books. "Uncover" document delivery and current awareness alerting service is available, and many articles are ready to be faxed in less than an hour (24-hour maximum turnaround time). Electronic Data Services include EDI (Electronic Data Interchange) for serials and book messages, ACCUSCAN for delivering data to your system via bar codes, and MARC with Books, which delivers LCMARC or UNIMARC records to your OPAC.

Blackwell North America
http://www.blackwell.com

"Specializes in the supply of U.S. and Canadian books and bibliographic support products to academic, research, and leading public libraries throughout the world. We are the market leader in combining traditional bookselling expertise with the latest developments in library technology." Became a full NACO member in 1995, contributing records derived from the authority control editing they perform each year on more than 25 million records sent to them by clients. Blackwell's Connect System offers World Wide Web access to their monograph and serials databases, and access to their order and subscription records. Each year, Blackwell upgrades almost 20,000 CIP records three to six months before the Library of Congress, so that their clients can enter complete bibliographic records to their local systems (approximate cost, $1.50/record). For a review of Blackwell's outsourcing services, see Karen Wilson's article "Outsourcing Copy Cataloging and Physical Processing: A Review of Blackwell's Outsourcing Services for the J. Hugh Jackson Library at Stanford" at *http://blackwell.com/news/issues/outsourcing.htm*. Records can be enriched with Blackwell's inventory and fund information and/or with table of content information. MARCwithBooks supplies LC-MARC records to accompany all titles ordered through Blackwell. Finally, their CD complete service (established January 1996) offers customers advice and information on all aspects of CD-ROMs, including technical support and training.

Book Dealers (Africana)
http://www-sul.stanford.edu/depts/ssrg/africa/afrbook.html

Offers information on the largest African book dealers here, including the African Book Collective and African Imprint Library Services. Also links to the African Publishing Home Page at *http://wn.apc.org/mediatech/publish*.

Dawson Europe Home Page

http://www.dawson.co.uk

"Europe's largest journal subscription agent and corporate and academic book supplier." New owners of Faxon.

EBSCO Information Services

http://www.ebsco.com

"The largest subscription agency in the world. A major vendor to libraries and organizations through 30 regional offices on six continents." Offers customized serials management services, EDI interfaces with most automated library systems, EBSCO/RETRO retrospective conversion service, EBScan bar code date input service, and EBSCONET Online Subscription Service. EBSCO Publishing and OCLC are collaborating to create a database of full-text article images. EBSCOhost is an online system that allows users to search dozens of citation and full-text databases and order documents through the Internet. The enhanced version complies with the Z39.50 standard and provides abstracts for nearly 4,000 periodicals. EBSCODOC is a full-service document delivery pioneer, working on cooperative and electronic document sourcing. Finally, see current and back issues of *At Your Service*, which include preliminary price projections for subscriptions and other news of interest to subscribers.

FAXON Company Home Page

http://www.faxon.com

"Serial publication subscription agency providing librarians and businesses with consolidated billing and publication information, and publishers with consolidated payment and preprocessing of claims for missing issues." Provides the annual Preliminary Subscription Price Projections (they're projecting an approximate overall increase of 9.5 percent in 1997 for a "typical collection"). FAXON helped to establish and maintains ANSI NISO standard Z39.56. FAXON Finder FlashTOC is a table of contents database, going back to January 1990, available via the Web. FlashTOC currently accesses 5 million article citations and over 300,000 TOC's. Up to ten authors from each article are included (cost: $10.00/year per FlashTOC search profile). *FAXON PubUpdate* (a quarterly publication providing new title information) is now available via the Web or e-mail delivery. FAXON makes available the full *NISO Catalog of Standards and Standards-Related Publications*. Finally, FAXON maintains a large list of publishers on the Internet at *http://www.faxon.com/Internet/publishers/pubs.html*.

Ingram Book Group

http://www.ingrambook.com

"Provides wholesale distribution of books, periodicals, multimedia, and spoken audio to booksellers, librarians, and specialty retailers." Check out the Book Kahoona's suggestions.

ISA Australia

http://www.design.net.au/isa/welcome.htm

Medium-sized general subscription agency servicing any library anywhere in the world, but focusing primarily on Australia. They produce the hard-copy directory *Periodicals in Print: Australia, New Zealand, and the South Pacific.*

James Bennett Home Page

http://www.pegasus.oz.au/~bennett

"Book supplier to Australia and the world." "Serves libraries, government, and the corporate sector with a high-quality supply line to published works. We source published works from all over the world, with particular strengths in Australasian material." Global network partners with the Blackwell Group.

Midwest Library Service (A Book Jobber to Libraries)

http://www.midwestls.com/brochure/index.html-ssi

Their database contains over 20,000 publishers.

Pan Asian Publications

http://www.panap.com

Full-service Asian materials distributor. Beautifully illustrated site.

Readmore, Inc.

http://www.readmore.com

Award-winning home page. Contains an extensive list of publisher's links, as well as an information collection which includes library science e-journals, lists, and sites. ReadiCat is a "web-accessible database of over 100,000 journals, periodicals, and CD-ROM titles with the latest bibliographic and price information" (available only to Readmore clients and users with guest accounts).

Provides access to BACKSERV, the BACK issues and Duplicate Exchange SERVice. BACKSERV has both lists and web/gopher services. Catalogs of back-issue dealers are also searchable. ROSS, Readmore's Online Serials Service allows clients to enter claims according to actual shipping data for individual issues. A DOS-based demo of ROSS is available for downloading. REMO, a microcomputer-based automated serials management system with the ability to print SISAC bar-code symbols as part of the check-in process, also has a demo available for downloading. Don't miss Readmore's Information Library—A Collection of Resources for Serials and Acquisitions Practitioners. Readmore's page is an excellent example of how useful a concise, carefully selected collection of links can be.

Retrieve

http://www.cais.net/sberner

"A consolidated book acquisitions service . . . For 25 years, we have filled individual, multiple, standing, and subscription orders for clients in the U.S. and 31 other countries." They also promise to "break through the complex maze of U.S. government and other Washington-based publication sources."

RoweCom

http://rowe.com

New kids on the block (established in 1994). Order and pay with a click of the mouse. Publisher payments, together with verified digital signatures, are sent over an encrypted Internet connection. The annual subscription fee is $95, no matter how large your collection. "The client-library uses RoweCom-developed software to request a subscription, which travels over the Internet to a Banc One server . . . the server then forwards order information to the publisher and payment information to Banc One, which provides the automated clearinghouse piece (debiting the buyer's bank and crediting the sellers)." RoweCom's costs are 75 percent less per subscription than those of traditional service agencies, so total cost for subscriptions and agency fees should be five to seven percent lower. Read more about RoweCom's services at **Subscribe 97** (*http://rowe.com/subscribe.html*). Rowe says "Anyone who is looking to reduce the cost of acquisitions has got to love it."

Swets and Zeitlinger

http://www.swets.nl/index.html (Head Office, Lisse, The Netherlands).

"Major international library supplier and information provider." They provide SwetScan, a table of contents service covering over 13,000 scholarly journals and SwetsInfo, which covers confirmation of orders, cancellations, and claims. Their online newsletter entitled *Network* is available here. Also check out Swet's Backsets Service.

WLN Acquisitions System

http://www.wln.com/wlnprods/onlinedb/acq.htm

"Generate online orders to participating vendors, maintain a standing orders file, do fund accounting . . . automatic claiming, etc."

Yankee Book Peddler

http://www.ybp.com

One of the most innovative vendors on the Web. YBP is "an international full-service bookseller specializing in U.S. academic book approval plans and library technical processing." In February 1996, YBP joined OCLC's Cooperative Upgrade Program for Cataloging-in-Publication (CIP) Data from LC. YBP will upgrade CIP records to full MARC records as newly

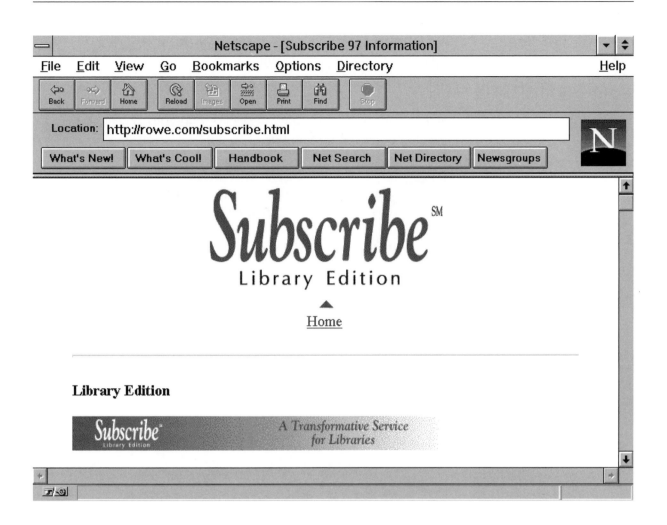

Figure 1.5
RoweCom

published material arrives, and will then send them to OCLC. These titles can then be searched on PromptCat and selected for purchase using OCLC Selection. See *http://www.oclc.org/oclc/press/960219c.htm* for more details. Subscribe97 "enables subscription orders, payments, claims, and responses to be transferred between libraries and publishers, bypassing traditional subscription agencies." A University of California at San Diego pilot project with Yankee Book Peddler will print UCSD's Innopac purchase order number as a bar-code on the slips inserted in the books shipped. This means that the correct order record can be accessed and received right out of the box. GOBI (Global Online Bibliographic Information) replaced their FOLIO product at the end of 1996. GOBI provides daily updates of the database and services for monographic firm orders, approval, and continuations customers by rapidly adding table of content information. More details are at *http://www.ybp.com/ gobinote.htm*.

1.2.2 GENERAL PUBLISHERS, BOOKSTORES, AND ORGANIZATIONS

No matter how wonderful jobbers are, you still must acquire some materials from other sources. The publishers and bookstores listed in this section are either extremely large single operations or they have combined with other publishers to offer you a dizzying array of materials to choose from. Remember those old acquisitions departments with an entire wall filled with publisher's catalogs, all kept in alphabetical order? Nowadays, many publishers can no longer afford to distribute paper catalogs; they will either advertise over their home pages or distribute electronic availability notices via e-mail, discussion lists, usenet, etc. Many are now offering to send you an e-mail notice when new materials in your field of interest become available. Look at the world through publishers' eyes—it can be a highly interesting and entertaining viewpoint.

Academic Book Center

http://www.acbc.com

Apply for log-in privileges and a password, and search to your heart's content.

AcqWeb's Directory of Publishers and Vendors

http://www.library.vanderbilt.edu/law/acqs/pubr.html

One of the best subject-specific lists on the Web.

Amazon.com Books

http://www.amazon.com

"One million titles, consistently low prices." Enables readers to submit their own book reviews, complete with ratings from 1–10. Authors may also advertise their material with such enticements as "Visit my home page and read the first three chapters free" (offers John Spencer Hill of his book, *The Last Castrato*). Check out Eyes and Editors, a personal notification service at *http://www.amazon.com/exec/obidos/subst/eyes-eyes.html*. Eyes is a "fully automated anthropomorphized search agent." Editors is "a group of real humans, our department editors, who preview galleys, read reviews, pick especially great books, and tell you about just those that fall into the genres and subject areas that interest you. And you get a discount on those books." Sounds just like what I used to do for patrons when I ran a small public library branch.

Association of American University Presses Combined Online Catalog/Bookstore

http://aaup.princeton.edu

Plans call for approximately 100 scholarly presses to participate in this combined online catalog/bookstore. Search titles of a single press or search combined presses.

Book Data
http://www.bookdata.co.uk
  Covers the U.K., Europe, the U.S., Australia, New Zealand, and South
  Africa.

Book Industry Communication's Bookish Home Page
http://www.bic.org.uk/bic/bic.html
  Some wonderful information here. Check out EDI for the Book World
  by Editeur at *http://www.bic.org.uk/bic/infopak.html* and Reports of the
  Library EDI Implementation Group. A listing of over 100 U.K. publishers is also available.

Book Stacks Unlimited
http://www.books.com/scripts/news.exe
  "Your local bookstore—no matter where you live." Over 465,000 titles
  available. For a good listing of publishers, see Publisher's Place.

Book Zone
http://bookzone.com/bookzone
  This site is set up to give you a browsing-the-aisles bookshop kind of
  feeling. Click on a subject (biography for example) to get treated to a
  great synopsis, and to view the cover.

Bookpages, Your Personal British Bookstore
http://www.bookpages.co.uk
  "Power search" over 900,000 titles.

Books On-line: Titles
http://www.cs.cmu.edu/Web/booktitles.html
  Browse by first letter of title or by a word or phrase in the title.

Bookstore at intertain.com
http://www.intertain.com/store/welcome.html
  This huge bookstore has over 500,000 titles available and promises to
  ship 90 percent of their orders within two working days. Search by subject or create a profile of your interests. Updated daily.

BookWeb—Homepage of the American Booksellers Association
http://www.ambook.org
  Guide to thousands of U.S. book stores and the latest information on
  books and the book industry. "Author tours," discussion groups, live chats,
  and more.

BookWire
http://www.bookwire.com

"The most comprehensive guide to the book-related resources of the Internet." This is one of those sites that could be surfed for hours. Don't miss Online Resources for Book People at *http://www.bookwire.com/index/Book-Resources.html*. Download entire books free in the BookWire Reading Room.

Borders Books/Music/Cafe

http://www.borders.com

Check out this blurb: "Today, Borders has the most sophisticated computer inventory system in the book retailing business. As each store's purchases are recorded, the system uses artificial intelligence technology to constantly adjust the store's inventory. It adds more books on topics that are selling and eliminates books on topics that aren't." Daily reviews of books, disks, and videos.

Canadian Publisher's Council

http://www.pubcouncil.ca

Active since 1910 as Canada's main English language book publishing trade association. Represents 34 publishing companies. Maintains a FAQ. Highly recommended: Publishing: A View from the Inside and This Little Book Goes to Market: A Cautionary Tale of Canadian Book Publishing and Pricing.

Children's Literature Web Guide: Internet Resources Related to Books for Children and Young Adults

http://www.ucalgary.ca/~dkbrown/index.html

Wow! Charlotte's World Wide Web. This site is incredible, containing everything related to children's literature. Provides book award lists, information about movies based on children's books, and much, much more.

Chosen for Children: The Perfect Way to Select Picture Books for Children

http://www.chosenforchildren.com

They're not lying—it's fun, it's colorful, it's legally addictive.

H. W. Wilson

http://www.hwwilson.com

Reader's Guide is now available as full-text in Mega and Mini Editions. Don't miss Rettig on Reference for reviews of adult reference books, and NewsFlashes/Libraries, which is updated Monday through Friday.

iBS (the Internet Book Shop)

http://www.bookshop.co.uk

"The Largest Online Bookshop in the World." (Have you noticed they ALL say this?) Catalogs of selected academic and trade publishers. They also make available British Books in Print, a searchable version of Whitakers, for online searching—*http://www.bookshop.co.uk/search.htm*. Search by title, author, subject, publisher, or by complete ISBN.

International Book Information Center, Inc.
http://sunsite.unc.edu/ibic/guide.html
>"The IBIC guide to book-related resources on the Internet." Also known as "The World-Wide Web Virtual Library: Literature."

International Thomson Publishing's thomson.com
http://www.thomson.com
>"Global confederation of publishing companies operating under one umbrella." thomson.com's attempt to organize the Internet is known as CyberHound Online—*http://www.thomson.com/cyberhound.html*. Gale's editors index a site under more than 75 different fields. Their rating criteria is based on content, design, and technical merit not "coolness."

Internet Road Map to Books
http://www.bookport.com/b_roadmap.html
>A common home page for book-related sites on the Internet. Search for any publisher on the Web by name or topical keyword. Just click on the map and go.

KBC On-Line Book Store List
http://kbc.com/html/bookstor.htm
>Offers listings of new and used bookstores on the Web. Bookstores from all over the world and many specialty stores are listed.

North South Books
http://www.northsouth.com
>"Fine children's books. Includes guides for teachers and parents, profiles and essays about authors and artists, and much more."

Publishers' Catalogs Home Page
http://www.lights.com/publisher
>Northern Lights Internet Solutions from Saskatoon, Canada, has compiled a great international listing of publishers' catalogs. Forty-nine countries are currently represented.

Publishers Marketing Association
http://www.pma-online.org
>Hundreds of links to member pages.

Publishers: The World Wide Web Virtual Library
http://www.comlab.ox.ac.uk/archive/publishers.html
>This site functions as a resource page FOR publishers.

Publishing Companies Online

http://www.edoc.com/ejournal/publishers.html

When last browsed, this list had almost 700 entries, divided into academic, computer books, sci/tech/medical/electronic publishing companies, online publishing projects, and more.

PUBNET

http://www.pubnet.org

Publishing industry's daily update. PUBNET formed in 1987 to give publishers and booksellers a cost-effective method of ordering books electronically. Trade bookstores, library jobbers, and distributors are also invited to join. Check out their new ordering table.

Readers Ndex

http://www.ReadersNdex.com

Specializes in literary information from the publishing industry. Besides providing information on authors, publishers, titles, and book reviews, Readers Ndex also provides Windows software for publishers to create their own home page. Browse by subject. Fill out their mailing list notification form, and you will receive a biweekly custom newsletter of new additions.

rec.arts.book FAQ Homepage

http://www.zmall.com/bmm/books-faq/homepage.html

Usenet's guide to books, bookstores, and book genres. Highly specialized pages, like Book Stores in Various Asian Cities or The Robin Hood Booklist, as well as reading lists from other newsgroups are available here.

Scholarly Electronic Publishing Bibliography

http://info.lib.uh.edu/sepb/sepb.html

Extremely useful listing of selected pertinent books, articles, and electronic documents concerning publishing on the Internet since 1990. Search by Word or Acrobat File.

Small Publishers Association of North America–SPANnet

http://www.SPANnet.org

Organization of self-publishers, independent presses, authors, and vendors in the U.S. and Canada.

Time Warner Pathfinder

http://pathfinder.com/welcome/?navbar

The largest publishing conglomerate on the Web. Great for the Java-enabled.

TitleNet

http://www.titlnet.com:8204

"A commercial area on the Internet created by Inforonics for publishers to present information about their products and services, and for users to request further information from publishers."

United States Government Printing Office (GPO)

http://www.access.gpo.gov

"Serving the printing, binding and information dissemination needs of the U.S. Government." On December 1, 1995 the Printing Office discontinued all of its fee-based subscriptions to core databases and began free access to all electronic products provided through GPO Access. This page includes free connections to The Congressional Record, The Federal Register, Congressional Bills, The Monthly Catalog of U.S. Government Publications, and much, much more. Search for local information from the Electronic Federal Depository Libraries using either a two-letter U.S. Postal service code or a three-digit telephone area code.

View of Midwinter by a Vendor/Librarian

http://www.lib.utk.edu/litanews/summer95/vendor.html

By Amira Aaron (*LITA Newsletter*, Summer 1995, vol. 16, no. 3).

Yahoo!'s List of Booksellers on the Web

http://www.yahoo.com/Business_and_Economy/Companies/Books

Yahoo!'s List of Publishers on the Web

http://www.yahoo.com/Business_and_Economy/Companies/Publishing

1.2.3 SPECIALTY PUBLISHERS AND SOURCES

Specialty publisher pages are frequently colorful, informative, and well worth a visit. Alternative presses are useful to many special collections departments, and genre publishers and bookstores that cater to possibly the most popular sections in your local public library. Special libraries will find the legal, medical, and music sites of interest (as will other librarians who like to listen to sound bytes, see some marvelous 3–D graphics, or feel the need to consult a lawyer!).

1.2.3.1 Alternative Publishers and Sources

Atomic Books
http://www.atomicbooks.com
> "Literary finds for mutated minds." It's colorful, it's fun, it's . . . . MU-TATED!

Broken Pencil—the Guide to Alternative Publications in Canada
http://www.io.org/~halpen/bpenal.html

Church of the SubGenius—Brain Toolkit and Surreality Reboot
http://sunsite.unc.edu:80/subgenius
> "Pornological Dementertainment—works from your computer out—it's better than life!" This site is really fun. Enter the Stark Fist of Removal and see for yourself.

Dark Horse Press
http://www.dhorse.com
> Premier comics publisher, with such titles as *Concrete*, *Star Wars*, and the *Godzilla* and *Aliens* series. First publisher to bring Japanese manga to the U.S. (manga are adult comics with violent and sexual themes). Their special issue *Aliens vs. Predator #0* broke all records and sold over 400,000 copies—more than any other comic book ever issued by an independent publisher.

Golden Quill Bookshop
http://www.goldenquill.com

Gutter Press
http://www.salzman.com/gutter
> "Dangerous fiction and radical literature."

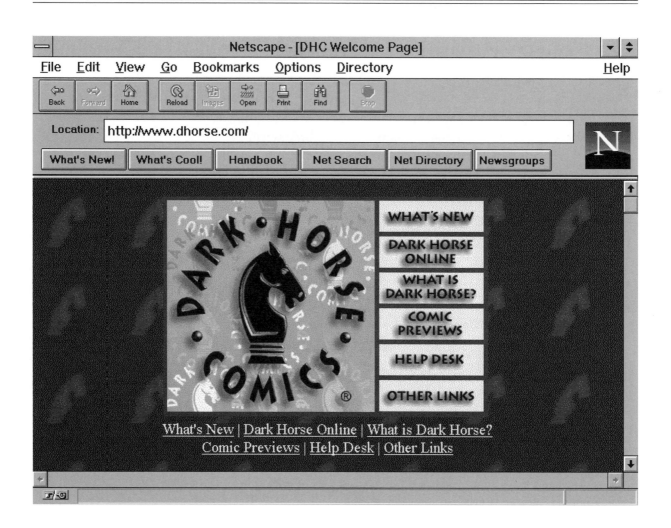

Figure 1.6
Dark Horse Press

Loompanics Unlimited

http://www.loompanics.com/contents.htm
> Unusual titles available, such as *The Beggar's Handbook* ("Beggars can make up to $200/day tax free"); *Secrets of a Super Hacker* by the Knightmare; *How to Bury Your Goods*; *Escape From Controlled Custody*; *How to Steal Food From the Supermarket*; *Curious Punishments of Bygone Days*; and finally *Bad Girls Do It! (An Encyclopedia of Female Murderers)*.

Monkeywrench Press

http://fletcher.iww.org:80/~monkeywrench
> "Devoted to publishing anti-authoritarian material of interest to working people."

Sources of Cool Books

http://www.io.org/~gutter/spn.html
> Links to small alternative press publishers, such as Gutter Press, Alternative X, Fringeware, and Golden Quill.

The Space Between—New and Used Books

http://www.tagsys.com/Ads/SpaceBetween
> "Our listings feature thousands of titles dealing with suppressed or alternative information."

Utne Online

www.utne.com
> Free chat café and classic alternative literature.

Verso Press

http://www.bookshop.co.uk/verso
> "Largest English radical publisher in the world."

1.2.3.2 Audio, CD-ROM, Micrographic, Multimedia, and Video Publishers and Sources

AcqWeb's Directory of Audio Books and Tapes, Publishers, and Vendors
http://www.library.vanderbilt.edu/law/acqs/pubr/audio.html

Audio Booksource
http://www.webcom.com/absource
   "Safe" online ordering.

Audio Publishers Association
http://www.audiopub.org
   Check out Audiobook FAQs and a comprehensive set of links to audio books.

Be Macro-Informed about Micrographics
http://nyslgti.gen.ny.us/nystate/associations/nyalgro/macro.html
   By Steven Walker.

Bowker-Saur CD-ROM Catalogue
http://www.worldserver.pipex.com/service/cdrom/contents.html

Canadian Institute for Historical Microreproductions
http://www.nlc-bnc.ca/cihm
   Bilingual (French-English) program to locate and preserve early printed Canadian materials.

CD-ROM Information Website
http://www.interaccess.com/uscchi/cdrom/index.html

CD-ROMs Online
http://www.cdromsonline.com
   Telnet connection.

CD-ROMs Plus
http://www.mediawhse.com/cdplus/cdplus.html
   Find FAQ files and don't miss What's New in CD-ROM Technology.

Creative Multimedia
http://www.creativemm.com
   "Leading developer and publisher of interactive multimedia information."

Discount Laser Disc
Portland, Oregon
http://www.teleport.com/~dld

Dolphin Disks
http://www.library.upenn.edu/vision/dolphin
> "Experimental electronic publishing project of the University of Pennsylvania library, consisting of Web-enabled CD-ROMs distributed by the library. These CD-ROMs are linked to an active Web site and just may be the wave of the future.

Facets Multi-Media Home Page
http://www.facets.org
> "One of the largest distributors of foreign, art, cult, and hard-to-find videos." Better yet, they are a nonprofit organization.

Laser Discs
http://www.discount-train.com/laser-disks

Mega Media-Links Main Menu@ Omnibus: Eye
http://omnibus-eye.rtvf.nwu.edu/links/submenu.html
> Find videotape and laser disc distributors, films, videos, multimedia—it's all here.

Nedbook
http://www.nedbook.nl
> International scientific booksellers and subscription agents and specialized CD-ROM agents. One of the first CD-ROM suppliers in Europe. Site has information available in English or Dutch.

OmniMedia
http://www.omnicorp.com
> "Multimedia publisher specializing in music, movies and kid's CD-ROMs."

Piglet Press Audio Books
http://www.halcyon.com/piglet
> Wonderful site dealing in audio books and CD-ROM books for children. Listen to characters from audio books in fast-loading .au files.

Terry's World of Audiobooks
http://www.wgts.org/audiobooks
> Lists other audio book sites, with e-mail addresses or toll-free numbers for those without home pages. Smiley icons mark those publishers who rent audio books. Reviews of audio books can be found at AudioFile— The Monthly Magazine of Audiobook Reviews at *http://www.idsonline.com/terraflora/Audiofile/main.html*.

UMI (University Microfilms Inc.)
http://www.umi.com

More than 27,000 newspapers and periodicals, and over 1.4 million dissertations in microform. Can provide xerographic copies of more than 140,000 out-of-print books. See the Books on Demand FAQ. Also check out the UMI Serials in Microform Catalog at *http://wwwlib.umi.com/ sim/gateway* ProQuest Digital Dissertations will be available in mid-1997. However, a permanent microfilm archive will still provide support for the digital library.

Updata Publication's On-Line Catalog of CD-ROM Databases
http://www.updata.com

One of the most comprehensive collections of CD-ROMs available. Updated quarterly.

Video Online Express—Selling Laser Discs, Videos, Audio Books, and Games
http://www.videoexpress.com

"60,000 VHS tapes, 10,000 laser discs, 5,600 audio books, 200 games." Customer ratings and reviews available.

Wholesale CD-ROMs Distributor Catalog
http://www.global-impact.com/a4.html

Over 10,000 CD-ROMs available, at rock-bottom prices.

1.2.3.3 Foreign/Bilingual Monograph Sources

Alapage (French Virtual Bookstore)
http://www.alapage.tm.fr
  "Milliers et milliers de livres d'une simple touche."

APNET Academic Press List of International Bookstores
http://192.215.52.3/222/ap/int/str.htm

Bilingual Books for Kids: Multicultural Connections y Cosas Hispanicas
http://www.mhv.net/~bilingbk/cgi-bin/make-a-store.cgi

BookServe, The International Internet Bookstore
http://www.bookserve.com
  Choose titles from BookServe USA (English), BookServe Deutschland (German), or BookServe Netherlands (Dutch) or Spanish. Books can be delivered to any country. The USA Page offers a search for a million books in English, Spanish, German, or Dutch. If you ask them to perform a custom search, a representative will answer your request within 24 hours during the work week.

Casalini Libri (Florence, Italy)
http://ww.caselini.com
  Read about the contributions of one of the largest Italian vendors. See Casalini Libri to Add Italian Records to the OCLC Online Union Catalog at *http://www.oclc.org/oclc/press/960126a.htm*.

China Books and Periodicals Inc.
http://www.chinabooks.com
  Largest distributor of Chinese language material since 1960.

Deutschsprachige Verlage im Internet
http://www.german-business.de/verliste.htm
  Links to German publishers.

DK Agencies—Indian Book Suppliers
http://www.dkagencies.com/page2.htm
  Search over 100,000 Indian titles in the English language alone, and more in Sanskrit, Tibetan, Hindi, and other vernaculars.

East View Publications, Inc.
http://www.eastview.com
  "World's largest clearinghouse for information products and services from the Ukraine and other former Soviet republics."

Editeurs Francophones (French and French-Speaking Publishers)
http://www.chu-rouen.fr/documed/edi.html

Editoriales y Librerias Espanolas
http://dalila.ugr.es/~felix/g2/a5.htm
   List of Spanish bookstores.

Extensive Worldwide List of Islamic Booksellers
http://www.msa-natl.org/resources/Bookstores.html

Foreign Acquisitions Background Paper
http://arl.cni.org/aau/Global.html
   See Research Libraries in a Global Context: an Exploratory Paper.

Foreign Book and Serial Vendors Directories, v.1: Book and Serial Vendors for Asia and the Pacific: Results of a Survey of ARL Libraries
gopher://ala1.ala.org:70/00/alagophxiii/alagophxiiialcts/alagophxiiialctsasia/50921007.document
   Well, at least you know, if you get to this page, that you are an excellent and accurate typist. Actually, you'll be glad you made the effort.

Foreign Monograph Book Vendors
http://weber.u.washington.edu/~acqdiv/forvend.html/
   Very thorough listing, complete with addresses. Updated frequently.

Frustration and Fun: Problems in the Acquisitions of Special Collections Materials: South Asia
http://poe.acc.virginia.edu/~pmgk/libsci/soAsCol.dos. By Philip F. McEldowney.

GBM Buch und Medien
http://buchhabdel.de/fhome.htm

GEIST—German Encyclopedic Internet Service Terminal
http://www.geist.spacenet.de/verlag-E.html
   Contains links to publisher's catalogs from German-speaking countries, profiles of publishing companies, and the Web site Humanities and Culture in Internet.

Icelandic Bookstores
http://www.treknet.is/reykjavik/bookstores.html

Indian Books Centre—Sri Satguru Publications
http://www.indiamart.com/ibc

International Specialized Book Services
http://www.teleport.com/~isbs
> Specialties include Australian, Irish, and Islamic studies, and Judaica.

Internationale Buchhandlervereinigungen
http://www.buchhandel.de/ebf-ibf.htm

Internet Chinese Librarians Club: Volunteer Services in Chinese Materials Acquisitions
http://www.lib.siu.edu/swen/iclc/chinacq.htm
> Find here a list of Chinese bookstores, online catalogs, Chinese materials vendors, and several e-mail addresses specifically for Chinese materials acquisitions consultation.

Japanese Bookstores
http://192.215.52.3/www/ap/japanstr.htm

Latin American Book Store, LTD.
http://www.latinamericanbooks.com
> Located in Ithaca, New York, this publisher has provided books to U.S. and Canada since 1982. They change theme sections quarterly.

Leon Sanchez Cuesta
http://www.globalcom.es/saculib
> Madrid, Spain vendor.

List of Chinese Bookstores
http://darkwing.uoregon.edu/~felsing/ceal/johnk.html
> Includes bookstores in China and Hong Kong.

Online Islamic Bookstore
http://www.sharaaz.com
> Books, audio visuals, software, and CDs related to the Muslim world and Islam.

Pages de France
http://www.planete.net/~jcroul
> "Number one online French bookstore on the Web." Books, CDs, and CD-ROMs available.

Puvill Libros
http://www.oclc.orgloclc/press/951127b.htm
> Read about this large Spanish book vendor at OCLC: Puvill Libros to Add Spanish Records to the OCLC Online Union Catalog, Enriching the OCLC PromptCat, PromptSelect, and Prism Services. More than 38,700 titles online.

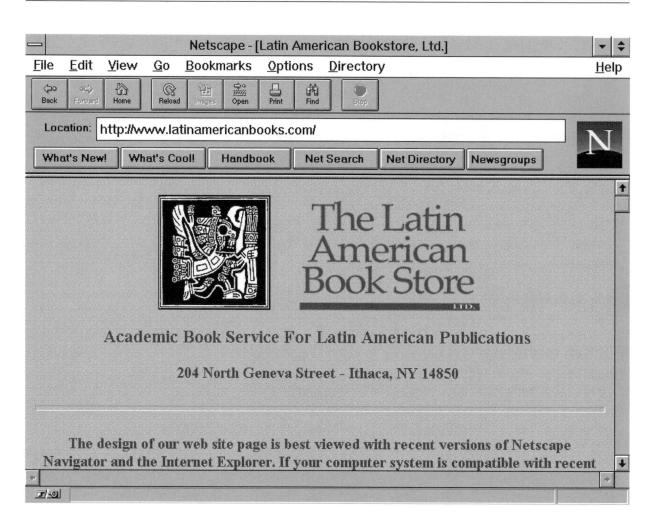

Figure 1.7
Latin American Book Store, LTD.

Russian Bookstores and Publishers
http://132.236.21.132/Russian.web/other/bookstor.htm

SALALM Home Page (Seminar on the Acquisition of Latin American Library Materials)
http://latino.lib.cornell.edu/salalmhome.html
   Includes Acquisitions Trip Notes and Latin American Bookseller Pages and conference information. Check out the Directory of Vendors of Latin American Library Materials—*http://latino.lib.cornell.edu/salalmvendors.*

Schoenhof's Foreign Books
http://www.schoenhofs.com
   "Comprehensive source for the world's languages (285 of them)."

Task Force on Acquisition and Distribution of Foreign Language and Area Studies Materials
http://arl.cni.org/aau/FA.html
   Focuses on trends in foreign acquisitions for major North American research institutions. Major sections discuss the historical perspectives of foreign acquisitions, a program for the distributed collection of foreign acquisitions, proposals for the coordinated development of Latin American studies resources, Japanese language scientific and technical serials, and German resources.

1.2.3.4 Legal Publishers and Sources

AcqWeb's WWW Resources for Law Librarians in Acquisitions and Collection Development
http://www.library.vanderbilt.edu/law/acqs/law.html

American Bar Association (ABA Network)
http://www.abanet.org
> "World's largest voluntary professional association." The ABA Virtual Store contains books, newsletters, CD-ROMs, video/audiotapes, and more. Sitetation highlights a legal-oriented site or mailing list each week.

Butterworths Canada
http://www.butterworths.ca
> Excellent site, mirrored by sister sites in Australia, New Zealand, South Africa, and the U.K.

Carswell Legal Center
Thomson Professional Publishing
http://www.carswell.com/legcen.html
> Peruse issues of the Law Book News Index from March 1995 to the present.

Dickinson School of Law Library Acquisitions Policy for Information Resources
http://www.dsl.edu/acq.html

Ediciones Andrade
http://www.jurisnet.com.mx/andrade.html
> Mexican legal materials.

General Code Publishers (U.S.)
http://www.generalcode.com
> Producers of PC Codebook for Windows.

Kluwer Law International
http://www.kli.com
> "World's largest publisher dedicated solely to providing international information and resources."

Law Book Network
http://lawbook.com
> "Buy and sell law books on the WWW." International focus.

Lawyers Cooperative Publishing Home Page

http://www.lcp.com

"One of the nation's oldest and largest legal publishers." Check out the vast Legal List for law-related Internet resources at *http://www.lcp.com/ The-Legal-List/TLL-home.html*.

LEXIS-NEXIS Communication Center

http://www.lexis-nexis.com/lncc

"World's premier online legal, news, and business information services." Lexis-Nexis adds more than 9.5 million documents weekly to the more than 1 billion documents online.

Martindale-Hubbell

http://www.reedref.martindalecom

Law directories available in print, on CD-ROM, and on Lexis-Nexis. Martindale-Hubbell assigns ratings for over 60,000 lawyers a year.

Matthew Bender and Co., Inc.

http://www.bender.com/bender/open

Publisher of nearly 500 print and electronic format titles. Check out "Inside Matthew Bender," a quarterly audio newsletter (printed text available here)—*http://www.bender.com/bender/open/webdriver?MItab-site Pages+MIral=newframe*

Michie

http://www.michie.com

"The nation's leading publisher of state codes." Text and CD-ROM publications. Full text available on some publications, and sample chapters of others available. Check out Michie's Diskette Library.

Monash University Law Library Acquisitions List

http://www.lib.monash.edu.au/newbooks/law/law.html

Monash is the largest Australian university law library. It maintains updated weekly and monthly acquisitions lists.

Nolo Press Self-Help Law Center

http://www.nolo.com

"Easy-to-use books and software on consumer law subjects, such as wills, small claims court, divorce, and debt problems." Maintains a regularly updated list of lawyer jokes.

Oceana Publications

http://www.oceanalaw.com/textonly/home.htm

International legal texts. Lack of graphics makes this site a superfast loader.

Shepard's
http://www.shepards.com

"Full-service, multimedia publisher, developing legal information products for today and tomorrow." Began in 1873 with Shepard's Citations—a record of court rulings on a gummed label that could be pasted inside law books. They provide a daily update service and Shepard's CD-ROM News.

West Publishing
http://www.westpub.com

One of the first companies to provide computer research services to the legal profession with WestLaw. They offer "Find a Lawyer," a free search through West's Legal Directory. West is involved with creating home pages for more than 800,000 lawyers listed in this directory.

William S. Hein and Co., Inc.
http://lawlib.wuacc.edu/hein/heinper1.htm

"World's largest distributor of legal periodicals." Also own back stock and exclusive reprint rights to over 500 law journals and reviews.

1.2.3.5 Medical Publishers and Sources

American Medical Association Publications Web Site
http://www.ama-assn.org/register/welcome.htm
Tables of contents and abstracts for many leading medical journals, including *JAMA*, *Archives of Internal Medicine*, and *Archives of Surgery*. Free full-text access is provided for the JAMA HIV/AIDS Information Center at *http://www.ama-assn.org/special/hiv/hivhome.htm*

BMJ Publishing Group (British Medical Journal)
http://www.bmj.com/index.html
Contains selected articles from the weekly BMJ.

Doody Publishing Health Sciences Book Reviews
http://www.doody.com/home_to.htm
Although full access to reviews of more than 5,000 new health sciences titles published since 1993 is available by paid subscription, free information is still available via the Medical Books News and Views Bulletin, as well as a directory of health sciences publishers.

Humana Press Inc. Scientific, Medical, and Trade Publishers
http://humanapress.com
Specializes in neuroscience, molecular biology, medicine, and cancer research. Download free articles from JMN Online.

Library Acquisitions Guidelines for Academic Visual Science Libraries
http://www.opt.indiana.edu/guideline/main.html#LAC

Lippincott—Raven Publishers
http://www.lrpub.com
Specialists in nursing, allied health, and medical publications. One of the largest health science publishers in the world. Recently purchased the American Journal of Nursing Company (AJN).

Login Brothers Book Company
http://www.lb.com
"One of the largest distributors of medical, nursing, and allied health books, and electronic products in North America."

Majors Medical, Scientific, Technical, Business, and Law Book Distributor
http://www.majors.com
"One of the oldest medical book distributors in the U.S." See their listing of medical bookstores and libraries at *http://www.majors.com/whrmed.html*

Medical Libraries on the WWW
http://msl-www.tamu.edu/msl/otherml.htm

MedWeb: Biomedical Internet Resources
http://www.cc.emory.edu/WHSCL/medweb.html
    Search this large list by country, keyword, or region.

Merck and Co., Inc.
http://www.merck.com
    Search the Merck Manual free of charge.

Mosby
http://www.mosby.com/Mosby/index.html
    "World's leading publisher of books, journals, and serial publications in
    the health sciences—medicine, nursing, allied health sciences, dentistry,
    veterinary medicine—and selected collection disciplines—health, physi-
    cal education, nutrition, and chemistry."

National Library of Medicine (U.S.)
http://www.nlm.nih.gov
    Let HyperDOC take you by the hand and lead you through a myriad of
    medical publications and databases. Check out their Preservation and
    Collection Management sections, or search Internet Grateful Med for a
    modest fee.

New England Journal of Medicine Online
http://www.nejm.org/scripts/surveyproc.cgi

OSA OpticsNet (Optical Society of America)
http://www.osa.org

Readmore Collection of Top Medical Publishers
http://www.readmore.com/medserv/pubmed.html
    When completed, this will be the most extensive searchable medical pub-
    lisher listing on the Web.

Rittenhouse Book Distributors
http://www.rittenhouse.com
    The *Rittenhouse Quarterly Report* is now available on the Web.

Thieme Medical and Scientific Publishers
http://www.thieme.com/index.htm
    "Major publishing force throughout Europe and the market leader of
    publishing companies in Germany." Publisher of books, journals, and elec-
    tronic products.

U.S. Pharmacopeia
http://www.usp.org
  Publishers of the *USP Quality Review*.

1.2.3.6 Music Publishers and Sources

Aardvark's Archive of Musical Styles
http://www.stl-music.com/genre.shtml
> Links to every imaginable style of music, from alternative rock, to barbershop quartet, blues, ginza (from Japan), Celtic Christian, country, flamenco, hiphop, new age, reggae, samba, and ska.

Africasette Music
http://www.africassette.com/~rsteiger/index.html
> African and world music available on CD, cassette, and video.

Allegro's On Ramp to the Information Super Highway
http://graffiti.cribx1.u-bordeaux.fr:80/PRESENT/MUSIC/ALLEGRO/allego.html
> "Largest independent distributor of classical music in America" as well as jazz, blues, new age, country, bluegrass, world music, and more. Also hear sound bytes.

All-Music Guide (AMG)—A Complete Online Database of Recorded Music
http://205.186.189.2/amg/music_Root.html
> Search by artist name, album title, music type (rock and roll, blues, cajun/zydeco, rap) and then by decade. Browse the Hypertext Music News, a list of new releases and a music glossary, or add new artists and albums to the list.

BMG Classics World
http://www.classicalmus.com
> Very colorful site, with links to performers, composers, "Nipper's Newest" (Nipper appears to be the famous puppy gazing into the Victrola horn of RCA Victor fame), Broadway, live appearances, and opera synopses (in English, German, French, and Italian).

Commercial World of Music
http://www.music.indiana.edu/music_resources/industry.html
> Extensive directories available.

Compact Disc Connection
http://www.cdconnection.com
> Search and order online from the largest distributor of new compact discs. They offer "more than 150,000 imports, domestic releases, and hard to find compact discs." Also, 135,000 ratings and reviews are offered.

European American Music Distributors Corporation
http://www.eamdc.com/Welcome.html
> U.S. representative for a variety of international classical music publishers.

G. Schirmer Inc./Associated Music Publishers Inc.
http://www.schirmer.com
> Receive weekly listing of updates via e-mail. Site contains permission request forms to copy out-of-print music or to quote music in a book, journal, or dissertation. Specialties are popular and classical sheet music. Schirmer also publishes rock and pop books through their Omnibus Press.

Harrassowitz Score Approval Plan Profile
http://www.lib.duke.edu/intop/casst/harrassm.html
> Very interesting list of contemporary composers included on the plan.

Indie Centre: an Independent label information site—
http://www.csd.net/~muji/indicentre.html

International Lyrics Server
http://www.lyrics.ch
> Find lyrics to 50,000 songs.

Internet Music Shop
http://www.musicsales.co.uk
> Service of the Music Sales Group, "one of the world's largest publishers of sheet music, music books, new media and music software." Download such sheet music GIF samples as the "Ave Maria (Bach-Gounod)" for organ, the "Maple Leaf Rag," or "Liberty Bell" (the Monty Python theme song).

Jaymar Music Limited
http://www.jaymar.com
> "Classical music for serious musicians." Choose "send me the latest" and be notified via e-mail when relevant new publications are released or when the selection of Viewable Scores has been changed.

John Gibbs Home Page
http://weber.u.washington.edu/gibbs
> An absolutely incredible selection of links compiled by John Gibbs, Music Librarian, University of Washington.

Juilliard Book Store
http://www.bookstore.juilliard.edu

Legal Deposit of Music in Australia

http://www.nla.gov.au/nla/staffpaper/phaddad2.html

   By Peter Haddad for the Music Reference Group, July 1996.

Mammoth Music Meta-List

http://www.vibe.com/vibe/mmm/music.html

   You'll love this site. Search special artists, recording labels, or local specialized geographic areas. All genres are represented. For a good example,
   see the Little Russia in San Antonio, Texas Music Page at *http://
   mars.uthscsa.edu/Russia/Music*

Mario's Music Links

http://www.goldtech.com/musicpages

   I would estimate that thousands of music publishers are listed here.

Mel Bay Publications

http://www.melbay.com

   Playing and performance instruction and chord books since 1947. One
   freebie sheet music selection available for downloading each month. More
   than 25 million guitar books sold.

Music Selection Resources on the WWW

http://www.halcyon.com/aseaberg

   Anna Seaberg, King County Library System, provides a wonderful listing
   of tools to verify sound recordings, books, and scores, as well as other
   pertinent music resources.

Music Publisher's Association of the United States

http://www.mpa.org

   One hundred-year-old company. Browse their Directory of Music Publishers at *http://www.mpa.org//publist.html*.

Music Search: The Internet's Music Only Search Site

http://musicsearch.com

   Over 50,000 hits per day.

National Music Publisher's Association

http://www.nmpa.org/

   This 80-year-old company is "dedicated to the protection of music copy-
   right across all media and across all national boundaries." See quarterly
   issues of *News and Views* at *http://www.nmpa.org/nmpa/news.html* and
   search the HFA SongList.

Norris-Whitney Communications

http://www.vaxxine.com/nwc

Specializes in book and journal publishing in the music and audio fields. Browse Music Books Plus and Bestsellers List.

NPR (National Public Radio) Transcripts, Tapes, and More
http://www.npr.org

Pepper Music Network
http://www.jwpepper.com
"Your Internet server for printed music of all publishers." Large and varied site offering sheet music and several hundred sound clips.

Rough Guides to Music
http://www.roughguides.com/RG_WWW/rgmusic.html
Contribute to an annotated illustrated directory of over 1,100 rock bands. Written by fans, but still a very worthwhile site to explore.

Sunhawk Corporation
http://www.sunhawk.com
Digital sheet music.

University Music Editions
http://chelsea.ios.com/~johnp3/ume/index.html
Over 220,000 pages of music scores in their catalog, published in a microfiche format in binders with eye-readable contents guides.

World Music Distribution Inc.
http://worldmusic.com
"The latest and greatest international music, sound samples, artist information, CD covers, exciting links, and more!"

World Music Recordings: Sources and Selection Tools
http://www.halcyon.com/aseaberg/worldbib.html

Worldwide Internet Music Resources
http://www.music.indiana.edu/music_resources
Fabulous list compiled by the William and Gayle Cook Music Library, Indiana University. You absolutely cannot beat this site for maximum music information. Be prepared to linger.

Yahoo! Music
http://www.yahoo.com/Entertainment/Music

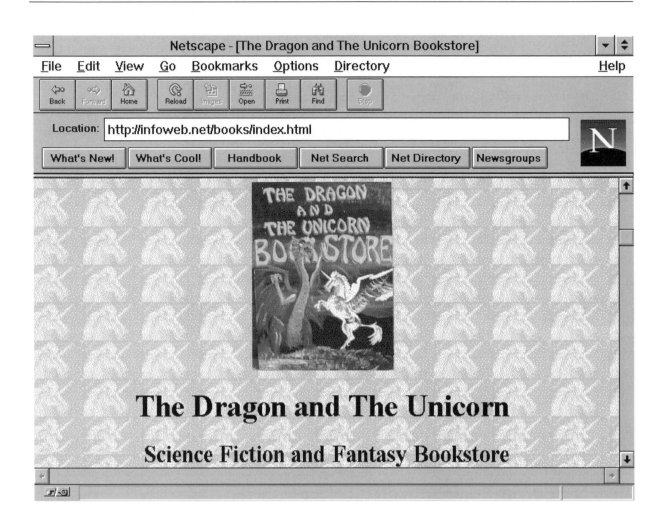

Figure 1.8
Dragon and the Unicorn Book Store

1.2.3.7 Science Fiction, Fantasy, Mystery, and Horror Publishers and Sources

Adventures in Crime and Space Bookstore
http://www.eden.com/~acs

Baen Books
http://www.baen.com
  Great, colorful fantasy and science fiction site. Read preview chapters.

Basement Full of Books
http://www.sff.net/bfob
  Cool site created by Vonda McIntyre, so the majority of titles are science fiction and fantasy authors. Books are available directly from their authors, and there's no charge to authors or readers for a listing. What a great opportunity to obtain both out-of-print books and autographed copies inexpensively.

Bloody Dagger Books
http://home.earthlink.net/~bloodydagger/index.html

Booked for Murder Ltd., the Mystery Reader's Paradise
http://www.infohiway.com/way/booked

Circlet Press—Erotic Science Fiction and Fantasy
http://www.apocalypse.org/circlet/home.html

Dangerous Visions Bookstore
http://www.readsf.com/index_im.html
  Turn on frames or leave them off. Browsing is fun in this "new, used, and out-of-print science fiction, fantasy, and horror" bookstore.

Dark Echo's Horror Web
http://www.darkecho.com
  "For those who seek the darker side of fiction…" Links to over 100 horror writers and much more. Have you guessed that the background color is black?

Del Rey Books: Science Fiction and Fantasy
http://www.randomhouse.com/delrey
  Check out the generous sample chapters and the FAQ files. Complete archives of the *Del Rey Internet Newsletter* (February 1993–present).

Dragon and the Unicorn Book Store
http://infoweb.net/books/index.html

Science fiction and fantasy bookstore with 10,000 new and used titles.

Feminist Science Fiction, Fantasy, and Utopia
http://www.uic.edu/~lauramd/femsf

Future Fantasy Bookstore
http://futfan.com
Lavishly illustrated, lots of information.

Ideology and Utopia: Better Worlds in Speculative Fiction—
http://www.changesurfer.com/Acad/SFBib.html

Janus Books, Ltd.
http://janusbooks.com
"Detective, mystery, suspense fiction . . . Sherlockiana."

Mysterious Home Page
http://users.aol.com/bchrcon97/mysteris.htm
Compilation of books, lists, home pages, awards, etc. You name it, they've got it. Links to such newsgroups as alt.books.nancy-drew and accompanying FAQ or the Lovejoy Mystery Page compiled by Jan Steffensen of Aalborg, Denmark.

Mystery Books On-Line
http://www.Killerbooks.com
"It's a killer idea for a bookstore." Over 18,000 mysteries in stock. They also offer signed first editions, Crime and Nourishment Gift Baskets, and novelty items like a gloss black Maltese Falcon.

Necro Publications
http://members.aol.com/necrodave/necro.html
"Publishers of hardcore horror."

Other Change of Hobbit—A Science Fiction and Fantasy Bookstore
http://www.dnai.com/~ochobbit
Hope they never change their introductory graphic. It's a fabulous drawing of a black cat perched on a stack of books gazing through a window at an alien world and at an interesting cat in a spacesuit looking back at her!

Pandora's Books Ltd.
http://portal.mbnet.mb.ca/pandora
"Mail-order-only bookstore, which has specialized in out-of-print science fiction, fantasy, horror, and mystery books since 1973."

SFF Net (Science Fiction and Fantasy)
http://www.sff.net/sff/index.htp

Tor Science Fiction and Fantasy
http://www.tor.com
New York-based publisher committed to science fiction and fantasy literature. "We annually publish what is arguably the most diverse line of science fiction and fantasy ever produced by a single English-language publisher." Sample chapters available.

Yahoo Business and Economy: Companies: Science Fiction, Fantasy, Horror
http://www.yahoo.com/Business/Corporations/Books/Science_Fiction_Fantasy_Horror

1.2.4 ONLINE DIGITAL PUBLISHERS

The World Wide Web is drastically transforming the older, established forms of publishing, especially the process of journal publications. Current trends indicate that, although print copies of journals are still strong, rising paper and vendor costs are forcing many libraries to either cancel their print subscriptions or resort to shared ownership via a consortium of libraries. There is a foreseeable time when paper publishing will diminish, and libraries will purchase access rights to the entire database of a journal publication, instead of maintaining a current paper collection and archival copies. If this thought depresses you, just keep in mind that books and serials did NOT disappear when radio, film, and video came along. They also will not disappear because online publishing and downloading are on the scene. Today's students and the public require full-text information online to facilitate research without having to access and then store a physical object. Many of us work in libraries that are physically bursting at the seams. Digital publishing is one very important method we have to preserve materials for the future. New technologies allow you to choose the font size, color, etc. of the digital book you are reading, as well as accessing beautiful color illustrations.

Alix of Dreams
http://www.primenet.com/~ciaran
> A beautifully illustrated novel by B. Clifford Shockey available free on the Web. Don't pass up this opportunity. Voted "Sublime Site of the Week," among other accolades.

Amebis d.o.o. Slovenian Online Publisher
http://www.amebis.si

Anamnesis Press
http://ourworld.compuserve.com/homepages/Anamnesis
> "Small but cutting-edge electronic publishing company devoted to the preservation of poetry and literary nonfiction on the electronic frontier. We use state-of-the-art electronic publishing techniques to produce hypermedia books on disk for the Windows and MS-DOS environment." They also produce virtual HTML books.

Arachnoid Writer's Alliance: Books Online
http://www.vena.com/arachnoid
> "A collection of books for sale by independent and self-published authors."

Automated Pen
http://users.quake.net/~autopen/autopen.htm
> Mystery, fantasy, and romance online.

B and R Samizdat Express
http://www.samizdat.com
> Don't miss the fantastic *Internet-on-a-Disk*, a monthly free newsletter listing electronic texts and Internet trends.

Bartleby Project (Columbia University, New York)
http://www.columbia.edu/acis/bartleby
> Offers free public access to public domain materials.

BiblioBytes
http://www.bb.com
> Purchase books online utilizing ICE—the Internet Creditcard Encryptor.

Bibliomania Classic Fiction Library
http://www.bibliomania.com/Fiction

Books On-Line: Authors
http://www.cs.cmu.edu/Web/bookauthors.html
> Browse by first letter of author's last name to find texts available online.

Boson Books
http://www.cmonline.com/boson
> "A good book in 10 minutes." Download your favorite title. A section of Serialized Novels offers a free chapter of a novel every two months.

Dial-A-Book
http://dab.psi.net/dialabook
> Offers complete books for download delivery to your hard disk. Browse first chapters of many titles.

Digital Books
http://www.digitalbooks.com
> Fiction, nonfiction, technical, and hypermedia books.

Digital BookWorld
http://www.digitalbookworld.com
> It's new, it's colorful, and it's extensive.

Electronic Book Aisle
http://www.bookaisle.com
> Pay-per-view—by the page, by the recipe, etc.

Electronic Journals for Latino/as
http://scuish.scu.edu/SCU/Programs/Diversity/ejlatin.html
> Links to English, Portuguese, and Spanish e-journals concerning both the Latino/a community in the U.S. and Latin Americans in general.

Electronic Paperless Publishing
http://www.awa.com/nomad/intro.html

Electronic Texts and Publishing Resources
http://lcweb.loc.gov/global/etext
   A Library of Congress Internet resource page. Especially useful when searching for home pages relating to single authors.

Enchanted E-Books
http://205.230.201.36
   Free samples, bookmarking, "enchanting" demo available.

Etext Archives
http://www.etext.org
   "From the sacred to the profane, from the political to the personal."

Grolier Electronic Publishing Online
http://www.grolier.com
   Download Shockwave and enjoy this interactive site.

Macmillan Computer Publishing Online Books
http://www.mcp.com/3316680954417/mcp/online_books
   Fifty online books available.

Mind's Eye Fiction
http://www.infohaus.com/access/by-seller/Minds_Eye_Fiction
   "A new concept in reading short stories on the Web. Try a story. If you like it, buy it." How does this work? Take, for example, the Martian fantasy *All the Angles* by Jack Nimersheim. Read the first 3,135 words free; the ending 2,343 words are $1.00.

OmniMedia Electronic Books
http://www.awa.com/library/omnimedia
   All titles are formatted specifically for Windows 3.1 and Windows 95 systems. Some have full-text search capability. Each page also offers the ability to request a sample copy.

Online Bookfair—Frankfurt Book Fair Homepage
http://www.online-bookfair.com
   Links to more than 8,000 publishers from 100 countries exhibiting.

Open Book Systems (OBS)
http://www.obs-us.com
   Previously the Online Book Store, this site offers online books and facilitates "online distributive publishing thinking" in four languages.

Project Gutenberg's Archive
http://uiarchive.cso.uiuc.edu/pub/etext/gutenberg

YOU, the dedicated reader/librarian have input the titles. Support this noble effort, fellow librarians. The history and philosophy of Project Gutenberg is available at *http://chaos.mur.csu.edu.au/itc125/pub/history.html*

Virtual Bookshelf
http://www.islandmm.com/islandmm/cgi-bin/sitemshomepg.pl? from home page=yes

Register your own bookshelf, which saves the books you add, and re-members your stopping place and any other customized settings in the books you read here.

Yahoo! Electronic Publishing
http://www.yahoo.com/Business_and_Economy/Companies/Publishing/Electronic_Publishing

1.2.5 OUT-OF-PRINT, RARE BOOKS, AND BACK ISSUE VENDORS

Here's a large section especially for bibliophiles. Many collections have gaps—caused by issues becoming lost in the mail, vendor mix-ups, theft, or a severe financial crunch that causes you to cancel periodical subscriptions after long and glorious complete runs. Financial gifts are frequently assigned to collecting those rare or out-of-print materials that will augment and enhance our collections. There are many out-of-print dealers who will search your "want list" free of charge, and other dealers who will offer "remaindered" materials at 85–90 percent discount. These home pages are well worth a browse.

Abracadabra Booksearch International
http://www.abrabks.com
> "We offer an intensive international booksearch and specialize in completing collections . . . We are able to locate approximately 65 percent of all titles searched."

Advanced Book Exchange
http://www.abebooks.com
> "The Internet's most popular service for buying and selling out-of-print, used, rare, and antiquarian books." Create a free account for yourself and save up to 100 items you desire on it. Or download version 1.1 of HomeBase, a bookstore inventory and client management system for PCs and Macs.

Alfred Jaeger, Inc.
http://www.ajaeger.com
> Back volume vendor offering an inventory of over 40,000 titles and access to a vendor network to locate out-of-print titles at wholesale prices.

Antiquarian Book Network
http://www.antiquarian.com
> Use their search engine, the Antiquarian BookWorm. Geared towards dealers and collectors.

Antiquarian Booksellers Association of America Book Net (ABAA)
http://www.abaa-booknet.com
> Specialties are rare books, maps, and prints. Also provides extensive book fair information. More than 200 book dealers are available online, accessible by U.S. regions. Searches also available by subject, by geographical state map, or by two-letter state abbreviations.

Bibliocity
http://www.bibliocity.com
> "Most excellent rare and collectable books on behalf of merchants of

distinction with a most sophisticated engine of discovery and instantaneous ordering by electronic post . . . handling of wants by a fully automatic mechanism."

BiblioFind
http://www.bibliofind.com
   Search out-of-print titles in English, French, German, Italian, or Japanese.

BookDotOrg, Inc.
http://www.book.org
   Nonprofit organization that allows students to trade used textbooks.

Books Out of Print (Reed Reference Publishing)
http://www.reedref.com/boop.html
   Internet edition, free to anyone requesting a password.

Bookshelf (Bibliophile Mailing List)
http://www.auldbooks.com/biblio/index.html
   "Maintained for the benefit of sellers and/or collectors of rare, out-of-print, scarce books in all subject areas." Browse their annotated list of book sellers and collectors (you can add your name and special interest here). Dont miss Identifying a First Edition at *http://www.auldbooks.com/biblio/other/forum/firsts.html*

C.I.R.T.—International Center for Retrieval of New, Ancient and Rare Books
http://italia.hum.utah.edu/gruppo/volta/cirt.html
   Ancient texts and manuscripts searched at no cost since 1950.

DEU-L Duplicate Exchange Union List
http://Niord.shsu.edu:70/1gopher_root%3a%bIDxSEL.DEV%5d
   List and archives of the ALA/ALCTS Duplicates Exchange Union.

Euroback Courier electronique
http://www.obspm.fr/cgi-bin/f-mail to/EUROPACK@UM1.vlg.ac.be/subject
   Archives for French language listserver concerned with the exchange of monograph and serial back issues among European libraries.

Fine Press Bookshop Online
http://www.tdigital.com/finepress/
   Shop for limited and private press items from hundreds of publishers.

International League of Antiquarian Booksellers
http://www.clark.net/pub/rmharris/ilab/english.html
   This page (in both French and English) has addresses of antiquarian booksellers, colorful country flags, and seals. Descriptions also mention which bookseller association each member belongs to.

Powell's Technical Books
http://www.technical.powells.portland.or.us
   Out-of-print science book dealer.

Pulpless.com
http://www.pulpless.com
   Treat yourself to pulpless fiction or nonfiction, or even download the
   Pulplettes singing their radio jingle.

Quick BookStop
http://www.quickbookstop.com
   Stop in and read everything in the Slush Stop. Then vote. Votes will be
   tallied, and if there are enough, then the book will be published.

Rare Books and Special Collection Links
http://aultnis.rutgers.edu/pgrbms.html
   This is a superb collection of links compiled by Peter Graham, of interest
   to the rare books acquirer/cataloger/conservationist.

RSB Rare and Secondhand Books
http://www.rsb.ch
   Free for customers. Booksellers pay ten percent of the selling price to
   RSB.

Setmaker
http://www2.gol.com/users/steve/f_books.htm
   "Odd volumes and incomplete sets—reunited at last." Free online public
   service.

Special Collections Resources on the Web
http://info.lib.uh.edu/specoweb.html

Verband Deutscher Antiquare E.V.
http://www.antiquare.de
"Die vereinigung von buchantiquaren, autographen—und graphikhandlern."

Virtual Bookshop
http://www.virtualbookshop.com
   "Specializing in rare, first edition, antiquarian, collectible, and fine books."

World Wide Wessex
Menlo Park, California
http://www.wessex.books.com
   First edition books, searchable by author. Also of great use is their links
   to 150+ author web pages.
   http://www.wessexbooks.com/authors.htm

1.3

Other Useful Internet Sources for Acquisitions

Communications ranging from late-breaking news affecting acquisitions work to rants about discount schedules can be found on the Internet. This section covers everything from acquisitions listservs to Web pages dedicated to postal rates. This may, in fact, be the part of this *Directory* you enter into your bookmark file first!

1.3.1 E-JOURNALS, LISTS, LISTSERVS, AND NEWSLETTERS

Acquisitions staff needs to keep current, as well as communicate with their colleagues about changes. Discussion lists such as SERIALST and ACQNET can be lifesavers when it comes to discussing an absolutely meaningless title change, or in claiming , or obtaining back issues of an esoteric title. More discussion lists are devoted to serials acquisitions, since serials differ considerably from monographs acquisitions, and are generally more confusing and time consuming. See this section to learn how to benefit from others' experiences and to save time.

ACQNET
The Acquisitions Electronic Network
http://www.library.vanderbilt.edu/law/acqs/acqnet.html
> Premier acquisitions-related managed list founded in 1990. "Aims to provide a medium for acquisitions librarians and others interested in acquisitions work to exchange information, ideas, and to find solutions to common problems." Keyword search ACQNET archives from 1991 to the present at *http://www.lib.ncsu.edu/stacks/a/acqnet*

Acquisitions Librarian
http://caroline.eastlib.vfl.edu/libsu/acqlib.html
> Check out most current tables of contents.

Against the Grain Electronic: "Linking Publishers, Vendors, and Librarians"
http://www.against-the-grain.com
> Published in paper format five times yearly. The Web site contains the complete 1995 and 1996 Tables of Contents and a listing of some Memorable Articles, Interviews, and Profiles.

BIC—EDI Discussion Group
http://www.bic.org.uk/bic/bicedi.html
> Join the list of the Book Industry Communication (BIC) group discussing Electronic Data Interchange (EDI).

BLAB, the Biomedical Library Acquisitions Bulletin
University of Southern California—Norris Medical Library
http://www.ghsl.nwu.edu/BLAB/BLAB_home.html
> BLAB is "a more or less monthly electronic newsletter covering selection and acquisition of materials in biomedical libraries." Items for the *Bulletin* are sent in by subscribers, and issues are available from January 25, 1995 to the present.

Book-Arts-L Archives

http://palimpsest.stanford.edu/Architext/AT-bookartsquery.html
Archives available from 1994 to the present for this unmoderated list of bookbinders, book artists, marblers, paper makers, printers, collectors, and curators.

Citations for Serial Literature

http://www.readmore.com/info/csl.html
"An electronic index which publishes the tables of contents, when available, for articles related to the serials information chain." Archives available from December 13, 1992 to the present.

Collection Management

http://bubl.ac.uk/journals/lis/ae/colman/index.html
Tables of contents from 1993 to the present.

Conservation DistList Archives

http://palimpsest.stanford.edu/byform/mailing-lists/cdl
Archives for all postings since 1988, as well as complete issues of the *DistList Newsletter*. Browse by year.

DOCDEL-L

http://www.ebscodoc.com/html/docdel-l.htm
EBSCO's Listserv, created "to promote discussion on the world of document delivery."

Exlibris—Rare Books List

http://palimpsest.stanford.edu/byform/mailing-lists/exlibris
"An electronic news and discussion group for those interested in rare books and special collections." Unmoderated. Individual messages available in monthly logs from April 1991.

GIFTEX-L

http://www.uvm.edu/~bmaclenn/backexch.html
Subscription information for this list which is devoted to gifts and exchange librarians. This list discusses theory and is not used for actual exchanges.

Library Acquisitions: Practice and Theory

http://bubl.ac.uk/journals/lis/kn/lapat/index.html
Tables of contents from 1992 to the present.

lis—acq

http://www.mailbase.ac.uk/lists-k-o/lis-acq
U.K. list for serials discussions.

lis-medjournal-duplicates

www.mailbase.ac.uk/lists-K-o/lis-medjournal-duplicates
"To facilitate journal exchange between U.K. medical libraries, by allowing librarians to post lists of journal duplicates and wants."

Needs and Offers-L

http://ftplaw.wuacc.edu/listproc/needsandoffers-l
Legal materials exchange list archived by thread.

New Law Books–L

http://ftplaw.wuacc.edu/listproc/newlawbooks-l

Newsletter on Serials Pricing Issues

http://sunsite.unc.edu/reference/prices/prices.html Editor, Marcia Tuttle.
Complete archives available from 1989 to the present.

SERIALST

Serials in Libraries Discussion Forum
http://www.uvm.edu/~bmaclenn/serialst.html
Moderated list. Since 1990 "an informal electronic forum for most aspects of serials processing in libraries. Appropriate topics include . . . acquisitions, collection management, serials budgets and pricing concerns, binding, preservation, microfilm, and other nonprint serials media." More than 2400 subscribers in 36 countries. Searchable archives available at *http://list.uvm.edu/archives/serialst.html*

VPIEJ-L Archives

http://borg.lib.vt.edu/ejournals/vpiej-l/vpiej-l.resource.html
"Discussion list for electronic publishing issues, especially those related to scholarly electronic journals." Searchable archive available. Usenet newsgroup available at *news:bit.listserv.vpiej-l*

1.3.2 NON-LIBRARY WEB SOURCES THAT SAVE ACQUISITIONS TIME AND MONEY

Finally, I'm sure you'll be interested in the latest developments in the Currency Rates section and the Addresses, Postal Information, and Telecommunications section. These home pages will simplify your life by allowing you to track packages, verify incomplete addresses, and find area-codes, toll-free numbers and nine-digit zip codes in a minimal amount of time. Time is money, or so they say, and hopefully these home pages will save you and your library both time AND money.

1.3.2.1 Addresses, Postal, and Telecommunications Information

555-1212.com's FastArea Code Look-Up for the U.S and Canada
http://www.555-1212.com/aclookup.html
> Easy as pie. There's an area code list by number (New Jersey is first with 201; Dallas, last with 972) or you can look up area codes by sState or province.

AmeriCom Long Distance Area Decoder: An Area/City/Country Code Lookup Service
http://www.inconnect.com/~americom/home.html
> I love their disclaimer: "Don't worry about spelling accuracy. The DECODER will usually know what you mean."

AT&T Toll-Free Internet Directory
http://www.tollfree.att.net
> Search by category (I chose libraries) and get a list of approximately 50 toll-free library service numbers (like the City of Austin Library Department Inter-Library Loan). Choosing Publishers is even better—there's a zillion of them.

Big Yellow: Your Yellow Pages on the Web
http://s6.bigyellow.com
> Over 16 million U.S. businesses listed. Links to a white pages search (Four11), an e-mail search, or search around the world with Big Yellow Global.

Canadian Postal Code Lookup
http://www.mailposte.ca/english/pclookup/pclookup.html
> French and English.

FedEx

http://www.fedex.com

Download free FedEx Tracking and Shipping Software to verify a package online, track it wherever it is headed, and print bar-coded shipping labels on plain paper using your laser printer. "One of FedEx–Ship's useful new features is FedEx e-forms, e-mail templates which allow the customer to send shipment information to the recipient by indicating shipment date, type of service, method of payment, and tracking number." Check out What the Postal Service Doesn't Tell You.

Foreign Postal Services

http://www.philately.com/transportation/postal_codes.htm

Find out about Australian postal codes, Swiss telecom, the Lithuania postal service, and more.

Four11.com

http://411.com

Internet white pages directory. "The most comprehensive and impressive people finder on the Net." Sign up for your free listing.

National Address Server

http://www.cedar.buffalo.edu/adserv.html

Enter an address. It will be rewritten in proper format, including the zip+4 code. Successful addresses can retrieve a Postscript or GIF file for printing with a bar code. Street maps are also available.

United States Postal Service

http://www.usps.gov

Choose from four local USPS home pages—the Atlanta, Georgia District, the Denver, Colorado Postal Business Center, Gainesville, Florida, or the Washington, D.C. Post Office. *Postal News* contains some interesting articles concerning parcel reform. View beautifully illustrated Stamps Online. Find out about modified marking standards for mail processed under classification reform. Track express mail or use the postage calculator.

UPS Package Tracking

http://www.ups.com/tracking/tracking.html

Fill in your tracking number (no dashes or spaces) and click. See the Guide to UPS Services. The UPS Quick Cost Calculator (available for downloading) helps estimate charges for U.S. shipments. Also of interest is the Guidelines for Good Packaging.

Zipcode Lookup and Address Information from the U.S. Postal Service

http://www.usps.gov/ncsc

Just fill in a company name, city, and state, and they will provide a nine-digit zip code and include the county. Also has list of state suffixes and abbreviations (Alley is abbreviated ALY). Check the online most-wanted posters while you're here.

1.3.2.2 Currency Rates

Choose a Currency: Foreign Exchange Rates

http://www.dna.lth.se/cgi-bin/kurt/rates/foreign/websvcs.html

Choose a currency, then choose a second currency to compare with your first choice. Rates are provided by the Federal Reserve Bank of New York and are updated at the end of each working day. See Frequently Asked Questions about On-Line Currency Rates at *http://www.dna.lth.se/home/kurt/currency-faq.html* for more details.

Global Network Navigator/Koblas Currency Converter

http://www.sinica.edu.tw/mirror/econwpa.wustl.edu/other_www/EconFAQ/node47.html

Created by David Koblas.

Lists the most number of currencies. Bi-weekly updates.

Olsen and Associates Currency Convertor

http://www.olsen.ch/cgi-bin/exmenu

164 currencies; changed daily.

Universal Currency Converter

http://www.xe.net/currency

Great Canadian site. The Interactive Currency Table has a form which says "Show me a currency table in units of ____." Choose a currency, and it will compare it with all other currencies on one page.

PART II

WEB PAGES OF SPECIAL
USE FOR CATALOGERS

OVERVIEW

Today's catalogers are at a crossroad—attached to the past through a long history of providing access to library materials via card catalogs and online library systems—and linked inexorably to the future, with the advent of the World Wide Web, graphical user interfaces to other library's OPACs, and the ever increasing quantity of e-journals, full-text databases, and multimedia materials to be cataloged. Choosing the past is no longer an option because of dwindling funds, rising materials costs, and the necessity of sharing resources. Choosing the future (cataloging Internet resources, restructuring of traditional departments, mastering and manipulating new computer applications) is the only path we can choose to ensure our continued survival in this rapidly changing field.

A primary motivation in writing this guide is to demonstrate to technical services librarians in general, and to catalogers in particular, what home pages have already been created, what documentation already exists online that may be useful to your library, and what ideas are being discussed by colleagues around the world. The World Wide Web has opened the door of global communication and sharing. Do not be afraid to discover all the potential benefits awaiting you. It is now within each cataloger's grasp to be at the cutting-edge of their profession. We must embrace new technologies and new methods of doing things, while at the same time, maintaining our tradition of total service to our patrons. In this guide you will see what a magnificent array of cataloging-related sites are available to you right now via the World Wide Web.

2.1

Cataloging In General

Many libraries, small and large, have opted to create a cataloging home page for their libraries. Very small libraries might be content to simply list departmental staff, with a description of their responsibilites, and perhaps a link to their e-mail addresses. Medium-sized libraries that do not want to maintain their documentation online, might opt to list links that are of use to their own particular department. Larger libraries will probably want to have all of their documentation online, complete with hypertext links. A decision to keep some documents for inhouse use only is certainly an option that some of these sites have employed. However, the sites that have decided to put all of their procedures online are performing a real service to the cataloging community. Annual reviews, contracts with vendors, conference reports, and papers written by department staff are just some of the many wonderful ideas contained within the *Cataloging in General* section. By exploring these pages, a cataloger could find specific information on cataloging backlogs, discover a rotated index to the Library of Congress Rule Interpretations, or even browse the largest online catalogs in the world.

ALA /ALCTS Committee Documentation
http://www.pitt.edu/~agtaylor/ala/alac.htm
  Documents relate to subject analysis and form/genre.

Auburn University Libraries Cataloging Department
Auburn, Alabama
http://www.lib.auburn.edu/catalog
  Contains sections on Research Projects from Cataloging Department
  Personnel, a Pre-Processing Procedure Manual, and a Cataloging De-
  partment FAQ (Frequently Asked Questions). Click on a dot to answer
  "What is cataloging?" "What are call numbers?" (Although simplistic, this
  may be useful to cataloging neophytes.)

Auraria Library Cataloging Services Home Page
administered by Colorado University, Denver, Colorado
http://www.cudenver.edu/public/library/cataloging/cataloging.html
  Take a look at their Cataloging Procedures Manual.

Bibliographic Enrichment Advisory Team (BEAT) Annual Report
http://lcweb.loc.gov/catdir/beat
  Library of Congress group that develops tools to aid catalogers in locat-
  ing and creating information, and to enrich LC bibliographic record content. This page details Table of Contents Projects, Enhanced Library of
  Congress Subject Headings, Machine-Readable Classification Schedules,
  Text Capture and Electronic Conversion Initiatives, ClipSearch, and more.

**Bibliotheconomie et Sciences d l'Information : Traitement
Documentaire**
Services Documentaires Multimedia Inc., Quebec, Canada
http://www.cam.org/~sdm/xbitd.html
  Good listing of cataloging resources, classification and indexing sites, and
  electronic document cataloging.

Bibliotheque Nationale de France Cataloguing Page
http://www.bnf.fr/institution/anglais/catalgb.htm
  Discusses the historical aspects of French cataloging, from the seven-
  teenth century treatise Advis Pour Dresser une Bibliotheque to cataloging computerization in the 1970s and 1980s, to the situation today. Also
  discusses the French Union Catalog.

British Library National Bibliographic Service (NBS)
http://icarus.bl.uk/nbs
  "NBS provides online access to over 17 million bibliographic records in
  22 databases...The BLAISE-LINE databases include catalogues of British Library collections, the Library of Congress Catalogue and other major

bibliographic files." The *British National Bibliography* is available on three CD-ROMs. The Catalogue Bridge contains retrospective catalog conversion information as well as many other services.

Cabrillo College Basic Procedures for Copy Cataloging and Processing in Innopac
Aptos, California
http://libwww.cabrillo.cc.ca.us/html/techserv/tsprocedures.html

CASST, Cataloging and Searching Support Team, Duke University Libraries
Durham, North Carolina
http://www.lib.duke.edu/intop/casst

Although the Pre-Cataloging Team Page was not accessible, the Bibliographic Searching Team Homepage was quite interesting. Links to the BIP Availability Page, which describes all possible BIP's in print, and describes which titles to search, based on the language and year of publication date. Also links to the 100 Subdivisions of Dewey Decimal, a Most Frequently Used Language and Country of Publication Codes page, and the Student Welcome to CATSS Page, which provides procedural and administrative details for new student assistants.

Cataloging
St. Norbert College, De Pere, Wisconsin
http://www.snc.edu/library/cat.htm

Cataloging Documentation on the Web
University of Oregon
http://libweb.uoregon.edu/~catdept/tools/catdoc.html

Geared toward supporting the staff at the University of Oregon's Knight Library, this page divides resources into descriptive cataloging, subject cataloging, MARC, OCLC, and LC resources. Browse through Publications of Interest to Catalogers, listen to a Quicktime Welcome video introduction, and absolutely do not miss issues of *Q.A. : Question Authority*, the Department newsletter. Read about the Gonzo Review, a talent show site with a photo of the 1812 Kazoo Overture on Kazoos. Or how about Zucchini Festival memories? These catalogers have that sought after quality—a good sense of humor.

Cataloging Oasis
Massachusetts Institute of Technology (MIT) Libraries, Cambridge, Massachusetts
http://macfadden.mit.edu:9500/colserv/cat

Cataloging policies and procedures are keyword searchable. Local resources include Expansion Table Codes for the 949 Field, Standard Ab-

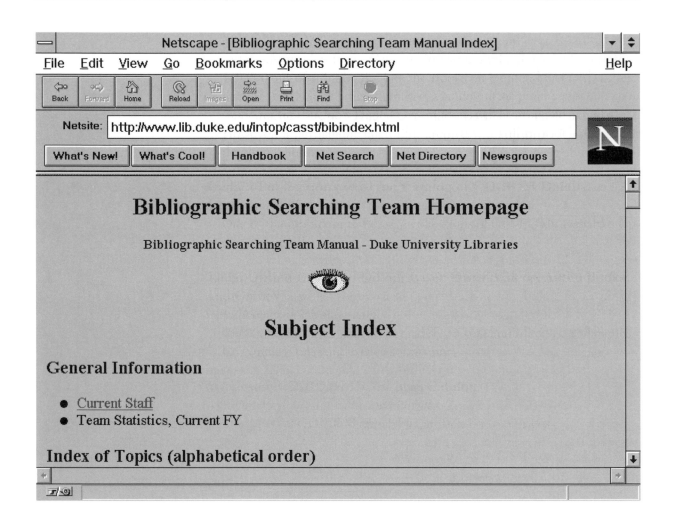

Figure 2.1
Duke Bibliographic Searching Team Homepage

breviations, Monographic Contributed Copy Guidelines, and a Passport for Windows Installation document. Country and language codes, cutters, OCLC, and MARC documentation abound. For a different viewpoint, look at MIT's Cataloging Barton Loader Team Page.

http://macfadden.mit.edu:9500/advance/team/cat.html
This team is responsible for loading bibliographic data from OCLC to Barton, their GEAC Advance Library System.

Cataloging Procedures
University of Nevada, Reno
http://www.library.unr.edu/~catalog/cathtml
　Discusses Government Document Call Numbers, Cataloging Electronic Resources, Cataloging Serials, and more.

Cataloging Resources
Indiana University Libraries, Bloomington, Indiana
http://www.indiana.edu:80/~librcsd/resource/library/cataloging
　"Arranged alphabetically, roughly." Search HYTELNET from this page and access the famous Cataloging Cheat Sheet. Originally written by J. McRee Elrod, and updated by Anna Kroll, this resource clearly defines correct MARC tag order, and what is contained in a typical monographic cataloging record. (Note: this predates format integration, so readers must look elsewhere for their 246, 538, or 856 fields.) All global changes are listed by month completed in Global Changes on IUCAT (updated weekly). Diacritics and Special Characters on OCLC and IUCAT is a useful comparative listing, as well as links to all OCLC Technical Bulletins.

Cataloging Tools
Clement C. Maxwell Library, Bridgewater State College, Bridgewater, Massachusetts
http://www.bridgew.edu/depts/Maxwell/cattools.htm

Cataloguer's Home Page, Al-Akhawayn University Library, Ifrane, Morocco
http://www.alakhawayn.ma/library/catalogr.htm
　Access Bibliographic Formats and Standards Online or look at the Descriptive and Subject Cataloging pages.

Cataloguer's Toolbox
Memorial University of Newfoundland, Queen Elizabeth II Library, St. John's, Newfoundland, Canada
http://www.mun.ca/library/cat
　Charley Pennell has created one of the finest, best-structured cataloging home pages around. The Departmental Policies and Procedures section

includes the highly recommended Field-by-Field View of MARC Policies and Procedures. The Shelflisting document "consists of an extremely condensed version of the Library of Congress's Subject Cataloging Manual: Shelflisting with alterations reflecting local practice." Division memos clarify analytic added entries and conference call numbers. Updated monthly statistics for 1996 are available. The Quick Reference Guide lists cataloging tools by format (computer files, maps, music, serials, etc.) or by subject (law, medicine). The quarterly Cumulated Library of Congress Weekly Subject Headings Lists begin with January-March 1995. Other sections of note are Local Tools, USMARC Documentation, and links to the National Library of Canada, OCLC, and the ISM Library Information Services (Information Systems Management Corp.). Finally, check out the Unicorn Toolkit: Tables, Guides, and Manuals for Use with Unicorn.

Cataloguing-In-Publication in the National Library of Australia
http://www.nla.gov.au/1/services/faq.html

Cataloguing Network in Pietermaritzburg (CATNIP) Annual Report of the University of Natal Library, South Africa
http://www.unp.ac.za/UNPDepartments/Library/catnann.htm

Cataloguing Policy Convergence Agreement
http://lcweb.loc.gov/catdir/pcc/converge.html
Details the cooperative relationship between the British Library and the Library of Congress.

Catpro: Cataloging Manual of the Resource Services Department, University of Florida Libraries
Gainesville, Florida
http://www.cis.ufl.edu/~sps/catpro.html
A new page with a substantial amount of documentation. Browse the Master Index for an idea of the great documents to come. Many items are already online. The Series section appears to be completed. Take a look at Minimal Level Cataloging Standards: Book Format, Quick Quick Cataloging, Series Policy for New Series, and Subject Headings/Call Numbers for UKM, Shared, DLC Enc Lvl 5, and DLC Enc Lvl 7 Records. Documents still to come include Processing Computer Files, Preservation Microforms Cataloging, and Caribbean Country Codes.

CIGS Archive: the Cataloguing and Indexing Scene in Scotland
http://www.almac.co.uk/business_park/slainte/slainte2/slainteg/2catani0/cigsarch/pascenei.html

Clemson University Libraries Catalog Unit Public Home Page
Clemson, South Carolina
http://www.lib.clemson.edu/cat/CatPage.html

Geared toward the general public. The Selected Glossary of Cataloging Terms is simply written, yet informative. The History of Cataloging at Clemson is enjoyable reading, and the Cataloging Statistics are potentially useful. Make sure to look at the Cataloging Language Resources on the Internet page, as well as the Pre-Processing Procedures Manual *http://www.lib.auburn.edu/catalog/pre-proc/toc.html*

COPAC
http://cs6400.mcc.ac.uk/copac

New online access to the largest university research libraries in Ireland and the U.K. Get online access to Oxford's Bodleian Library, Cambridge University, Edinburgh University, Glasgow University, and more. The database contains almost 4 million records and 5 million holdings statements.

Cornell University Library Technical Services Manual
Ithaca, New York
http://www.library.cornell.edu/tsmanual

Excellent example of a paper-based cataloging manual transformed into an electronic manual. Information is extensive. Highlights include large sections on cataloging electronic resources, format integration, Series Authority Record Document, and the Composition of RLIN and NOTIS Fixed Field Labels. CTS Procedures (*http://www.library.cornell.edu/CTS/ctsproc.htm*) discusses Collection-Level Cataloging, Treatment of OCLC Batch/Match Records, LC/NCCP Fast Cataloging, and much more.

CWRU University Library Bibliographic Services
Case Western Reserve University, Cleveland, Ohio
http://www.cwru.edu/CWRU/UL/cat.html

"To read is human, to catalogue divine." Good collection of links.

CWU Library Catalog Department Home Page
Central Washington University Library, Ellensburg, Washington
http://www.lib.cwu.edu/cat-dept

Simply done, but effective. Choose either a text-based or Web interface to access CATTRAX, their online catalog.

Eden-Webster Library Cataloging and Technical Services Departments
Webster Groves, Missouri
http://library.websteruniv.edu/cathome.html

Excellent selection of links.

ELEC-TECH: ELECtronic Documentation of Central TECHnical Services Cataloging Information
State University of New York at Buffalo
http://wings.buffalo.edu/libraries/units/cts/cat
Details the responsibilities of the Cataloging Maintenance Team, as well as providing an outstanding Authorities Section, a page especially for Cataloging Backlogs, and sections on Pamphlet and Paperback Bindings. The 1997 Bindery Shipment Due Date Schedule is excellent.

Exeter University Library, Library and Related Resources
Exeter, UK
http://www.ex.ac.uk/~ijtilsed/lib/wwwlibs.html
Excellent guide with a European focus, created by Ian Tilsed.

Florida International University Libraries Cataloging
University Park and North Miami, Florida
http://www.fiu.edu/~library/staff/catalog/cat1.html
New, clean looking page with a substantial selection of online documentation.

Format Integration Phase 2: Technical Bulletin #212
http://www.oclc.org/oclc/tb/tb212/toc.htm

Format Integration: the Final Phase
http://wings.buffalo.edu/publications/mcjrnl/v3n2/glennan.html
Articles by Kathryn P. Glennan. *MC Journal: The Journal of Academic Media Librarianship* v3#2, Fall 1995: 1–31.

Functional Requirements for Bibliographic Records
http://www.nlc-bnc.ca/ifla/VII/s13/frbr/frbr-toc.htm
Draft report for world-wide review. Recommended by the IFLA Study Group, May, 1996.

Georgetown University Lauinger Library Cataloging Department
Washington, D.C. Metropolitan Area
http://gulib.lausun.georgetown.edu/dept/catalog
Highlights include the Copy Cataloger's Manual, the Policy and Procedures Manual, statistics, and their beautiful illustrations.

Glossary of Cataloguing Terms
Griffith University Library, Brisbane, Australia
http://www.gu.edu.au/gwis/ins/library/glossary.html
Example entries include: AUSMARC—"The Australian standard format for the exchange of records (bibliographic and authority) in machine-readable form. Based on the original MARC." Or Moys Classification

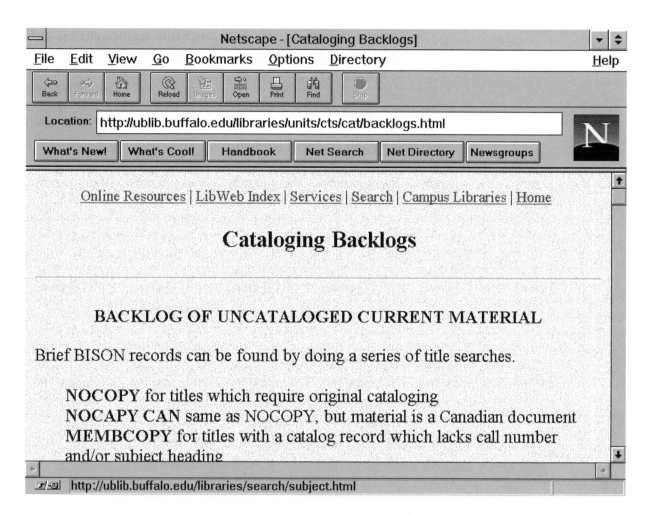

Figure 2.2
Cataloging Backlogs (ELEC-TECH)

Scheme—"a system for classifying legal material, based on jurisdictions whose legal systems are similar to English Common Law, and legal systems of all other modern jurisdictions."

Johns Hopkins University Milton S. Eisenhower Library Cataloging Department

Baltimore, Maryland

http://milton.mse.jhu.edu:8001/library/cat/hompg.html

Discusses organization, computer files, books, serials, videos, and other non-book cataloging.

Library of Congress Cataloging Directorate Home Page

Washington, D.C.

http://www.loc.gov/catdir/catdir.html

This page contains the most up-to-date links at the Library of Congress. See Modes of Cataloging Employed in the Cataloging Directorate for specific information outlining Full, Enhanced Collection Level Cataloging (CLC+), Collection Level Cataloging, and Minimal Level Cataloging. Then go directly to the five year Progress Report on Subject Subdivisions conference recommendations. The Program for Cooperative Cataloging's (*http://lcweb.loc.gov/catdir/pcc*) goals are to catalog quicker, more effectively, and to make records more widely available for sharing. This program has a name authority component (NACO), a subject authority component (SACO), a bibliographic component (BIBCO), and a serials component (CONSER). Their current focus is on simplifying descriptive cataloging and subject cataloging and to resolve name versus authority issues. Core level cataloging exceeds that of minimum cataloging but does not necessarily equal that of full-level cataloging. Through shared cataloging, the PCC has managed to increase name authority records submitted by 38.9 percent in three years, series authority records by 314 percent, and subject authority records by 288 percent. Browse the Books and Serials Section, or Videos and Other Non-book Cataloging. Also see their Accomplishments page. It's impressive. The Cataloging Policy and Support Office (CPSO) issues pages like the Brief Guide to LC Policy and Practice for Format Integration: Books: Fields 246, 505, 525, 538, 546. The text of subclass ZA (Information Resources) is also available here.

Library of Congress Online Services

http://lcweb.loc.gov/homepage/online.html

LOCIS, the Library of Congress Online System, contains approximately 30 million records for items owned by LC that are publicly accessible, and other records from selected research institutions. LC now provides four different methods for searching their catalogs. LOCIS Search Guides are available at *gopher://lcweb.loc.gov/11/locis/guides/. LOCIS* can be accessed by using this URL: *telnet://locis.loc.gov* and is invaluable for catalogers to verify bibliographic data and authority headings. A Z39.50 Gateway provides simple name or title word searches. Go to Browse to search by subject, author, conference, series, title, LC classification number, or Dewey Decimal number. Finally, the Experimental Search System utilizes relevancy ranked searching. LC MARVEL—*gopher://marvel.loc. gov:70* (the Library of Congress Machine-Assisted Realization of the Virtual Electronic Library)—is a CWIS (Campus-Wide Information System) that provides access to electronic resources and information about the Library of Congress. It presents plain ASCII text, for the most part, to accommodate all types of equipment. Find here all LC Subject Heading Weekly Lists and information on USMARC format and documents of international standards. The Library of Congress FTP file is available 24 hours a day (*ftp://ftp.loc.gov/pub*).

Liens pour Catalogage/Repechage
Bibliotheque Paul-Emile-Boulet, Universite du Quebec a Chicoutimi, Quebec, Canada
http://www.uqac.uquebec.ca/biblio/referenc/bibo_ca1.htm
> Many Canadian and U.S. links. See Cartotheque P-E-Boulet Classification des Cartes Suivant LC.

LION (Librarian's Information Online Network) Cataloging Resources for School Libraries
Philadelphia, Pennsylvania
http://libertynet.org/~lion/cataloging.html
> This wonderful page includes links to Books for School Library Catalogs, Abridged Dewey, CD-ROMs for School Libraries, links to cataloging-related topics discussed on LM-NET (a mailing list for school librarians), and much more.

National Agricultural Library Cataloging Branch's "Cattleloging" Superhighway
Beltsville, Maryland
http://www.nal.usda.gov/cataloging
> Beautifully arranged site. Click on Who We Are and get treated to 1936 and 1996 staff photos, and a wonderful, large-print synopsis of their activities then and now. Over 18,000 bibliographic records are created annually, both in English and in over 30 foreign languages. Unique agriculturally related names and subject heading authorities are contributed to the Library of Congress Authority File. Search ISIS, their online public catalog and journal citation database.

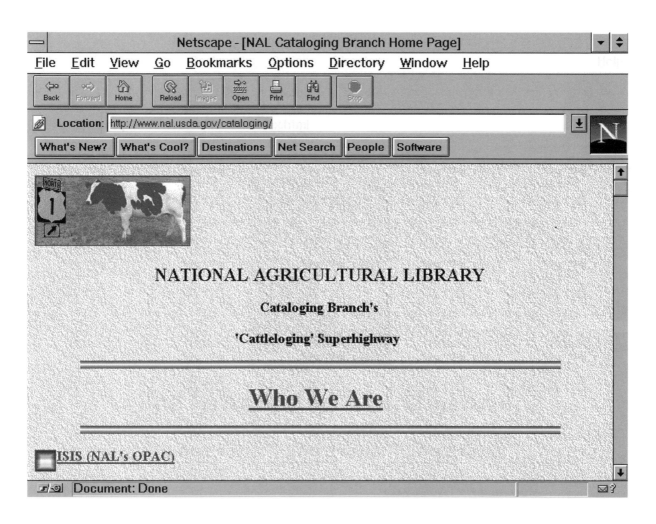

Figure 2.3
National Agricultural Library "Cattleloging" Superhighway

National Assembly Library Cataloging and Classification

Seoul, Korea

http://www.nanet.go.kr/nal/1/libe1–45.htm#b

Korean cataloging rules for description are used. A modified Dewey Decimal Classification scheme is followed.

National Library of Australia (Canberra, Australia)

http://www.nla.gov.au

Some wonderful information here. Check out Cataloguing in WORLD 1 by Julia Trainor at *http://www.nla.gov.au/nla/staffpaper/trainor1.html/*. WORLD 1 is a collective effort between the National Libraries of Australia and New Zealand to provide cataloging assistance and access to worldwide networked information and services of all kinds. WORLD 1 will replace the existing ABN (Australian Bibliographic Network) and Ozline, a network of Australian bibliographic directories and research databases.

National Library of Canada (Ottawa, Ontario, Canada)

http://www.nlc-bnc.ca/ehome.htm

The NLC has revised their levels of cataloging treatment. Effective April 1, 1996, the NLC began using three cataloging levels (full, minimal, and abbreviated) instead of the previous five (full, partial, enhanced minimal, minimal, and abbreviated). Read about AMICUS, the National Library's Bilingual System of more than ten million bibliographic records. Although AMICUS is currently a fee-based service ($40 every three months for Canadian libraries), resanet, a subset of the AMICUS database, containing brief records, is now available electronically at no charge sometime in the near future. CIP (Cataloguing in Publication) describes the Canadian CIP program in detail. There's a FAQ Page and a User Guide, as well as forms and examples of CIP cataloging records. Check out Virtual Canadian Union Catalogue: Myth or Reality? by Carrol D. Lunau (*http://www.nlc-bnc.ca/resource/vcuc/elunau.htm*). Very engaging report, first published in Feliciter, November/December 1995. Catalogers are working together to create a super virtual catalog. Read about Catalogue Record Syntax, Implications of Adopting Common Data Conventions, and more.

National Union Catalog of Manuscript Collections (NUCMC)

Library of Congress, Washington, D.C.

http://lcweb.loc.gov/coll/nucmc

Free-of-charge cooperative cataloging program operated by the Library of Congress. Catalogers create records in RLIN; the tapes are then purchased and loaded by LC. Eligible repositories must be located in the U.S. and its territories, and not have access to either RLIN or the Library of Congress.

Northwestern University Library Catalog Procedures and Organization in Brief
Evanston, Illinois
http://www.library.nwu.edu/catalog/orgbrief.html
> Succinct, bulleted page covers department functions, in-process control, input, record modification, authority file, cooperative union catalogs, and cataloging of professional level catalogers. Major revisions of Edition 21 of the Dewey Decimal Classification (DDC) system are also discussed in detail.

Oberlin LCRI (Library of Congress Rule Interpretations Index)
http://www.oberlin.edu/~library/lcri/

OCLC Passport for Windows
http://www.oclc.org/oclc/passport/passport.htm
> The authoritative source for all Passport information. Check out the Frequently Asked Questions, Tips, and Enhancements and Repairs.

Penn State University Libraries Cataloging Department
State College, Pennsylvania
http://www.libraries.psu.edu/IASWEB/CatsWeb/index.htm
> Very colorful and organized. General Information includes an organizational chart and a history of cataloging at Penn State. Their Cataloging Department Meeting Schedule is outstanding. Other highlights include their Dictionary Page, Internet Authoring Page, Rare Books' Table of Roman Numerals, and Maps Cataloging Team Page.

Princeton University Libraries Catalog Division Home Page
Princeton, New Jersey
http://infoshare1.princeton.edu/katmandu/cathome.html
> Extraordinary amount of information. The Cataloging/DBMS Documentation includes RLIN for Windows and NOTIS hints (logging-on instructions, diacritics, printing, etc.), Music Cataloging, HTML, MARC, NOTIS, Recon, and RLIN documentation, subject cataloging (Specific Guidelines for Subject Subdivisions), and statistics (including New Titles, Items Added, and New Authority Records). A useful page is Cataloging CD-ROMs and Compuer Disks (*http://infoshare1.princeton.edu/katmandu/comp/comfil.html*), which highlights and simplifies the MARC format for computer files. A Statistical Portrait of Princeton Cataloging for 1995 is also included, as is Team Documentation of the Slavic/Germanic and Science-Technology/Social Sciences Cataloging Team.

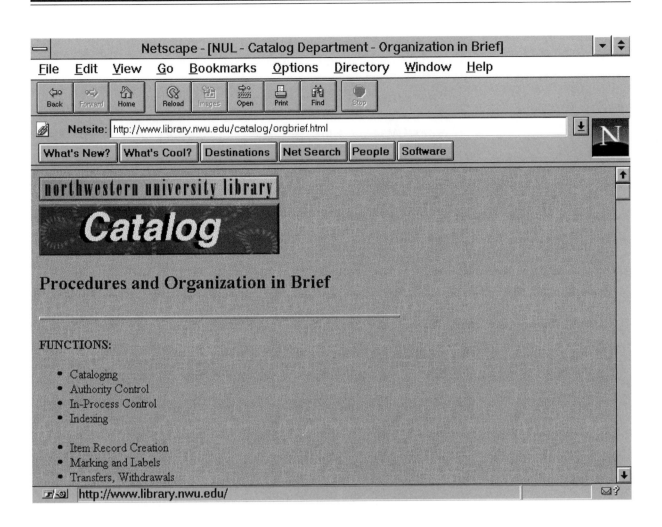

Figure 2.4
Northwestern University Library Catalog Procedures and Organization in Brief

QTECHWeb Home Page (Queen's University Libraries, Ontario, Canada) Cataloguing Resources Page
http://130.15.161.74/techserv/qcatalog.html

Many cutter pages here. Procedures and user's guide for ISM CATSS, links to legal and medical cataloging-related pages, and much more. QTECHWeb's patrons may access the Library of Congress, the National Library of Canada, and the U.S. National Library of Medicine with ease. Only the best sites have been linked. New sites are appropriately marked. Truly a gem among web pages for its clarity and comprehensiveness.

Resources for Cataloging (Iowa State University)—
http://www.lib.iastate.edu/ts/cat.htm

Link to Gabriel (the gateway to Europe's National libraries), HYTELNET on the World Wide Web, LC Marvel, and more.

Ressources des bibliothecaires: Catalogage
Canadian Forces College, Canada
http://www.cfcsc.dnd.ca/links/lib/catf.html

French and English links to resources.

Shared Cataloguing: IZUM
Institut informacijskih znanosti, Slovenija
http://www.izum.si/info_eng/catalouging.html

"In the process of Shared Cataloguing the data is entered on local computer systems...whereas on the computer system of the IZUM/COB/SS bibliographic utility...the union (cooperative) bibliographic COB/B database is created."

Southern Illinois University at Carbondale Cataloging and Order Department
http://www.lib.siu.edu/swen

A rich assortment of cataloging memos includes Main Shelflist Verification/Cleanup, Video Cataloging, and Processing of Certain Nonbook Materials (Software, Compact Discs, CD-ROM Databases, and Cassettes/Kits/Reel-to-Reel Tapes). CatMe File Transfers (using the Windows version FTP application) can be found at *http://www.lib.siu.edu/sfurtwen/ftp/ftp.htm*.

St. Joseph County Public Library Cataloging Department Home Page
South Bend, Indiana
http://sjcpl.lib.in.us/homepage/cat.html

The first public library in the U.S. to have a home page. Access their OPAC and Dial-A-Cat, connect to OCLC's home page, or browse a few online bookstores.

Stanford University Libraries Cataloging Services
http://www-sul.stanford.edu/depts/catdept

Stanford provides Guidelines for Creating Bibliographic Records for Automated Copy Searching. "These guidelines are written with a view to maximizing matching potential of bibliographic records against RLIN (Diogenes) or OCLC." Their Cataloger's Reference Shelf includes a link to the Electronic Maps Collection at the University of Texas at Austin (*http://www.lib.utexas.edu/Libs/PCL/Map_collection/Map_collection.html*).

SUNY Cortland Memorial Library
State University of New York College at Cortland, New York
http://www.cortland.edu/www/libwww/tech/cat_proc.htmlx

"Informal" cataloging procedures include Add-ons (multiple copies), Call Numbers for Bibliographies, Preparation of Member Copy for Cataloger Review, and Proofreading Skills. The Cataloging Department policies are very well done. Check out Realia, Games, and Other Type R Material, Cataloging Two-Dimensional Nonprojected Graphic Material, or Cataloging Videotapes. Internet Resources for Catalogers are also worth looking into. Finally, check out MARC Review Analyses of SUNY Cortland's OPAC by Johanna Bowen, Janet Selby, and Jonathan Jiras.

SWRLSS Cataloging Manual
Southwest Regional Library Service System, Colorado
http://www.colosys.net/swrlss/catalog.htm

A Colorado-based consortium discusses member library cataloging, profiles, procedures, etc.

TPOT (Technical Processing Online Tools) Cataloging
University of California at San Diego
http://tpot.ucsd.edu/Cataloging/catdept.html

One of the finest, if not *the* finest Cataloging Department site around. The Policies and Procedures section contains Guidelines for Formatting and Submitting Documents to TPOT: Cataloging by George Janczyn, TPOT Manager, and an extensive section on bibliographic and item records. A few highlights of this section are pages on Workflow for Copy Cataloging of Japanese Language Monographs, a table of Editing Guidelines for OCLC Records: Books, a section on Exporting Bibliographic and Authority Records from PRISM, a Revised Procedure for Automated Statistics, and my Web page, the Top 200 Technical Services Benefits of Home Page Development. The Cataloging Department's Administrative/Technical section includes departmental goals and objectives, annual reports, meeting schedules and contingency plans (Is OCLC down? Innopac or InnovAcq down?) There are large Innopac and OCLC sections, and a fantastically detailed new Format Integration Page. Don't miss Crystal

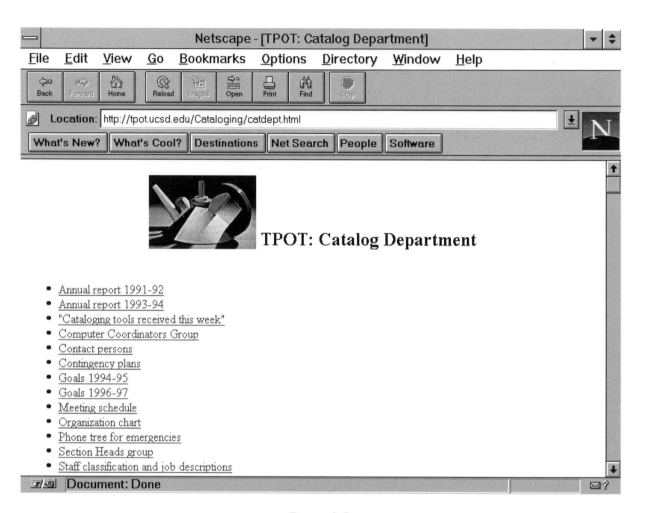

TPOT: Catalog Department

- Annual report 1991-92
- Annual report 1993-94
- "Cataloging tools received this week"
- Computer Coordinators Group
- Contact persons
- Contingency plans
- Goals 1994-95
- Goals 1996-97
- Meeting schedule
- Organization chart
- Phone tree for emergencies
- Section Heads group
- Staff classification and job descriptions

Figure 2.5
TPOT Cataloging

Graham's Format Integration: Major Changes for Printed Serials and Major Changes for Books. Special collection cataloging procedures are also here. Check out the Program for Cooperative Cataloging (PCC) Record Identification Agreement (*http://tpot.ucsd.edu/Cataloging/ Bib_records/bibco.html*). "International cooperative effort aimed at increasing access to library collections by providing useful, timely and cost effective cataloging that meets mutually accepted standards." Initiated in February 1995, 203 libraries were participating by October 1995. Find out about Specs for the Core Level Record. Finally, keyword searching of TPOT is now available (*http://tpot.ucsd.edu/tpotsearch.html*).

Unidad de Catalogacion
Biblioteques de la UPC, Barcelona, Spain
http://escher.upc.es/st/sp_cat.html
   Lists combined functions of several cataloging departments.

UNILINC Cataloguing Manual
http://www.unilinc.edu.au/catmanual/contents.htm
   Non-for-profit Australian organization formed in 1978 to introduce sophisticated library technologies to the higher education sector in Australia. Sections on Chinese Language Transliteration, Quick On-the-Fly Records, Related Works vs. Accompanying Materials, and much more.

University of Canterbury Cataloguing Department Home Page
Christchurch, New Zealand
http://www.canterbury.ac.nz/libr/cat/libr.htm
   Very likable smaller cataloging page, with links to a detailed Department Staff Page and to their online catalog.

University of Colorado at Colorado Springs Library Cataloging Information
http://www.uccs.edu/~library/cat.html
   Good collection of LC, OCLC, MARC tags, and cutter links.

University of Melbourne Library Cataloguing Resources
Melbourne, Australia
http://www.lib.unimelb.edu.au/catalogues/catres.html#worktools

University of Michigan Original Cataloging Page
Ann Arbor, Michigan
http://www.lib.umich.edu/libhome/ocu
   Well-organized site. Language Skills in the Original Cataloging Unit is a potentially useful chart for any library. The Current Original Cataloging Special Projects Page links to the CIC ARTFL Cataloging Project: Guidelines concerning a special one-year collaborative cataloging project. The

cataloging department houses and coordinates the In-Process Locator Service, which facilitates rush cataloging and processing of in-process materials. The Library Documentation Place Holder Page contains the Monograph Cataloging Division Mission Statement and various cataloging policies and procedures. Finally, be sure to see the Brief Record Cataloging Page, developed in 1984 to reduce an extensive backlog of uncataloged material.

University of Minnesota Libraries Cataloging Resources
Minneapolis, Minnesota
http://www.lib.umn.edu/ts/resource.html#cataloging
Original Cataloging page contains some interesting project reports. An example is Title II-C Project to Catalog: Ames Library of South Asia Rare Materials. Another project discusses the "description of collections of original manuscripts and illustrations for 100 prominent authors/illustrators of children's books held in the Kerlan collection."

University of South Australia Library Cataloguing on the Internet
http://136.169.62.185/library/techser/catalog/catlinks.htm#cattool
Excellent collection of links.

University of South Carolina Cataloging Department Home Page
http://www.sc.edu/library/catalog/catalog.html
The Cataloging Manual contains documents for Authorities, Locations, and Workflow. Also available are a University Policies and Procedures Manual and a good selection of links.

University of Toronto Faculty of Information Studies: Bibliographic Elements and Displays Project
http://www.fis.utoronto.ca/research/displays/index.htm
Very interesting evaluations of Web displays of bibliographic records. These displays are then matched with client preferences. Also of interest is the Monographs in Academic Libraries: Checklist of Bibliographic Elements in Items.

University of Virginia Library Cataloging Services Department
Charlottesville, Virginia
http://www.lib.virginia.edu/cataloging
One of the premier cataloging pages. Their Cataloging Procedures Manual is extensive and contains chapters on original and copy cataloging of monographs, serials and rare books, videorecordings, slides, realia, maps, and microforms. Their Computer Files Cataloging section is probably the most extensive available. Links to cataloging related sites are numerous and well-organized.

University of Washington Libraries Original Cataloging Division
Seattle, Washington
http://staffweb.lib.washington.edu/catdiv/index.htm
> Exceptionally clear procedures, well-written steps to searching OCLC,
> Pre-MARC Era Imprints, Printout /Workform Preparation, Authority
> Work, and more.

**Vanderbilt University, Jean and Alexander Heard Library
Cataloging Team**
Nashville, Tennessee
http://www.library.vanderbilt.edu/rs/cataloging.html
> Descriptions of the original, copy cataloging, and verification teams. See
> the Mission Statement for the Original Cataloging Team (adopted May
> 1996).

**Wayne State University Libraries Technical Services Manual:
Cataloging**
gopher://gopher.libraries.wayne.edu:70
> Select Technical Services, Technical Services Manual, and then Catalog-
> ing at this newly revamped site.

**Widener Library Cataloging Services Department Cataloging
Documentation**
Harvard University Libraries, Cambridge, Massachusetts
http://www-hcl.harvard.edu/wid-cat/cd.html
> Procedures here for Cataloging Photocopies of Monographs, Classed-
> Together Series, and an extensive Transfer Procedure Manual. Also avail-
> able is a description of LC's Cataloger's Desktop and the ISSN Compact.
> A very interesting memo is Software Configurations for the Technical
> Services Workstation (*http://www-hcl.harvard.edu/wid-cat/
> n960227.html*).

Yale Catalog Librarians Homepage
New Haven, Connecticut
http://www.cis.yale.edu/test/libtemp.html
> Temporary cataloging page which is sure to be revamped in the future.

2.2

Authority Control

Authority control, perhaps more than any other cataloging activity, has legitimized and standardized cataloging bibliographic records throughout the world. Uniform standardization of bibliographic records is more crucial than ever, now that anyone can browse library catalogs throughout the world from the comfort of their home. The sites listed here discuss the full gamut of authority control, vendor-related services, collection development, and maintenance policies for online authority work. Certainly some of you remember searching frantically for a location name in the BGN (United States Board on Geographic Names). Now you can simply direct yourself to the Geographic Name Server or Canada's Geographical Names Page to resolve your problems.

Ancestry Home Town
http://www.ancestry.com
Genealogy, news, lessons, and databases.

Arabic NACO Manual Table of Contents
http://infoshare1.princeton.edu/katmandu/cp20/aranatoc.html
Excellent sections concerning variant romanizations, unused surnames, and much more. For additional Princeton information, see the entry entitled Name Authority NACO Information.

Authority Control
State University of New York at Buffalo
http://wings.buffalo.edu/libraries/units/cts/ac
An excellent authorities page. Provides a basic glossary of terms, examples, and procedures for personal, corporate, and geographic names, subjects, and series authority control. Authority Control: Full Bibliography, compiled by Stacy Snyder and Ellen Greenblatt, is an extensive resource, which can be searched alphabetically or by author.

Authority Control in the NDIS
National Documentation and Information Service, National Library of Australia
http://www.nla.gov.au/2/abn/comittees/abnsc dm.html#nine
Overview of authority control by Julia Trainor that recommends continuing usage of LCMARC, modified by Australian additions and changes, and ideas about the integration of AUSMARC and LCMARC.

Authority Control in the 21st Century: an Invitational Conference: Proceedings, 1996
http://www.oclc.org/oclc/man/authconf/procmain.htm
What a smorgasbord of excellent papers! Read about Identifying Personal Name Headings with Cross References in a Public Database, Characteristics of Member-Established Headings in the OCLC Database, Authority Work and Control in Germany, and so very much more.

Authority Records in NOTIS
http://www.library.nwu.edu/catalog/notis/notis9.html
Northwestern University Library's *NOTIS User's Manual* describes searching strategies to obtain authority records, an example of an authority record, and how to exit an authority record.

Automating Heading Correction in a Large File: Harvard's Experience
http://www.oclc.org/oclc/man/9391ausy/wendler1.htm
By Robin K. Wendler, Bibliographic Analyst, Harvard University.

Describes the experience of correcting headings resulting from the merger of 45 autonomous historical catalogs containing approximately 5 million records.

Biography (A & E)
http://www.biography.com
Search 15,000 names, past and present, for substantial biographical information.

Blackwell North America Authority Control Services—Appendix H
http://www.blackwell.com/services/techserv/ach.HTM
Here is an example of the extensive information contained in an Authority Control Profile Form. Other appendices cover authority control notification service, record processing, manual review, and correction.

Canadian Geographical Names—Natural Resources Canada
http://ellesmere.ccm.emr.ca/cgndb/english/Home.html
"Where is Tsiigehtchic? Which is further west ... Edmonton or Calgary?" Information on national or regional maps. Search by current or historical names, and then download the desired data. Over 500,000 names available. Find out about the Canadian Permanent Committee on Geographical Names, and don't forget to have fun at the World of the Weird and the Wonderful page (*http://ellesmere.ccm.emr.ca/cgndb/english/schoolnet/ weird.html*).

Cataloging Bulletin ODE2—Overseas Office Name and Series Authority Record Upload Now in Production
http://lcweb.loc.gov/catdir/odenar.html
Discusses how bibliographic records which were previously handled manually are now loaded automatically into LC MUMS.

Change and Continuity in Subject Authority Control
http://www.oclc.org/oclc/man/9391ausy/mandle.htm
By Carol Mandel, Deputy University Librarian, Columbia University.
   Speculates on the creation and contents of an LCSH-based national subject authority file.

Collection Development and Maintenance Policies for Authority Records
Maddux Library, Trinity University, San Antonio, Texas
http://www.trinity.edu/departments/maddux_library/tsauth.html
This site is of particular interest to NOTIS users. Discusses personal and corporate names/subjects, series and uniform titles, topical subjects, duplicate, and orphan authority records.

Figure 2.6
Canada's Geographical Names/Natural Resources Canada

Future Is Now: Reconciling Change and Continuity in Authority Control

http://www.oclc.org/oclc/man/9391ausy/toc.htm

Proceedings of the OCLC Symposium, ALA Annual Conference, June 23, 1995.

Geographic Name Server

http://www.mit.edu/geo

Searchable index provides name, country, state, or province, latitude, longitude, and elevation. Mostly U.S. material. Uses information from the geographic nameserver database at *martini.eecs.umich.edu*.

GNIS (Geographic Names Information System)

http://www-nmd.usgs.gov/www/gnis

Developed by the USGS (United States Geological Survey) in cooperation with the U.S. Board on Geographic Names (BGN). Contains information on approximately two million federally recognized names of physical and cultural geographic features in the U.S. Search for details on the name and location by state, county, and geographic coordinates of beaches, basins, canals, caves, cemeteries, forests, levees, streams, and wells.

Greater New Orleans Archivists Name Authority Project

http://www.gnofn.org/~nopl/links/archives/gnoa.htm

Example of a local information project to build up an unofficial personal name authority file. For use in "processing and cataloging materials produced or collected by individuals connected to the New Orleans area."

Instructions for Creating an Authority Record

http://www.library.cornell.edu/tsmanual/Authority/inst.html

Cornell gives clean, well thought out instructions for authority record creation. See NACO Searching Instructions Examples.

International Standards in Authority Data Control: Costs and Benefits

http://www.nlc-bnc.ca/ifla/IV/ifla62/62–dana.htm

By Alan Danskin, Head of Authority Control, The British Library, Boston Spa.

Latin American Authors: Country Listing

http://www-lib.usc.edu/~calimano/bib_control/paises.html

An excellent resource for Latin American catalogers. Authors are arranged by country, by LC classification number, and by cutter.

Library of Congress Name Authority File (via PALNI **(Private Academic Library Network of Indiana) WWW to Z39.50 Gateway**

http://www.palni.edu/palniwww/Z3950/LC_Names.html

Quick and easy searchable form permits searching of title, author, and subject keywords contained in 3.4 million authority records.

Library of Congress Rule Interpretations
http://www.library.nwu.edu/iesca/rules/lcri25.html
Find the text of Chapter 25, Uniform Titles and a complete index.

Library of Congress Subject Headings for Aboriginal and Torres Strait Islander People
http://www.nla.gov.au/dnc/aboriginal/martin.html. By Giles Martin, State Library of South Australia, May 4, 1995.
Discusses the North American bias of the Library of Congress Subject Headings, and discusses variations employed by the Australian Bibliographic Network.

LTI Authority Control
http://www.librarytech.com/a-aint-b.htm
Library Technologies Inc. offers "name and subject authority control based on the Library of Congress name and subject authority databases" plus over 1 million LTI-created records. A good overview of authority control is included.

NACO Authority Guidelines from the Library of Congress
gopher://marvel.loc.gov/11/services/cataloging/coop/faq
Frequently Asked NACO Questions, Frequently Asked Questions about Joining NACO, List of NACO/PCC Liaisons, and more.

NACO Procedure for Changing Existing National-Level Authority Records
http://tpot.ucsd.edu/Cataloging/Auth_records/nacochange.html

Name Authorities NACO Information
Princeton
http://infoshare1.princeton.edu/katmandu/cp20_/headtoc.html
Originated in the mid-80s as a local version of LC's DCM Z1. Continually revised and updated. A particularly useful section is the Use of Reference Sources in NACO Works, which discusses specific situations (persons not primarily known as authors, surname alone on chief source, etc.). Other items of interest include a section on Requesting Class Numbers From the Library of Congress, the Quick Guide to LC in RLIN, Pre-AACR2 Headings in the Name Authority File, Near East Holdings in Non-Near East Cataloging, and Dividing up the World: Headings for Certain Entities.

Name Authority File: the British Library National Bibliographic Service (NBS)
http://icarus.bl.uk/nbs/recs/cbridge/naf.html

Contains all name headings created for the British National Bibliography since 1981. Available by FTP, dial-in transfer, and various other magnetic media. Downloading available from the Catalogue Bridge (*http:// icarus.bl.uk/nbs/recs/cbridge/overview.html*)

NameBase
http://ursula.blythe.org/NameBase/.quickie.html
Searchable proper name index, containing names of individuals, corporations, and groups. NameBase contains book reviews (but no subject access) of people in the news related to the military, organized crime, intelligence agencies, scandals, terrorism, UFOs, and other topics of interest.

Names of Printing Towns
Cathedral Libraries Catalogue, Canterbury, England
http://crane.ukc.ac.uk/semls/cathlibs/towns.htm
Find English and other vernacular forms for Latin names of printing towns listed in early printed books.

National Imagery and Mapping Agency GEOnet Names Server
http://164.214.2.53/gns/html/index.html
Check here for authoritative foreign geographic feature names. "Information in this database has been used to prepare and publish the series of foreign country gazetteers approved by the U.S. Board on Geographic Names." Offers links to the Digital Gazetteer of Bosnia and Herzegovina, and the Defense Mapping Agency (DMA), among others.

Non-Western Name Conventions
gopher://liberty.uc.wlu.edu/00/library/human/eashum/nameconv.
By T. W. Tan and Peter K. W. Tan, National University of Singapore.
   "Provides very interesting comparisons among cultures on the use of surnames and given names."

Notable Citizens of Planet Earth Biographical Dictionary
http://www.tiac.net/users/parallax
Includes concise biographical information on over 18,000 notable figures, past and present. Provides birth and death years, professional awards, literary and artistic works, and more. Index is searchable by any keyword or expression, not just the name of a person. Updated frequently.

OCLC Authority Control Questions and Answers
http://www.oclc.org/oclc/promo/9438auth/9438.htm
Discusses the software that has made "more than 5.6 million corrections to headings in OLUC (Online Union Catalog) bibliographic records." Corrections are made to personal and corporate names, series, LC subject headings and MeSH headings. This software works automatically to

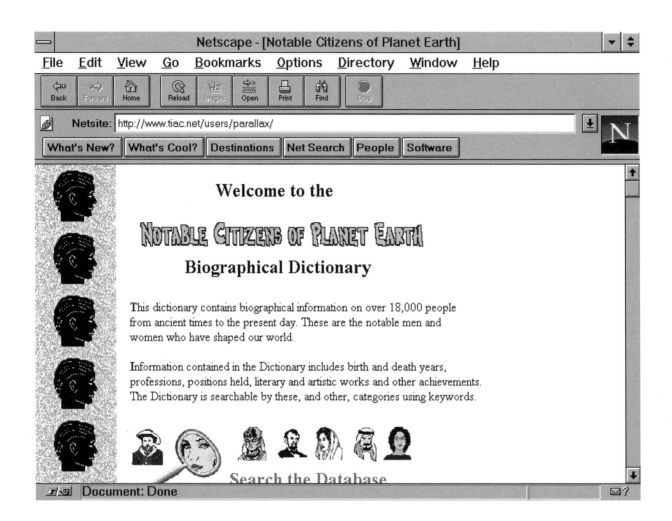

Figure 2.7
Notable Citizens of Planet Earth Biographical Dictionary

locate and resolve frequently occurring patterns of heading errors. Can be included with OCLC's RETROCON and TECHPRO services.

Onomastikon (Dictionary of Names)

http://www.fairacre.demon.co.uk

Proper names, surnames, and their meanings. Search Celtic, Early and Modern England, Medieval Europe, the Ancient World, Former Soviet Union, the Americas, and many more.

PCC (Program for Cooperative Cataloging) Task Group on Name Versus Subject Authorities

gopher://marvel.loc.gov/00/services/cataloging/coop/coop_cncl/divworld

"Established to re-examine and recommend policies for content designation and formulation of headings for entities with characteristics common to both names and subjects, especially events, works of art, and geographic names, with the goal of regularizing practices between LCSH and AACR2, and among the variant practices of the cataloging community."

Project DELICAT

Data Enhancement of Library Catalogues

http://portico.bl.uk/gabriel/en/projects/delicat.html#what

"Aims to create an expert system capable of automatically detecting errors in library catalogues, and drawing these to the attention of library staff." Full partners in this development are the Biblioteca Nacional (Spain), Bibliotheque Royale Albert 1 (Belgium), Fraunhofer Gesellschaft (Germany), and the British Library (U.K.).

Project Helen: Transliteration Schemes Used by European Libraries and Name Authority Issues

http://alcyone.cc.uch.gr/~kosmas/Helen/helen_schemes.html

Paper by Evelyn Cornell discusses issues in Greek transliteration, AACR2 rules concerning Greek name authority, and actual practice in European libraries.

Reframing the Authority Control Debate

http://www.oclc.org/oclc/man/9391ausy/younger.htm. By Jennifer A. Younger, Assistant Director, Technical Services, Ohio State University.

Discusses the "reasons why it is important to examine the values and goals underlying the practices of authority control as we know them" and the need to "increase productivity in authority control while maintaining effective information retrieval."

Series Procedures: Series Verification in the Name Authority File (NAF): LC AACR2R Copy

http://infoshare1.princeton.edu/katmandu/series/lcaacr2.html

Procedures are also available for member copy cataloging and original cataloging. Includes Princeton's Authorities Corner Archive.

Series: Traced and Untraced, Controlled and Uncontrolled: the Next Frontier?

http://www.oclc.org/oclc/man/authconf/kaplan.htm.
   By Michael Kaplan, Harvard College Library, Cambridge, Massachusetts.

Standard for Machine-Proposed Authority Records

http://lcweb.loc.gov/catdir/pcc/strawn.html
   By Gary L. Strawn, Northwestern University Library.

Subject Authority Cooperative Program

Library of Congress
gopher://marvel.loc.gov:70/00/services/cataloging/coop/saco
   Learn how to submit subject headings and classification numbers to the Library of Congress. Read the Statement of Expectations for SACO Participants.

Tools for Authority Control: Subject Headings

http://lcweb.loc.gov/cds/lcsh.html
   LC's Cataloging Distribution Service offers Library of Congress Subject Headings, Classification Plus, and CDMARC Subjects. For name headings, there is CDMARC Names—(3.1 million records; the entire LC Name Authority File on four compact discs), the Name Authority Cumulative Microform, and the NACO Participant's Manual.

TPOT Cataloging—Authority Records

http://tpot.ucsd.edu/Cataloging/auth.html
   Contains NACO procedures for creating new records or editing national level records. Examples of 670 fields, local fields and notes for authority records, and Prism authority highlights.

21st Century Authority Control: What Is It and How Do We Get There?

http://www.oclc.org/oclc/man/9391ausy/tillet.htm
   A very interesting paper by Barbara B. Tillett, Chief, Cataloging Policy and Support Office, Library of Congress.

United States Board on Geographic Names (BGN)

http://www-nmd.usgs.gov/www/gnis/bgn.html
   This federal board has served as the definitive authority on all domestic and foreign geographic name usage since 1890. Librarians may request the Board to render decisions on proposed new names, name changes, or conflicting names. Snail-mail requests only.

2.3

Classification and Indexing

This Classification and Indexing section should be of primary interest to catalogers today. The immense chaotic knowledge base that we call the World Wide Web is in need of indexing, description, and categorization. Lately there have been discussions on Autocat and on other cataloging-related lists, as to whether we are indeed catalogers or indexers, and what is the difference? Yahoo! hires catalogers who provide subject-access to approximately 3,000 pages daily. This is certainly an admirable figure, and it would be impossible for them to do more, but . . . is this cataloging? Or indexing? With the plethora of search engines and web-robots that go out gathering new sites faster than the speed of light, can we possibly hope to apply traditional MARC-based cataloging to each site invented? And the unfortunate truth is that many Web pages are like dreams—they are there one time you search and gone the next time, never to be found again. Where do these pages go? That's a metaphysical question, which I doubt even those of you involved with meta access would be hard pressed to answer.

Alcuin
http://library.ncsu.edu/drabin/alcuin
> Database of Internet resources designed by North Carolina State University Libraries to practice collecting, organizing, and classifying Web resources. The underlying database consists of MARC records driven by DRA-designed software. This prototype experiment was developed in 1994 and updated in March 1995. Also includes a very good listing entitled Other Areas of Classification Research Interest.

Alphabetical Index to Sections (Dewey Decimal Classification)
http://ivory.lm.com/~mundie/DDHC/Dewey_index.html

American Society for Information Science (ASIS) Special Interest Group/Classification Research
http://cait.cpmc.columbia.edu/www/asis
> "Concerned with organizing information and includes indexing, index construction, indexing language, thesaurus construction, classification of information in any form, and testing and evaluating the effectiveness of these products."

American Society of Indexers Home Page
http://www.well.com/user/asi/index.html
> "The index is the key." With mounting confusing over whether Yahoo! and other Web sites are cataloging or indexing their home pages, or whether in fact catalogers are indexers or vice-versa, this site should be of interest. ASI is the "only professional organization in the U.S. solely devoted to the advancement of indexing, abstracting, and database construction."

Australian Society of Indexers
http://godzilla.zeta.org.au/~aussi
> Indexes provided are comprehensive. Tables of contents and abstracts of the Indexer are available from April 1992 to the present.

Beyond Bookmarks: Schemes for Organizing the Web
http://www.public.iastate.edu/~CYBERSTACKS/CTW.htm
> Absolutely indispensable listing of Web sites which have either used standard classification schemes or controlled vocabulary in order to provide enhanced access to Internet resources.

Brief Guide to the Bliss Classification Scheme (Birkbeck College Library, London, England)
http://rs306.ccs.bbk.ac.uk/Departments/Library/classif.html

BUBL WWW Subject Tree
http://bubl.ac.uk/link/subjects
   Arranged by Universal Decimal Classification.

Classification Research Group and the Theory of Integrative Levels
http://edfu.lis.uiuc.edu/review/summer1995/spiteri.html
   By Louise F. Spiteri, Faculty of Information Studies, University of Toronto.
      Discusses the origin and contributions of the U.K.-based Classification Research Group.

Classification Society of North America (CNSA)
http://5100.dium/nho.pt/~fln/Boston 95/boston95.html
   Information on the *Journal of Classification*, distribution lists, and Usenet newsgroups of interest to classification research.

Classifying Internet Objects
http://s700.di.uminho.pt/~fln/Boston95/boston95.html
   By F. Luis Neves and Jose N. Oliveira, Departamento Informatica, Universidade do Minho, Braga, Portugal.

Cuttering Numbers for Specific Computer, Programming Languages, Specific Computers, and Specific Computer Programs, Parts 1 and 2
http://www.lib.siu.edu/swen/vernlis1.htm
   Expands the Dewey Decimal classification scheme.

Cutter-Sanborn Three-Figure Author Tables
http://www.bibl.ulaval.ca/info/cutternd.html

CyberDewey: A Guide to Internet Resources Organized Using Dewey Decimal Classification Codes
http://ivory.lm.com/~mundie/DDHC/CyberDewey.html
   An interesting concept—attempting to organize Web pages by broad Dewey Decimal Classification numbers. Outside of the U.S., Dewey commands a 70 percent market share. "Dewey is a faceted system, meaning that its codes are constructed from meaningful subunits" and is more consistent than LC.

CyberStacks
http://www.public.iastate.edu/~CYBERSTACKS
   A "centralized, integrated, and unified collection of significant WWW and other Internet resources." Categorized using the Library of Congress classification scheme, all resources are full-text, hypertext, or hypermedia. Subjects are broken down by broad classification, then within

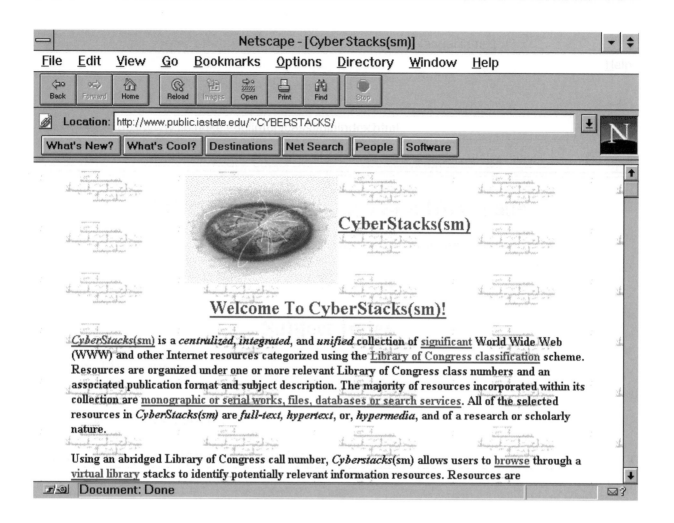

Figure 2.8
CyberStacks

narrower subclasses, and finally listed under a specific classification range and associated subject division.

Dewey Decimal Classification: A Practical Guide
http://www.oclc.org/oclc/man/9353pg/9353toc.htm
By Lois Mai Chan, John Phillip Comaromi, and Mohinder Partap Satija.
Includes Chapter One, the Life and Mind of Melvil Dewey, in its entirety. The Basic Plan of the Classification, Structure and Organization of the Schedules: Notes and Instructions, and Synthesis of Class Numbers or Practical Number Building are also included.

Edinburgh Engineering Virtual Library (EEVL)
http://eevl.icbl.hw.ac.uk
Classification project utilizing UDC (Universal Decimal Classification) to organize engineering information on the Web. A search system is provided for an archive of news articles from approximately 125 engineering news groups. Another UDC-based project is the NISS Directory of Networked Resources (*http://www.niss.ac.uk/subject/index.html*). "Universal Decimal Classification is an international standard library classic, invented as a way of describing every possible subject in a universal library." For a succinct description, see UDC in Brief (*http://www.niss. ac.uk/resource-description/udcbrief.html*).

Faceted Access: A Review of the Literature
http://www.music.indiana.edu/tech_s/mla/facacc.rev. By Amanda Maple.
Presented at the Music Library Association Annual Meeting, February 10, 1995. Sponsored by the Working Group on Faceted Access to Music. Traces faceted access from Ranganathan through its use in WWII, to discussions of precis, thesauri, and terms such as equivalence, hierarchical, and affinite/associative.

Fiction Indexing Policy
British Library Fiction Group
http://portico.bl.uk/nbs/marc/655polc.html

Future Indexing Developments in World 1
http://www.zeta.org.au/~aussi/hendersons.html
By Sandra Henderson, National Library of Australia.

Geographic Cutter Table for U.S. States and Regions (In One Alphabetical Arrangement)
http://www.lib.siu.edu/swen/uscutter.htm

IFLA Section on Classification and Indexing: Review of Activities, 1994–1995
http://www.nlc-bnc.ca/ifla/IV/ifla61/61–dund.htm

Donna Duncan of McGill University, Montreal, Canada discusses the activities of the Working Group on Principles Underlying Subject Heading Languages and the State of the Art Survey of Subject Heading Systems.

Internet Cataloguing-in-Publication
http://www.lm.com/~mundie/CyberDewey/ICIP.html

By David A. Mundie.

The suggestion here is for the Web to adopt the CIP model. "Smart worms" could take over the task of generating subject-oriented catalogs of net resources. An ICIP form would generate ICIP and MARC records automatically.

Internet Resources in Dewey Decimal Order with DDC Subjects
Mid-Continent Public Library, Independence, Missouri
http://www.mcpl.lib.mo.us/dewey.htm

Klassifikationsskemaer
Royal Library of Denmark
http://www.kb.dk/kb/rex/uask

LC (Library of Congress) Classification Schedules: A Short List
http://tpot.ucsd.edu/Cataloging/Subj_analysis/lc.sched.html

Compiled by Arlene Taylor, Associate Professor, School of Library and Information Science, University of Pittsburgh, Pittsburgh, Pennsylvania.

LCEasy for Windows and Macintosh 2.0
http://www.lightlink.com/kish

Training for the Library of Congress Classification system for new library assistants, produced by Mary L. Kish.

Library of Congress Classification: Subclass ZA—Information Resources
http://webdoc.sub.gwdg.de/edoc/aw/lccn/1996/lccn4_4.htm

Library of Congress Classification System Tip Sheet
http://www.hccs.tx.us/Library/TipSheets/Lcclass.html

Library of Congress Cutter Tables
www.mun.ca/library/cat/lccutter.htm

Basic, P Class, biography, and translation tables.

**LION (Librarians Information Online Network) Internet
Resources Classified by Dewey Numbers**
http://www.libertynet.org/education/schools/lion/internet-by-dewey.html
   An eclectic selection of links employing Dewey Classification for Internet
   resources.

Materials Organized by Mathematical Subject Classification
http://www.ams.org/mathweb/mi-mathbyclass.html
   Probably quite useful to mathematicians.

Moys Classification Scheme as Used in the Law Library
University of Newcastle Library, New South Wales, Australia
http://wwwlib.newcastle.edu.au/faculty/law/app1.html

National Library of Medicine Classification Scheme
Annette and Irwin Eskind Biomedical Library, Vanderbilt University, Nashville, Tennessee
http://www.mc.vanderbilt.edu/biolib/classification.html

**Nordic WAIS/World Wide Web Project: Subproject—Automatic
Classification of WAIS Databases**
http://www.ub2.lu.se/autoclass.html. By Anders Ardo and Traugott Koch.
   Automatic classification according to UDC, English medium edition.

**Novelist: Unreal-How HCL (Hennepin County Public Library)
Catalogs Fiction**
http://www.carl.org/nl/n/news0297.html. By Sanford Berman, Head Cataloger.
   Must reading for those interested in providing additional access points to
   fiction titles. Fifty thousand adult fiction titles are currently listed. Over
   29,000 of these have either an annotation or a full-text book review.

OCLC Forest Press DDC Home Page
http://www.oclc.org/oclc/fp/fptxthm.htm
   The official Dewey Decimal Classification (DDC) Web Site. Announces
   DDC 21 workshops, provides ALA conference reports, as well as reports
   from the Decimal Classification Editonal Policy Committee. A new section links libraries using the DDC, as well as a tutorial on Dewey for
   Windows.

**Organizing Computer Resources: or, How I Learned to Stop
Worrying and Love the DDC**
http://ivory.lm.com/~mundie/DDHC/organizing_computers.html. By David
A. Mundie.

Superintendent of Documents Classification System
http://exlibris.colgate.edu/departments/govdocs/govdocs2.html
> Did you know that the SuDocs numbering system dates back to 1895–1903? Read about its history and structure here. A list of major SuDocs classes is also provided.

UDC—Universal Decimal Classification
http://www.niss.ac.uk/help/udc_help.html
> "Indexing and retrieval language in the form of a classification for the whole of recorded knowledge, in which subjects are symbolized by a code based on Arabic numerals." Learn how to utilize the UDC Subject Tree.

Unicode Home Page—*http://www.unicode.org*
> "The Unicode Worldwide Character Standard is a character coding system designed to support the interchange, processing, and display of the written texts of the modern world . . . in its current version, the Unicode Standard contains 38,885 distinct coded characters derived from 25 supported scripts." These characters cover the principal written languages of the Americas, Europe, the Middle East, Africa, India, Asia, and Pacifica.

World Wide Web Virtual Library
http://www.w3.org/hypertext/DataSources/bySubject/
LibraryOfCongress.html
> Major site using the Library of Congress Classification System for organization of Web resources.

2.4

Bibliographic Record Formats

Just as the MARC format revolutionized cataloging by facilitating exchange of records using a standardized format, HTML, SGML, and other newer formats are already forever changing the ways libraries can display our holdings for patrons. This section covers standards, code lists, and tutorials catalogers can use to understand and learn more about formats of all kinds of records.

2.4.1 MARC, AUSMARC, CANMARC, UKMARC, UNIMARC, USMARC, ETC.

The MARC section makes it perfectly clear that a worldwide MARC format is truly a necessity nowadays. Thank goodness an agreement was signed by the Library of Congress (USMARC), the National Library of Canada (CAN/MARC), and the British Library (UKMARC) on December 14, 1995 to create a Global MARC Format. The expected date of USMARC and CAN/MARC conversion is January 1998. UKMARC convergence is expected by January 1999.

CAN/MARC Changes for MARC Format Alignment
gopher://marvel.loc.gov:70/00/.listarch/usmarc/96–8rpt1.doc

Cataloguing with the MARC Editor
http://www.tkm.mb.ca/microcat-manual/c_editor.html

From MARC to Markup: SGML and Online Library Systems
http://www.lib.virginia.edu/speccol/scdc/articles/alcts_brief.html
  By Edward Gaynor, University of Virginia Library.

Introduction to MARC Format Integration
http://www.nlc-bnc.ca/pubs/netnotes/notes5.htm
  By Young-Hee Queinnec.
    From Network Notes #5, Information Technology Services, National Library of Canada, February 1995. Also available in French.

MARC Documentation Page
Princeton University Libraries
http://infoshare1.princeton.edu/katmandu/marc/marctoc.html
  This excellent page links to MARC Field Guides, all MARC Code Lists, and MARC Notes and News.

MARC Documentation Status: Network Development and MARC Standards Office
http://lcweb.loc.gov/marc/status.html
  Premier MARC site listing all changes to USMARC formats.

MARC of Quality
http://world.std.com/~tmq
  Offers a wide assortment of MARC products, including MARC Review and MARC Analysis. Download free software.

MARC Review: Database Inspector
http://www.bibfile.com/main/marcrevw.htm

DOS-based software examines and analyzes USMARC bibliographic and authority records to find anomalies, such as cataloging errors, misspelled words, materials requiring format integration updating, and more.

MARCIVE, Inc.

http://www.marcive.com

Library vendor based in San Antonio, Texas, that has specialized in converting catalog cards into MARC records for over 25 years. They offer the Ongoing MARC Record Service, providing MARC records to be loaded directly into your local system. They still offer cards, too—shipped within 24 hours of receipt of the order. Plus "depository libraries find MARCIVE to be the best source for GPO cataloging, both retro and ongoing." Read USMARC: That's Our Story and We're Sticking to It.

MARCMaker and MARCBreaker

http://lcweb.loc.gov/marc/marcutil.html

Two interesting products. MARCMaker accepts files from most text editors and word processors and converts properly formatted information into the MARC record structure. MARCBreaker converts structurally sound MARC records and reformats the information into an ASCII text file format.

OCLC-MARC Code Lists

http://www.oclc.org/oclc/man/code/codetoc.htm

On the MARC: A Program for Creating MARC Records

http://sscd2.loc.gov/ecip/onmarc.htm. By David Williamson, Senior Descriptive Cataloger, Library of Congress.

This program uses text capture and electronic conversion involving the Electronic CIP experiment at LC. LC produces LC MARC records from electronic data, utilizing screen captures of bibliographic records from OPACs which can be converted into LC records, or any text, in electronic form. This prototype program has now been replaced by a new program entitled ClipSearch.

PREMARC (Library of Congress Older Materials)

gopher://marvel.loc.gov:70/00/locis/guides/prem.loc

Cataloged by LC from 1898 to 1968. Now available for searching on OCLC in their unrevised format.

Setting the Record Straight: A Guide to the MARC Format

British Library National Bibliographic Service

http://icarus.bl.uk/nbs/pubs/srs2.html

An excellent and detailed overview by R. W. Hill of MARC, UKMARC, and UNIMARC.

Towards a Common MARC Format
British Library National Bibliographic Service
http://portico.bl.uk/nbs/marc/commarcm.html
> Proceedings of an open meeting held at the Library Association Headquarters, London, July 21, 1995.

Translation and Expansion of Classification Systems in the Arab Countries and Iran
http://www.nlc-bnc.ca/ifla/IV/ifla61–solp.htm
> By Poori Soltani, Senior Research Librarian at the National Library of Iran, Tehran.
>
> "Discusses the necessity for expanding the two most commonly used classification systems—the Library of Congress Classification and the Dewey Decimal Classification—to meet vernacular needs."

UKMARC Web Page
British Library National Bibliographic Service (NBS)
http://portico.bl.uk/nbs/marc/overview.html
> Links to news about the UKMARC Manual: A Cataloguer's Guide to the Format, 4th ed. (British Library, 1996). Data here includes history and development of the MARC format, as well as the structure and organization of a UKMARC record. Also contains a Guide to Fields, and a report of the July 20, 1995 meeting entitled Towards a Common MARC Format.

UNIMARC (Universal Bibliographic Control and International MARC Core Programme)
http://www.nlc-bnc.ca/ifla/VI/3/p1996–1/unimarc.htm
> IFLA provides UNIMARC: An Introduction, which describes differences between MARC and UNIMARC, and more.

USMARC Code Lists and Formats
gopher://marvel.loc.gov/11/services/usmarc/marcdoc

USMARC Machine-Readable Cataloging (MARC)
http://lcweb.loc.gov/marc
> "The MARC formats are standards for the representation and communication of bibliographic and related information in machine-readable form." Documents are keyword searchable. Check out MARC User Notes, the USMARC Code List for Languages: Changes and MARC DTDs (Document Type Definitions), as well as news, announcements, product information, and subscription information for the USMARC Forum.

2.4.2 HTML, HTTP, METADATA, SGML, STANDARDS, TEI, ETC.

A current hot topic concerns the inability of the MARC format to be useful for cataloging Internet resources, and the possible replacement of the MARC record by an SGML record (Standard Generalized Markup Language). Highly recommended is Edward Gaynor's article "From MARC to Markup: SGML and the Online Library Systems," http://www.lib.virginia.edu/speccol/ scdc/articles/alcts_brief.html. The section entitled Metadata, SGML, Standards, TEI, Etc. is for all you metadata enthusiasts. NISO standards, ANSI standards, the Text-Encoding Initiative, the SGML Primer are all here.

ALCTS Taskforce on Meta Access: Midwinter 1996 Meeting Minutes
http://www.lib.virginia.edu/alcts/about/min196.html
> Discusses many important issues, including our "current competition with other communities to define and describe bibliographic resources in digital form."

ANSI NISO Z39.56—Serial Item and Contribution Identifier (SICI)
http://www.faxon.com/Standards/Z3956–SICI-Intro.html

ASCII Code Charts
http://www.tbi.net/~jhall/ascii1.html
> Even, odd, space, and mark parity.

Automating the Structural Markup Process in the Conversion of Print Documents to Electronic Texts
http://www.csdl.tamu.edu/DL95/papers/palowitc/palowitc.html
> By Casey Palowitch and Darin Stewart.
>
> Here's an attempt to "construct a system for automatically identifying structural features and applying Standard Generalized Markup Language (SGML) tagging, based on the Text Encoding Initiative Document Type Definition (TEIDTD), to text captured from print documents via optical character recognition (OCR)."

Catalog Librarians and Networked Information: An Incomplete List of Relevant Projects, Programs, Papers, Presentations, Courses, Etc.
http://www.library.yale.edu/~mbeacom/internetcataloging.html. By Matthew Beacom, Yale University.

Catalogers and the Creation of Metadata Systems: A Collaborative Vision at the University of Michigan
http://www.oclc.org/oclc/man/colloq/butter.htm. By Kevin L. Butterfield.
  This visionary paper discusses the need for libraries to provide description and access to Internet resources by creating new "metainformational systems."

Cataloguing: Separate Metadata Record
http://www.ub2.lu.se/tk/metadata/cat-sept.html

CORE Project Overview
http://www.oclc.org:5047/oclc/research/projects/core
  An electronic library prototype providing network access to graphics and full text of the American Chemical Society Journals and associated chemical abstracts services indexing since 1980. Coded completely in SGML. Discusses the design and implementation of XSCEPTER, which provides "on the fly formatting of SGML as defined by configurable style guides, and a DTD, to provide rapid display of scholarly data."

DISA Home Page (Data Interchange Standards Association)
http://www.disa.org
  Discusses national standards development and EDI.

Dublin Core Metadata Element Set Home Page
http://www.oclc.org:5046/research/dublin_core
  Many relevant links here.

EAD Finding Aid Project
http://lcweb2.loc.gov/ammem/ead/eadhome.html
  Read about LC's "efforts to encode archival finding aids using the Standard Generalized Markup Language and the beta version of the Encoded Archival Description (EAD) Document Type Definition (DTD)."

Fred: The SGML Grammar Builder
http://www.oclc.org/fred. By Keith Shafer.
  "Fred is an ongoing research project at OCLC to study the manipulation of tagged text." Articles and lists of documents are available, as well as the binary code if you would like to install Fred on your computer for non-commercial use. Read about Grammar Reduction from a URL or Input Text.

From Books to the Web: To Digitize a Library
http://onix.com/tonymck/iwnickw.htm
  Great SGML information in this step-by-step guide.

GILS (Government Information Locator Service) Report to the Information Infrastructure Task Force
http://www.acl.lanl.gov/sunrise/RelatedInfo/GILS/gils.html
> GILS developed its own method for handling metadata in government resources. GIL uses ANSI Z39.50 standards and client-server technology to allow users to locate government information.

HTML and Web Page Design Aids
University of Virginia Science and Engineering Libraries
http://www.lib.virginia.edu/science/othersci/pagedesign.shtml
> This page contains a wealth of information concerning links on backgrounds, icons, style guides, and templates to construct great looking Web pages, as well as an extensive list of links to HTML documents.

HTML Basics
Stanford University Libraries and Academic Information Resources
http://www-sul.stanford.edu/tools/tutorials/html2.0/basics.html
> A lengthy and extremely well done tutorial focusing on tagging, whitespace, managing files and directories, and Uniform Resource Locators.

HTML DTDs (and Other Public Text)
http://www.w3.org/pub/WWW/MarkUp/html-pubtext

HTML: Proposed Collection Level Tags
http://www.oclc.org:5047/oclc/research/publications/weibel/collection
> Discusses Persistent Toolbar Panels, multifonts, collection stylesheets, and more.

HTML Tags
http://www.uth.tmc.edu/~snewton/irc/howto.html
> Discusses the four foundational tags, document tags, headers, links, and more.

HTML Validation Tools and Link Checkers
http://lcweb.loc.gov/global/internet/html.html#validate
> Links to A Kinder Gentler Validator, Weblint: Quality Assurance for Web Pages, MOMspider (Multi-Owner Maintenance Spider), lvrfy, Checksite, and more.

Hypertext Transfer Protocol (HTTP) Working IETF Group
http://www.ics.uci.edu/pub/ietf/http

Indexing the World
http://stork.ukc.ac.uk/computer_science/Html/Pubs/IHC10–94/TOC.html

By Ian Cooper, Computing Laboratory, University of Kent, Canterbury, Kent, England.

A clearly written overview of what is involved in indexing the Web. Cooper favors Uniform Resource Names, and suggests that "smaller indices linked to, from a huge virtual index space, provide a functional scalable method of indexing individual documents."

Internet Technology Standards and Organizations Page
http://www.nlc-bnc.ca/ifla/II/standard.htm
Probably the most comprehensive site for standards on the Web.

Introduction to HTML
http://129.79.33.62/jmdocs/htmlintro.html
Tutorial by Digital Libraries covers basic and advanced HTML and multimedia integration.

Introduction to HTML
http://www.utoronto.ca/webdocs/HTMLdocs/NewHTML/htmlindex.html
Thorough documentation of HTML, SGML, CGI, and HTTP by Ian Graham.

MARC Record Sample in SGML Markup
http://sherlock.berkeley.edu/asis_paper/sgmlmarc.txt

Metadata and Data Cataloging
http://lcgisn./lsu.edu/lcgisn/meta_ovr.html
Overview of the Federal Geographic Data Committee Metadata Standard.

Metadata and Data Management Information Page
http://www.llnl.gov/liv_comp/metadata/metadata.html
IEEE workshops, mail archives, and a bibliography concerning metadata.

Metadata, Dublin Core, and USMARC: a Review of Current Efforts
gopher://marvel.loc.gov/00/.listarch/usmarc/dp99.doc
MARBI Discussion Paper no. 99, Library of Congress, January 21, 1997.

Metadata: The Foundations of Resource Description
http://www.cnri.reston.va.us/home/dlib/July95/07weibel.html. By Stuart Weibel, Office of Research, OCLC Online Computer Library Center, Inc. *D-Lib Magazine*, July 1995.

Meta Language for Describing Internet Resources Using the Dublin Core Element Set
http://gea01.pangea.org/lnet96/a2/a2_2.htm

NISO: National Information Standards Organization
http://www.niso.org

"Nonprofit association accredited as a standards developer by the American National Standards Institute, the national clearinghouse for voluntary standards in the U.S." Find abstracts for a multitude of standards here.

OCLC/NCSA Metadata Workshop Report
http://www.oclc.org:5047/research/conferences/metadata/
dublin_core_report.html

Executive summary by Stuart Weibel, Jean Godby, and Eric Miller.

SGML Bibliography Update
http://www.sil.org/sgml/biblio.html

Exhaustive listing.

SGML PRIMER: SoftQuad's Quick Reference Guide to the Essentials of the Standard: the SGML Needed for Reading a DTD and Marked-Up Documents and Discussing Them Reasonably
http://www.sq.com/sgmlinfo/primbody.html

Simplified SGML for Serial Headers, Version 2(SSSH2)
http://www.pira.co.uk/sssh/sssh2.htm

Standard Generalized Markup Language and the Transformation of Cataloging
http://www.sil.org/sgml/berknasg.html. By Daniel V. Pitti, University of California, Berkeley.

Presented at the Annual Conference of the North American Serials Interest Group, June 1994.

TEI Guidelines for Electronic Text Encoding and Interchange (P3)
http://etext.virginia.edu/TEI.html

Searchable documents made available from the Electronic Text Center at the University of Virginia. Download a program for converting TEI-tagged bibliographic headers into MARC format called tei2marc (*ftp://etext.lib.virginia.edu/pub/tei2marc/tei2marc.tar*).

Text Encoding Initiative: Background and Context Edited
http://www.gca.org/stanpub/teiback.htm. By Nancy Ide and Jean Ve'ronis.

Text Encoding Initiative (TEI) Recommendations
http://www.ilc.pi.cnr.it/EAGLES96/spokntx/node13.html

"A chapter of the TEI Guidelines is devoted to the transcription of spoken texts. It describes the basic structure . . . header, text divisions—and defines ways to signal basic structural elements.

Uniform Resource Names: A Progress Report
http://www.dlib.org/dlib/february96/02arms.html
> By the URN Implementors. *D-Lib Magazine*, February 1996.

Unique Identifiers: A Brief Introduction
http://www.bic.org.uk/bic/uniquid
> By Brian Green and Mark Bide.
>
> Discusses "intelligent" and "unintelligent" numbers, Serial Item and Contribution Identifier (SICI), Publisher Identification Identifier (PII), Digital Object Identifier (DOI), Uniform Resource Names (URNs), Persistent Uniform Resource Locators (PURLs), and more.

Universal Resource Characteristics (URCs)
http://union.ncsa.uiuc.edu/HyperNews/get/www/URCs.html
> Get your metadata data here! URCs are related to URNs (Universal Resource Names) (*http://union.ncsa.uiuc.edu:80/HyperNews/get/www/URNs.html*).

"You Call It Corn, We Call It Syntax—Independent Metadata for Document-Like Objects"
http://info.lib.uh.edu/pr/v6/n4/capl6n4.html
> By Priscilla Caplan. *Public Access Computer Systems Review* 6, no. 4 (1995): 19–23.

Z39.50 Maintenance Agency
http://lcweb.loc.gov/z3950/agency

2.5

Cataloging Special Formats and Subjects

Cataloging nonprint materials and music is often scarier than cataloging monographs. Cataloging serials comes with its own special set of headaches. Here, you'll not only find Web pages with information on these special formats, you'll also find much needed help cataloging materials of all kinds in special subjects like law and medicine.

2.5.1 COMPUTER FILES

Cataloging computer files is daunting, you say? Not with such wonderful documentation like that found in the Computer Files section. In particular, the University of Virginia's Chapter XII: Computer Files Cataloging Applications and Module 31: Remote Access Computer File Serials must be read.

Cataloging Computer Files

Princeton University Library's Cataloging Documentation

http://infoshare1.princeton.edu/katmandu/comp/comtoc.html

> Catalog remote access computer file publications, as well as CD-ROMs and Internet resources.

Chapter XII: Computer Files Cataloging

University of Virginia Library, Charlottesville, Virginia

http://www.lib.virginia.edu/cataloging/manual/chapters/chapxii.html

Development of CONSER Cataloging Policies for Remote Access Computer File Serials

http://info.lib.uh.edu/pr/v7/n1/anderson.7n1

> By Bill Anderson and Les Hawkins. *Public-Access Computer Systems Review* 7, no. 1 (1996).

Fields for Describing Computer Files: the British Library National Bibliographic Service (NBS)

http://portico.bl.uk/nbs/marc/856guid.html

> Discusses the 258 Computer File Characteristics Field, the equivalent to the U.S. ISBD Type and Extension of File Area. Also contains a slightly modified (for UKMARC) Guidelines for the Use of Field 856.

MARC Format Computer Files

http://infoshare1.princeton.edu/katmandu/marc/mdfmarc.html

Module 31: Remote Access Computer File Serials

http://lcweb.loc.gov/acq/conser/module31.html

> By Melissa Beck, University of California, Los Angeles.
>
> Indispensable site for understanding what a remote access computer file serial is and how to catalog it.

2.5.2 FOREIGN LANGUAGES

The section on Foreign Languages is one that is close to my heart (being a Latin American cataloger responsible for Spanish, Portuguese, Nahuatl, Mayan, Catalan, Galician, etc.). As any language specialist knows, each language has special rules, characteristics, etc. which set it apart from other languages. Spanish names have double surnames—the father's family name first and the mother's family name second. Portuguese names are cataloged using the last surname, even if that last name is Junior! Russian names consist of the father's family name used as a middle name, with the appropriate suffix added to signify "son" or "daughter." Some languages use unusual symbols, dots, and "clicks." Two of the absolutely best home pages for cataloging foreign languages are Cynthia Bertelsen's Cataloging Foreign Language Material: Resources for Cataloging and Princeton's Slavic Cataloging Manual. In addition to these great sites, included here are dictionaries, linguistics sites that allow you to identify unknown scripts by asking pertinent questions about the narrative in hand, and much, much more.

Abbreviations of the Names of the Month by Language
http://infoshare1.princeton.edu/katmandu/bookser/months.html

Acronym Expander
http://habrok.uio.no/cgi-bin/acronyms
   Helpful when it does know the requested acronym, and very polite when it doesn't know the answer. For example, a search on the acronym SALALM (Seminar on the Acquisition of Latin American Library Materials) merited the reply: "I'm terribly sorry, but I haven't heard that acronym before."

All the Scripts in the World
http://idris.com/scripts/Scripts.html
   Here's where to take that book written in a language that no one can identify. Find samples of any of 6,000 or so languages in current use. Each script is accompanied by an explanatory paragraph. There are even examples of three invented scripts.

Arabic Script Cataloging on RLIN
http://www.sas.upenn.edu/African_Studies/Software/
RLIN_Arabic_10732.html

Autores Latinoamericanos/Latin American Authors
http://www-lib.usc.edu/~calimano/bib_control/paises.html
   Fantastic resource compiled by Ivan Calimano, which contains a list of countries with appropriate links to the literary authors for each country. Every author listed has an LC classification number and cutter assigned.

Cataloging Foreign Language Materials: Resources for Catalogers
http://www.vt.edu:10021/B/bertel/catalog.html

This remarkable page by Cynthia D. Bertelsen really exemplifies what the ultimate languages home page should look like. It's colorful, succinct, and yet overflowing with good information. Highlights include a large section on Africana Cataloging and Resources (see Issues in Cataloging Non-Western Materials: Special Problems with African Language Materials at *http://www.vt.edu:10021/B/bertel/africana.html*). Other sections are just as wonderful. Cataloging Tools has a fine selection, with new material clearly marked. The Cultural and Historical Resources section has links to the CIA World Fact Book 1995, and the Islamic Calendar Converter (*http://wwwcgi.umr.edu/cgi-bin/cgiwrap/msaumr/hijri*), and World Flags. Be prepared to wander through this site for a long period of time.

Chinese Character Pronunciations
http://www.webcom.com/ocrat/reaf

Here's a "JavaScript application for showing how to pronounce Chinese characters. If you have some Chinese text and you don't know the pronunciation, you can find out by using your mouse to cut and paste it into this application. For each character, the transliterated pronunciation is displayed." Choose either Mandarin or Cantonese.

Colibri Dictionaries Page
http://colibri.let.ruu.nl/html/dictionaries.html

comp-jugador
http://csg.uwaterloo.ca/~dmg/lando/verbos/forma.html

Conjugates all Spanish verbs.

Cyrillic Alphabet
http://www.colby.edu/librarybase/tech.serv/Working%20papers/Cyrillic.html

Large type version, especially helpful for searching OCLC for Russian titles.

East Asian Studies BI Clearinghouse
http://www.library.ucsb.edu/chiu/house.html

See Chinese Romanization Systems: Zhuyin versus Pinyin, parts 1–4.

ECHO-EURODICATOM
http://www.uni-frankfurt.de/~felix/eurodictautom.html

New web interface of a database of official and technical terms. Fill in your query—choose source language used and target language requested. (This supposedly works for English, French, German, Italian, Spanish, Danish, Dutch, and Portuguese.)

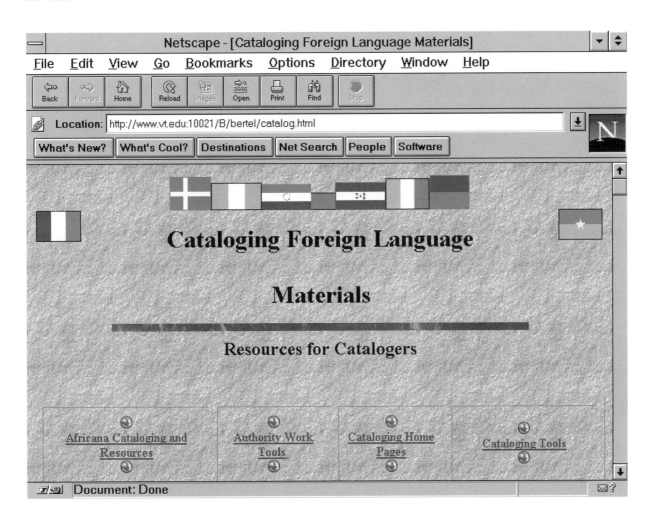

Figure 2.9
Cataloging Foreign Language Materials

English—Czech Dictionary
Anglicko Cesky Slovnik
http://www.fce.vutbr.cz/public/invrt/slovnik.html

English—Hungarian Dictionary
(Mta Sztaki Distributed Systems Department)
http://www.sztaki.hu/sztaki/elibrary/szotar.html

English—Russian Dictionary
http://public.elvis.ru/~denis/dict.cgi

English—Foreign Language Dictionaries of Common Computing Terms
http://www.css.qmw.ac.uk/CSS/foreign/intro.html
   Currently French, German, and Spanish, but more dictionaries will soon be added.

English to Italian Hypertext Dictionary (World Surfari)
http://www.supersurf.com/italy/ital-eng.htm
   Search by word or part of a word.

Ethnologue Languages of the World
Summer Institute of Linguistics, Inc., Dallas, Texas
http://www.sil.org/ethnologue/ethnologue.html
   Information by country or language family. Under Languages of Special Interest, there are 16 Gypsy languages, 27 Jewish languages, 79 Pidgin and Creole languages, and 103 deaf sign languages.

Foreign Language Resources on the Web
http://www.itp.berkeley.edu/~thorne/HumanResources.html
   Fantastic site. Gathers the best language pages in Arabic, Chinese, French (these sites are truly exceptional), German, Hebrew, Italian, Latin, Portuguese, Russian, Scandinavian, South Asian (Hindi, Nepali, and Urdu), Spanish, Swahili, Tagalog, Turkish, and Yiddish.

French–English Dictionary
http://humanities.uchicago.edu/forms_unrest/FR-ENG.html

Glossary of Bibliographic Information by Language
http://stauffer.queensu.ca/techserv/biblang.html
   From Danish to Swedish, with Latin and major European languages in between.

Greek and Latin Classics Internet Resources
a Library of Congress Internet Resource Page
http://lcweb.loc.gov/global/classics/claslink.html

Human-Languages Page
http://www.june29.com/HLP
> Translating dictionaries, online languages, and much more. "A focal point for language-related information on the net." Currently includes hundreds of links to spoken, written, signed, or invented languages.

Hypertext Webster Interface
http://lamb.connectnet.com/moto/websters.html
> Each definition is also a link.

Indonesian Multilanguage Machine Translation System—Chinese, Indonesian, Japanese, Malay, and Thai
http://nataya.aia.bppt.go.id/immts/immts.html

Internet Public Library Encyclopedia's Ready Reference
http://www.ipl.org/ref/RR/REF/encyclopedia-rr.html
> Get a free trial subscription to Britannica Online, check out Encyberpedia, the Encyclopedia Smithsonian, FAQ Finder (a guide to over 1800 FAQs), the Global Encyclopedia, and more.

Japanese–English Dictionary Gateway
http://www.wg.omron.co.jp/cgi-bin/j-e

Juergan Peus' Comprehensive Listing of Dictionaries on the Web
http://math-www.uni-paderborn.de/HTML/Dictionaries.html

Larry's Aussie Slang and Phrase Dictionary
http://www.uq.edu.au/~zzlreid/slang.html

Linguist's List: Dictionaries, Etc.
http://www.emich.edu/~linguist/dictionaries.html
> An exceptional collection of links. Browse through dictionary projects, thesauri, Turkish, Thai, Swedish, and Slovak dictionaries. Norwegian, Latin, Lakhota (Sioux), Greek, Estonian, Chinese—the possibilities are endless. There's also a large assortment of American English and British English dictonaries.

LingWhat?
http://idris.com/lingwhat/lingwhat.html
> This site asks pertinent questions about the unknown language in your hands, to narrow it down to a specific language. First question is: Does the language use the Latin alphabet? If your answer is no, then you will see this page: "Do you see any characters that look like the following?" This page is great fun. I can't wait to get hold of an unknown language to test it on.

List of Language Lists
Oxford University Language Centre, Oxford, England
http://info.ox.ac.uk/departments/langcentre/langlists.html
> Prepared by Bernard Comrie and Michael Everson.
>
> Potentially very useful site. For example, if I was cataloging an Aztec text and had a question, I could address it to the NAHUAT-L list, a Czech text question could be sent to the MUTEX list, and so on.

Logos Dictionary
http://www.logos.it/query.html
> Search 5 1/2 million terms in over 30 languages. Add or delete a definition, access someone pronouncing the word correctly, and link to dictionary lists from many different countries.

Martindale's "The Reference Desk" World Wide Overview— Dictionaries and Encyclopedias
http://www-sci.lib.uci.edu/HSG/Ref1.html#OVER2
> An extraordinary collection of language resources and dictionaries. Foreign Languages for Travelers contains over 20 languages: English-Finnish, English-German, English-Indonesian, etc.

Multilingual and Multiscript Issues in Cataloguing
http://www.nlc-bnc.ca/ifla/IV/ifla62/62–alij.htm
> By Joan M. Aliprand, Senior Analyst, Research Libraries Group, Inc.

National CJK (Chinese Japanese Korean) Service (National Library of Australia)
http://www.nla.gov.au/1/asian/ncjk
> Member libraries sharing data for CJK materials they hold.

Near East Technical Services Division (NETS)
http://infoshare1.princeton.edu/nets/deptnets.html
> Princeton is responsible for cataloging between 7,000–8,000 Near Eastern titles annually. Links to Arabic, Persian, Hebrew, Turkish, and Ottoman NACO procedures (Princeton only).

Non-Roman Core Record Task Group Final Report
gopher://marvel.loc.gov/00/services/cataloging/coop/coop_cncl/jackphy.fin
> Find out the PCC Core Record Elements required for records containing JACKPHY scripts.

OCLC CJK Users Group Home Page
http://sun3.lib.uci.edu/~oclccjk

On-Line Dictionaries
http://www.bucknell.edu/~rbeard/diction.html

Many dictionaries and thesauri listed here. Dictionaries that can be downloaded are available.

Pedro's Dictionaries
http://www.public.iastate.edu/~pedro/dictionaries.html

Portuguese Dictionary
http://www.public.iastate.edu/~pedro/pt_all/pt_dict.html/

Rivendell Online Language Dictionaries and Translators
http://rivendel.com/~ric/resources/dictionary.html
> Absolutely first-rate site, containing hundreds of multilingual and translation dictionaries. Links to dictionaries in approximately 75 languages, including Afrikaans, Chechen, Inuktitut, Gamilaraay (spoken by the Kamilaroi people of New South Wales, Australia), Latin, Rasta, and many others. On a scale of 1–4, this site merits a 5.

Romance Languages Resource Page
http://humanities.uchicago.edu/romance
> Browse this extensive list in French, Italian, Portuguese, or Spanish.

Slavic Cataloging Manual
Princeton University Libraries Cataloging Documentation
http://infoshare1.princeton.edu:/katmandu/sgman/smtocs.html
> Designed with the "experienced cataloger" in mind. Search alphabetically or by fields. For example, choosing "24.13 type 2" words gives us Slavic/Germanic Manual Corporate Bodies. Choosing "cities" results in Naming Changes for Cities of the Former Soviet Union. The Descriptive Cataloging section contains data on country of publication codes, titles, edition and series statements, and notes. Excellent authorities section. Another wonderful section is the Authority Number Section. Check call numbers for Czech, Polish, Russian, Slovak, Belarusian, and Ukranian authors. Or how about Names of Married Hungarian Women? Also take a look at Jim Weinheimer's Home Page: Slavic/Germanic Cataloger at Firestone Library (*http://www.princeton.edu/~jamesw/index.html*). This is a flawless example of what a subject specialist's page should look like. For an excellent overview, see Recent Trends in Slavic Cataloging at Princeton University.

Some Guidelines for Cataloguing Khojki Manuscripts
http://global.globale.net/~heritage/granths/guide.html
> By Dr. Ali S. Asani, Harvard University.
>> Hints on cataloging Ismaili literature in Indic languages. This is multilingual material employing several different scripts in one item.

TransWord Foreign Language Crossword Puzzles

ftp://ftp.dartmouth.edu/pub/LLTI-IALL/365german-news/tw/index.htm

OK, not exactly cataloging-related, but lots of fun. As the page says "Test your English, German, Spanish, French, Italian, Dutch vocabulary!"

Universal Survey of Languages

http://www.teleport.com/~napoleon

Alphabetic list of languages with audio samples.

Vernacular Designations

http://infoshare1.princeton.edu/katmandu/bookser/verntoc.html

Available in almost any language.

Virsoft

http://www.virsoft.com

Shareware version of a Spanish-English dictionary that attaches directly to Microsoft MS Word 7.0.

Web of Culture

http://www.worldculture.com

Award-winning site discussing world culture. Find lists of capitals, currency, gestures, holidays, languages, resources, religions, etc.

Web of On-Line Grammars

http://www.bucknell.edu/~rbeard/grammars.html

Find grammars and language instruction in 27 languages, including Speaking Chinese, an Integral Dutch Course, English for Russian Speakers, French Lessons with Real Audio Sound, Kurdish Grammars, Galician Morphosyntax, and Welsh Grammars.

Wordbot

http://www.cs.washington.edu/homes/kgolden/wordbot.html

This incredible page will change forever the way you search the Web. Load a page through Wordbot, choose a language dictionary, and every word on the page will now be an underlined link to the appropriate dictionary translation. This site is better using frames, since you can view the dictionary and the page at the same time.

Yahoo! Dictionaries

http://www.yahoo.com/Reference/Dictionaries

Yamada Language Center Non-English Font Archive

http://babel.uoregon.edu/yamada/fonts.html

Information about 103 languages. Contains 112 fonts for 40 languages. The font guides are very clear and are accompanied by language guides and links to related pages.

2.5.3 INTERNET RESOURCES AND DIGITAL DOCUMENTS

Internet Resources and Digital Documents is the section where new ideas, thoughts, and experiments abound. How do we catalog Internet resources? Which sites do we choose? What level of cataloging do we give them? Do we use Library of Congress or Dewey Decimal classification, or no classification at all? How often will we check our 856 fields for outdated, changed, transmogrified, or non-existent links? Will we use PURLs? It is perhaps daunting to think that some sources estimate a total of 10,000 new web pages are created daily. Even though the majority of these appear to be personal home pages, or commercial enterprises, there is still a number of academic, research, and library-oriented pages being created as well. If you must only investigate two sites in this section, I would recommend the Intercat site and the PURL (Persistent Uniform Resource Locators) page. But there's such an abundance of material here that I hope you will investigate all of these sites and begin to catalog Internet resources yourself. Only by all of us cataloging these sites will we learn how, why, which ones. All these questions are still up in the air and must be answered soon, and in a decisive manner, or our days of cataloging are numbered.

Ad-Hoc Classification of Electronic Clinical Documents
http://www.dlib.org/dlib/january97/medical/01aronow.html
By David B. Aronow and Fangfang Feng, *D-Lib Magazine*, January 1997.
Classification is based on INQUERY (*http://ciir.cs.umass.edu/inqueryhomepage.html*), which is an information retrieval system based on document indexing, query processing, query evaluation, and relevance feedback. There is also a Japanese version of INQUERY.

ALCTS Taskforce on Meta Access
http://www.lib.virginia.edu/alcts
Superb site. Very comprehensive listing under Internet Cataloging and Access Projects.

By the Lake: Cataloging Internet Resources
University of Wisconsin–Madison
http://www.uwm.edu:80/People/mrowe/cat.html
Mary Rowe's helpful list.

Cataloging Digital Images: Issues
http://lcweb.loc.gov/catdir/semdigdocs/gaynor.html
By Edward Gaynor, University of Virginia Library.

Cataloging Electronic Texts (Electronic Text Centers and Libraries)
http://www.ceth.rutgers.edu/info/news32/CATALOG.html
Procedures for cataloging electronic texts in MARC format through RLIN.

Cataloging in the Digital Order
http://csdl.tamu.edu/DL95/papers/levy/levy.html
By David M. Levy, Xerox Palo Alto Research Center.
  Wonderful paper written by a computer scientist, which "explores the nature of cataloging as it is now practiced." Mr. Levy talked to catalogers, observed one at work, read the seminal texts, and subscribed to library/cataloging Listservs to research his paper, which also theorizes on the future of cataloging.

Cataloging Internet Resources: a Beginning
http://www.lib.ncsu.edu/staff/morgan/cataloging-resources.html
  Not to be passed up. Eric Lease Morgan, of "Mr. Serials" fame, discusses former projects as well as current efforts to include Internet resources into library OPACs.

Cataloging Internet Resources: A Beginning
http://www.library.yale.edu/~mbeacom/clatalk/index.htm
  Matthew Beacom, Yale University Libraries, shares his comprehensive Power Point slides used for a presentation at the 105th annual Conference of the Connecticut Library Association, April 23–24, 1996.

Cataloging Internet Resources: A Manual and Practical Guide
http://www.cwru.edu/CWRU/UL/Manual.txt Nancy B. Olson, editor.
  Developed to assist those participating in the OCLC/U.S. Department of Education-funded project: "Building a Catalog of Internet Resources." Codes and tags follow OCLC MARC rather than USMARC format.

Cataloging Internet Resources (OCLC Samples)
http://www.oclc.org/oclc/man/9256cat/example.htm

Cataloging Internet Resources Project
http://ublib.buffalo.edu/libraries
  Contains guidelines, links, and more.

Cataloging Productivity Tools/I. Spectrum: A Web-Tool for Describing Internet Resources
http://www.oclc.org/oclc/research/publications/review94/part1/1spectr.htm
  Project Manager, Diane Vizine-Goetz, Consulting Research Scientist, OCLC.

Cataloging the Internet
http://ublib.buffalo.edu/libraries/units/cts/Internet/brugger.html
  By Judith M. Brugger.

Cataloging the Internet: Report from the Field
http://library.tufts.edu/~webtisch/cataloging/netsl/netsl.htm

Presentation prepared for the NETSL (New England Technical Services Librarians) spring meeting, April 12, 1996, Worcester, Massachusetts, by Rick J. Block. Discusses what and what not to catalog, and provides specially prepared work forms. Take a look at Internet Cataloging Procedures, as well.

Cataloguing and Indexing of Electronic Resources
http://www.nlc-bnc.ca/ifla/II/catalog.htm

Extremely helpful index of articles, mailing lists, periodicals, and Web sites pertaining to electronic resource cataloging.

Cataloguing and the Internet: Some Personal Thoughts
http://www.scit.wlv.ac.uk/wwlib/docs/thoughts.html

By Peter Burden, School of Computing and Information Technology, University of Wolverhampton, West Midlands, England.

Discusses the development of WWWlib, a "classified, searchable catalog of U.K. WWW pages."

Cataloguing Rules and Conceptual Models
http://www.oclc.org:5046/~emiller/misc/tillett.html

By Barbara B. Tillet, Library of Congress.

OCLC Distinguished Seminar Series, January 9, 1996.

Cataloguing the Internet: Pitfalls in the Quest for "Quality Links"
http://www.cfc.sc.dnd.ca/~aaron/paper.html

By Aaron Bradley, Canadian Forces College.

An all-around outstanding collection of links presented (in absentia) at the First International Workshop on the Future of Intrenet Services.

CATNET Project
University of Arizona Libraries Access Action Plan, 1996–1997
http://dizzy.library.arizona.edu/users/eagleson/catnet-w.htm

A substantial site, interested in cataloging and archiving campus-general knowledge.

Cheshire II System
http://sherlock.berkeley.edu/asis_paper/sectionstar3_2.html

For all those interested in the future of online catalogs and full-text information retrieval.

Dewey 2000: Cataloging Productivity Tools
http://www.oclc.org/oclc/fp/research/dwy2000/dwy2000.htm

By Joan S. Mitchell, editor, Dewey Decimal Classification, and Diane Vizine-Goetz, OCLC.

Digital Documents Cataloging and Its Professional Implications on Librarians

http://imlab9.landarch.uiuc.edu/~wu/Self/Spring95/lis475/Paper1.0.html
By Xin Wu.

"One-site centralized cataloging will be eliminated, because the original document is already machine readable and all the bibliographic information is imbedded in it. Cataloging will shift to more complicated knowledge relationship control."

Digital Image Collections: Cataloging Data Model and Network Access

http://www.columbia.edu/cu/libraries/inside/projects/diap/paper.html
By Stephen Paul Davis, Columbia University Libraries.

Discusses new methods of cataloging images, sound files, full-motion videos, composite documents, archival collections, and texts.

Does It Really Matter? The Cataloging Format, the Sequential Order of Note Fields, and the Specifics of Field 856

http://www.oclc.org/oclc/man/colloq/shieh.htm
Paper presented by Jackie Shieh, University of Virginia Library, at the OCLC Internet Cataloging Project Colloquium.

eJournals, Suchmaschinen und die Katalogisierung des WWW:
Max-Planck-Gesellschaft, Munich, Germany

http://www.gwdg.de/~hkuhn1/wwwcat/gfkl196v.html/
Excellent overview by Dr. Heinrich Kuhn.

"Vortrag gehalten auf der 20. Jahrestagung der Gesellschaft für Klassifikation in Freiburg am 7. Marz 1996."

Electronic Classification Schemes
http://orc.rsch.oclc.org:6109/classification

Electronic Journals—Cataloguing
http://library.uwaterloo.ca/ejournals/info/ej_cataloguing.html
"Listed here are projects or discussions relevant to cataloguing electronic journals or electronic resources in general."

Formas de se Classificar a Informacao na Web
http://www.psi.com.br/Sistemas_de_Procura/introducao.html

Guidelines for Cataloguing Online Resources
http://www.konbib.nl/kb/is/gedocarchief/edocarchief/olr.en.html
Dutch-English document detailing how online resources should be cataloged in a shared automated cataloging system. Extremely detailed document complete with many MARC field examples.

Guidelines for the Use of Field 856

http://www.loc.gov/marc/856guide.html

Revised March 1996. Prepared by the Network Development and MARC Standards Office.

Learn all about the USMARC bibliographic and holdings format used for electronic location and access, which contains the information needed to locate an electronic resource.

Information About Cataloguing Electronic Resources

http://www.englib.cornell.edu/needscataloging/etext.html

Compiled by Richard J. Pugh.

Many valuable links here, including Cornell University's Guidelines for Cataloging Electronic Resources on Servers.

Interactive Electronic Serials Cataloging Aid (IESCA)

http://www.library.nwu.edu/iesca

Provides a glossary of cataloging and computer terms, and contains cataloging rules, interpretations, and examples.

InterCat—A Catalog of Internet Resources

http://www.oclc.org/oclc/man/catproj/overview.htm

Searchable catalog of bibliographic records for Internet resources, selected and cataloged by libraries around the world. Project enrollment peaked at 225 libraries, creating over 4,000 bibliographic records, with a 2.7 percent URL failure rate in its last test. Search by author, title, uniform title, subject, publisher, notes, electronic access field, OCLC number, year, and more. Archives are available at *http://ftplaw.wuacc.edu/listproc/intercat/archive.html*

Internet Library for Librarians Cataloging

http://www.itcompany.com/inforetriever/cat.htm

Completely revamped resource, compiled by Vianne Tang Sha. An incredible listing of cataloging-related Internet resources. Sections include Organizing Internet Resources, Non-Cataloging Approach, Traditional Cataloging Approach, and a compendium of USMARC documents.

Internet Resources to Inform and Support Cataloguing Functions

University of Toronto Library

http://www.fis.utoronto.ca:80/library/cir/catnet.htm

University of Toronto Faculty of Information Studies Continuing Education Workshop. Discusses e-journals cataloged as part of the University of Toronto's Electronic Resources Project, the application of AACR2R to cataloging, and MARC Coding of Internet Resources. Samples of an OPAC record for PACS Review with and without MARC tags is included. "The purpose behind designing such a page for a cataloging depart-

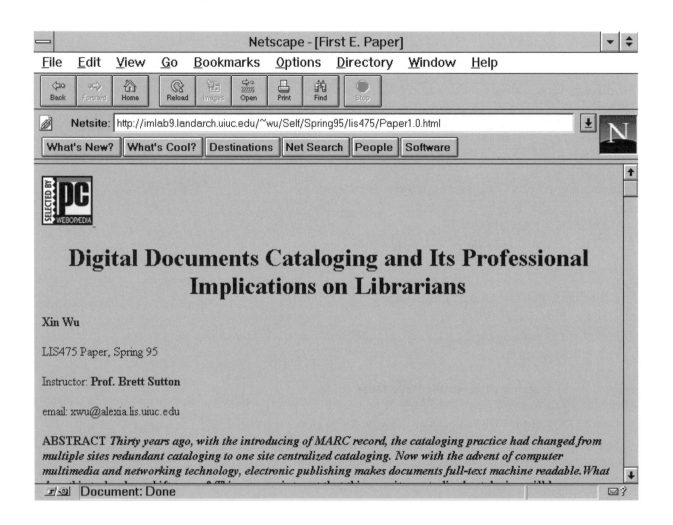

Figure 2.10
Digital Documents Cataloging and Its Professional Implications for Librarians

ment is to increase the efficiency of the cataloguing process and create more complete and accurate bibliographic records.

Modifying Cataloging Practice and OCLC Infrastructure for Effective Organization of Internet Resources
http://www.oclc.org/oclc/man/colloq/hsieh.htm

By Ingrid Hsieh-Yee, Assistant Professor, School of Library and Information Science, Catholic University of America.

After cataloging 160 Internet resources in two months, it became clear that some aspects of full-level cataloging did not work well with Internet resources, and so an augmented minimal-level cataloging standard is proposed.

OCLC's NetFirst (the Authoritative Directory for Internet Resources)
http://www.oclc.org/oclc/netfirst/netfirst.htm

Now available on OCLC's OLUC, Firstsearch, and EPIC. NetFirst "indexes all major Internet resource types, including WWW pages, discussion lists, Usenet newsgroups, FTP sites, journals, newsletters, gopher sites, library catalogs, and Internet-accessible services." Fifty-five thousand records to start, and 8,000 more added monthly. See the FAQ for more information. View a demo or browse some sample records. Each record includes an annotated abstract, host location, subject headings, and Dewey classification numbers. NetFirst (and FirstSearch) are not free. Check for pricing information and free trial offers.

Persistent URL Project (PURL)
http://purl.oclc.org

Persistent Uniform Resource Locators (PURLs) are markers that point to an intermediate resolution service instead of the oh-so-changeable URL. When the URL changes, "the PURL resolution service associates the PURL with the actual URL and returns that URL to the client." PURLs have been assigned to all cataloged records in the Internet Cataloging Project. This site explains PURLs, as well as allowing you to register and create your own PURLs for your site. PURL software can be downloaded, or join the PURL-L discussion list at *http://purl.oclc.org/OCLC/PURL/PURL-L*. An alternative prototype search is now available at *http://ss2.dev.oclc.org:4076/SecondSearch/Second.html*.

Proceedings of the OCLC Internet Cataloging Colloquium
http://www.oclc.org/oclc/man/colloq/toc.htm

Conference held in San Antonio, Texas, January 19, 1996. Very interesting collection of field reports and position papers. The *Ambivalent Librarian* by Mark R. Watson, University of Oregon Library, discusses the experience of his library with the Intercat Project; Amanda Xu, MIT Li-

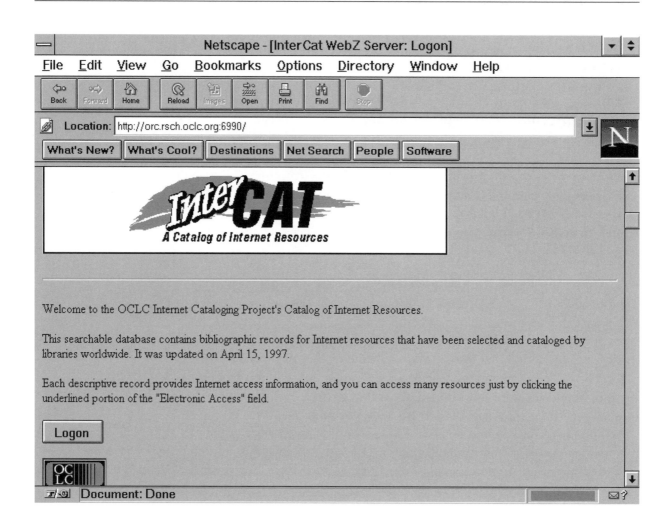

Figure 2.11
InterCat

braries, has written Accessing Information on the Internet: Feasability Study of USMARC Format and AACR. This large document discusses the use of TEI headers, the Dublin Core Metadata element set, the Uniform Resource Characteristic, and the USMARC format to describe Internet resources. Finally, check out Access to Networked Documents: Catalogs? Search Engines? Both? by Arlene G. Taylor and Patrice Clemson, University of Pittsburgh.

Proceedings of the Seminar on Cataloging Digital Documents, October 12–14, 1994, University of Virginia Library, Charlottesville, and the Library of Congress
http://lcweb.loc.gov/catdir/semdigdocs/seminar.html

> Lots of graphics, audio messages, and information from this groundbreaking seminar. Some of the difficulties involved in using MARC bibliographic records as a basis for indexing digital documents are discussed here. Catalogers are asked to be alert to the potential of providing access to bibliographic materials in innovative ways (i.e., without using MARC).

Project Aristotle: Automated Categorization of Web Resources
http://www.public.iastate.edu/~CYBERSTACKS/Aristotle.htm

> "A clearinghouse of projects, research, products, and services that are investigating or demonstrating the automated categorization, classification, or organization of Web resources."

Report of the Task Force on Cataloging Remote Access Electronic Serials
http://www.library.yale.edu/cataloging/netinfo/ejtfrpt3.htm

RLG Digital Image Access Project (DIAP)
http://www.columbia.edu/cu/libraries/indiv/avery/diap.html

> Link to Avery Images, a sample of Columbia's Stokes/DIAP images, along with PhotoCD versions of those same images. These images have been attached to Avery Library's RLIN MARC catalog.

Scorpion Project
http://orc.rsch.oclc.org:6109

> OCLC research project studying cataloging and indexing of electronic resources. The "primary focus of Scorpion is the building of tools for automatic subject recognition based on well-known schemes like the Dewey Decimal System."

Subject Tree, Library Service, and CATRIONA
http://bubl.at.uk/link/subjects

> CATRIONA was set up to "investigate the technical, organizational, and

financial requirements for the development of applications programs and procedures to enable the cataloguing, classification, and retrieval of documents and other resources over networks, and to explore the feasability of a library system supplier-led collaborative project to develop such applications and procedures and to integrate them with one or more existing library housekeeping systems and associated OPAC interfaces." This page discusses the development of CATRIONA and the Subject Tree (UDC) structure.

TPOT: Cataloging Internet/Electronic Resources
http://tpot.ucsd.edu/Cataloging/catinternet.html

As always, TPOT comes through with some exceptional links.

Using Library Classification Schemes for Internet Resources
http://www.oclc.org/oclc/man/colloq/v-g.htm

Diane Vizine-Goetz, OCLC Office of Research and Special Projects, provides an overview of online classification data, specifically Online Dewey and the Library of Congress Classification Schedules to catalog Internet resources.

Why are Electronic Publications Difficult to Classify? The Orthogonality of Print and Digital Media
gopher://arl.cni.org:70/00/scomm/edir/guedon.94

By Jean-Claude Guedon, Department of Comparative Literature, University of Montreal.

A seminal article, which originally appeared in the 4th edition of the Directory of Electronic Journals, Newsletters, and Academic Discussion Lists, May 1994.

Yahoo! Cataloging the Web
http://www.library.ucsb.edu/untangle/callery.html

Read all about Yahoo!'s subject hierarchy, and how and why it was designed.

2.5.4 LEGAL MATERIALS

A highlight of the Legal Materials section is the page developed by the Florida State University Law Library Cataloging Department. Much good documentation is available here, more than at any other legal library site known at the time of this writing. For the same reason, included are a few more general sites that will probably yield a much larger selection of cataloging-related home pages than was originally discovered.

Bodleian Law Library Cataloguing Report, 1985–1993
http://www.rsl.ox.ac.uk/mh/rpt/rpt93bll.html
   Discusses backlogs, total number of law cataloging records added, and much more.

Cataloging Department Procedures Manual, Charles B. Sears Law Library
State University of New York at Buffalo
http://wings.buffalo.edu/libraries/units/law/services/cataloging/proc_manual.html
   Excellent cataloging manual. Contains procedures for supplements, loose leaf formats, and multi-volume piece designators, as well as discussing the backlog and law location guides.

Cataloging Manual, University of San Francisco, School of Law Library
San Francisco, California
http://www.usfca.edu/law_library/ts/cat/tp.html
   Premier legal cataloging site. Check out Preparing the Materials for Cataloging, Actually Cataloging Materials, and the Cataloging Manual Revisions of Texts Decision Chart, which details how to choose the correct main and added entries for items that are revisions of other items. For some humor, see Quotes to Aid in Times of Cataloging Crises.

Charting the Web—Resources of Interest to Law Librarians
http://vls.law.vill.edu/library.info/inlib.htm

Copy Cataloging and Cooperative Cataloging
http://www.aallnet.org/sis/fcilsis/093kuper.html
   By Aaron W. Kuperman, Library of Congress. *FCIL Newsletter*, May 1995. Legal emphasis.

Florida State University Law Library Cataloging Department
http://law.fsu.edu/library/cat/catdept.html
   Extensive documentation available. Especially valuable is the Hypertext Assisted Technical Services: FSU Law Library Cataloging Procedures

Manual (*http://law.fsu.edu/library/cat/catman.html*), which covers everything from authority file maintenance to withdrawals. This document is helpful to any cataloger, especially those using a NOTIS system.

Foreign and International Law Web Page (ForIntLaw), Washburn University School of Law, Topeka, Kansas
http://lawlib.wuacc.edu/forint/forintmain.html
> See Cataloging Enhancements to Local Indexes, which details projects like the updating of ISSN fields in bibliographic records for ILP-indexed law reviews and journals for improved "hook-to-holdings" and many other local enhancements. Search international law by geographical region or by topic.

ILUG (Innovative Law Users Group)
http://ftplaw.wuacc.edu/ilug/ilug.htm
> Member-created documentation and more.

Law Library Catalogs
http://lawlib.wuacc.edu/washlaw/lawcat/lawcat.html
> Telnet to a multitude of law library catalogs.

LawCrawler: Legal WWW Search
http://www.lawcrawler.com/index.html

'Lectric Law Library
http://192.41.4.29/index.html
> Take a virtual tour. Stop at the Lawcopedia to search legal terms and topics. Use the 'Lectric Law Looker-Upper if you become confused. A handy guide to SuDoc numbers can be found at *http://www.lectlaw.com/files/lwr14*.

Legal Sources on the Internet
http://jcomm.uoregon.edu/~tgleason/Law_j202.html
> Many legal links of possible utility.

Legislative Indexing Vocabulary: the CRS Thesaurus (Library of Congress)
http://lcweb.loc.gov/lexico/liv/brsearch.html
> "Once you have located the correct LIV Index term by searching or browsing, you can find legislation relevant to that term by copying and pasting or typing the LIV Index term directly in the Search by Index Term box in THOMAS."

Lillian Goldman Law Library at Yale Acquisitions and Cataloging Tools

http://elsinore.cis.yale.edu/lawweb/techacq.htm

Helpful listing of useful sites. Search the GPO Monthly Catalog of U.S. Government Publications (MOCAT) at *http://www.access.gpo.gov/su_docs/dpos/adpos400.html*

Meta-Index for U.S. Legal Research

http://gsulaw.gsu.edu/metaindex

Anything can be searched here, including general search tools as well as specialized legal tools.

Russian Law: KL Schedules (Princeton Slavic/Germanic Manual Classification)

http://infoshare1.princeton.edu/katmandu/sgman/kl.html

Technical Services Law Librarian

http://www.aallnet.org/sis/tssis/tsll/tsll.htm

The latest five issues are available. Regular columns include Description and Entry, Internet, Preservation, Serials, Subject Headings, and more.

University of Oklahoma Law Center Directory of Library-Related Discussion Groups

http://www.law.uoknor.edu/lists.html#librar

Check out the archived messages of CALL-L (Canadian Academic Law Librarians), GOVDOC-L, Law-Tech, and more.

Use of Law Library Records

Yale University, Orbis Cataloging Manual

http://lsounix1.library.yale.edu/~lso/orbis_catman1/lawbibl.html

World List: Non-U.S. Law-Related Resources for Internet Users—

http://www.law.osaka-u.ac.jp./legal-info/worldlist/world.htm

WWLIA (World Wide Legal Information Association) Legal Dictionary

http://www.islandnet.com/~wwlia/diction.htm

It's clearly written and fun to use. See the legal definition of "zipper" for a good example.

WWW Resources for Law Librarians in Acquisitions and Collection Development (AcqWeb)

http://www.library.vanderbilt.edu/law/acqs/law.html

WWW Virtual Library: Law

http://www.law.indiana.edu/law/v-lib/lawindex.html

> Lists of law libraries, law journals on the Web, law search tools (like LawCrawler) (*http://www.lawcrawler.com*), which searches U.S. and foreign federal legal information), and the Legal Research Meta-Index.

Yahoo! Law

http://www.yahoo.com/Law

2.5.5 MEDICAL MATERIALS

There are many more medically-related home pages dealing with cataloging than I was able to find in the Medical Materials section. Do, by all means, check out the Harley E. French Library of the Health Sciences Library Statistical Portrait of Cataloging 1994–1995, as well as the National Library of Medicine site.

Adding Value: An Activity Analysis of the Cataloging Process of the University of the West Indies, Medical Sciences Library
http://yotrinidad.com/mpredhtm
   by Martha Ingrid Preddie

Brief Guide to National Library of Medicine Call Numbers
http://www.hslib.washington.edu/hsl/infoguid/nlmcall.html

CliniWeb (Clinically Relevant Search Results from Various Web Sites)
http://www.ohsu.edu/cliniweb/sites.html
   Developed at the Oregon Health Sciences University, this project indexes clinical Web pages using MeSH vocabulary.

Entrez MEDLINE Query
http://www.molbiol.ox.ac.uk/www/ewan/enform.html

Hardin Meta Directory of Internet Health Sources
http://www.arcade.uiowa.edu/hardin-www/md.html
"We list the sites that list the sites."

Harley E. French Library of the Health Sciences (University of North Dakota School of Medicine) Bibliographic Control Page
http://www.med.und.nodak.edu/depts/library/bibcontr.htm
   Check out the Statistical Portrait of Cataloging for 1995–1996, which lists new titles cataloged, changes to the online catalog, and a nice smaller selection of cataloging resource links.

How to Order Cataloging for Medical Titles (MARCIVE)
http://www.marcive.com/news0995.htm#howtoorder

How to Use "Index Medicus"
http://www.kumc.edu/service/dykes/TIPSHEET/indxmed.html

Internet Address for Technical Services Questions About Selection, Acquisitions, and Cataloging at the National Library of Medicine
http://www.nnlm.nlm.nih.gov/psr/lat/v4n3/netadtsd.html

Internet Grateful Med: New User's Survival Guide
http://igm.nlm.nih.gov/Html-Documents/splash/igm_20/
IGM.survival.guide.html
   Detailed document.

Medical Entities Dictionary (MED)
http://paella.med.yale.edu/medinf/med.html
   "A structured medical vocabulary developed at Columbia University."
   Although created for internal use, they have allowed the dictionary to be
   accessible by the public.

Medical Museum Without Walls
http://http2.Sils.umich.edu/HCHS/RetroSpex/RetroV3N1/retro3.1c.html
   By Denise Anthony, Artifacts Cataloger, Historical Center for the Health
   Sciences.

Medical Subject Headings: Annotated Alphabetic List
http://www.fedworld.gov/ntis/health/medann.htm
   Ordering information.

Medical Subject Headings Information: MeSH
U.S. National Library of Medicine
http://www.nlm.nih.gov/mesh/meshhome.html

Medicine Net Medical Dictionary
http://www.medicinenet.com/MAINMENU/GLOSSARY/Gloss_A.htm

MEDLARS (Medical Literature Analysis and Retrieval System)
http://www.wnet.org/mhc/Info/Resources/general.html
   The "computerized system of databases and databanks offered by the
   National Library of Medicine." Contact and telnet information available.

MEDLINE Database
http://sacredheart.len.net/medline.htm
   Free access to certain portions of the database.

MEDLINE MeSH Subheadings
http://info.gas.org/STNEWSPMAY/mesh.html

Medscape
http://www5.medscape.com
   Register the first time, then access an extensive Glossary of Medical Terms,
   thousands of free full-text articles, and search MEDLINE.

MEDWEB: Biomedical Internet Resources
http://www.cc.emory.edu/WHSCL/medweb.html

Merck Manual
http://www.merck.com
  Free searching available here.

Most Useful Fields When Cataloging Medical Artifacts
http://http2.sils.umich.edu/HCHS/ARTIFACTS/expfields.html

Multilingual Glossary of Technical and Popular Medical Terms in Nine European Languages
http://allserv.rug.ac.be/~rvdstich/eugloss/welcome.html

National Library of Medicine Cataloging-in-Publication (NLM/CIP Project)
gopher://marvel.loc.gov:70/00/services/cataloging/coop/coop_nlm

National Library of Medicine Call Number
http://206.102.94.200/tlc/crs/Auth0243htm

National Library of Medicine (NLM) Classification, 5th ed., 1994
http://www.tulane.edu/~matas/5intro.html
  Introduction and scope notes.

National Library of Medicine Classification Scheme for Books
  http://www.hap.man.ac.uk/lib/class.html

NLM Locator
http://www.nlm.nih.gov/databases/locator.html
  "Searches the book holdings database (CATLINE), the audiovisual holdings database (AVLINE), the journal holdings database (SERLINE), and
  the directory of information resources (DIRLINE) of the U.S. National
  Library of Medicine."

OMNI: Organizing Medical Networked Information
http://omni.ac.uk
  Database of resource descriptions containing titles, URLs, MeSH keywords, and NLM classification codes.

Rethinking Genres/Forms Divisions
http://www-mlatss.stanford.edu/InviteHoffmann.html
  By Christa Hoffmann, Head, Cataloging Section, National Library of
  Medicine.

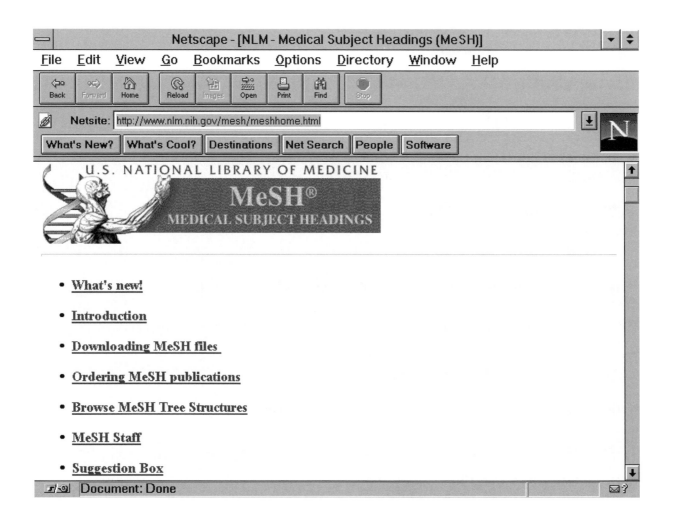

Figure 2.12
Medical Subject Headings Information (U.S. National Library of Medicine)

SEA Currents: Cataloging the Internet: Mission Impossible?
http://www.nnlm.nlm.nih.gov/sar/curr/96n4/catalog.html
> Discusses the experience of the University of Baltimore Health Sciences
> Library.

Unified Medical Language System (UMLS)
http://www.nlm.nih.gov/pubs/factsheets/umls.html
> Information on the Specialist Lexicon, an English lexicon of biomedical
> terms, and the Metathesaurus (concepts can be mapped to terms).

U.S. National Library of Medicine
http://www.nlm.nih.gov
> Connect to MEDLARS via telnet. Grateful Med for Windows is now
> available, as well as fact sheets, newsletters, reports, and ordering infor-
> mation.

2.5.6 MUSIC MATERIALS

Music cataloging is a special case unto itself. In addition to regular access points (author, title, subject), music cataloging records should provide access to composers, soloists, conductor, performance groups, etc. Frequently the material included is so varied that subject access becomes impossible. Another problem involved in cataloging music is the fragility of the various mediums. Sheet music disintegrates, vinyl scratches and warps—and, in order to adequately describe many pieces, the item must be listened to, increasing the wear and tear. Many sites are of interest in the Music Materials section, including two necrology indexes, but most of my praise is directed toward the Music Library Association's Working Group's site, Sheet Music Cataloging Guidelines. It's fantastic!

British Library Music File Service
http://icarus.bl.uk/nbs/recs/cbridge/music.html
> "Provides fortnightly sets of catalogue records for sheet music published in the United Kingdom and received under legal deposit as well as overseas publications acquired by the British Library." View a sample of the Music File Record.

CAIRSS for Music Database of Music Research Literature
http://www.einet.net/hytelnet/FUL064.html
> Search this huge bibliographic database of music research literature. Contains the full text of 18 primary journals and selected articles from 1,500 more.

Case for Composer Main Entry for Videorecordings of Musical Works
http://www.music.indiana.edu/tech_s/mla/gf.dt. By Grace Fitzgerald.

Cataloging Documentation (SIRSI)
http://library.vanderbilt.edu/sirsidoc/h-code-m.htm
> Holdings codes from NOTIS to SIRSI

Cataloging Music Theses
Princeton University Libraries
http://infoshare1.princeton.edu/katmandu/desc/thesmus.html

Clasicat for Windows
http://www.tdware.com/index.html
> Classical music cataloging program available in both 16-bit and 32-bit versions.

Common Music Dictionary
http://ccrma-www.stanford.edu/CCRMA/Software/cm/dict/Intro.html

By Heinrich Taube, Composition /Theory School of Music, University of Illinois.
Technically oriented dictionary which gives multiple definitions of such words as amplitude, pitches, and scales.

Composer Timeline
http://www.edinboro.edu/cwis/music/cordell/timeline.html
    Search by century.

Eda Kuhn Loeb Music Library, Harvard University
http://www.rism.harvard.edu/MusicLibrary/Welcome.html
    Especially interesting is the Library Classification Scheme, developed in the nineteenth century specifically for Harvard's collections and to facilitate browsing.

Faceted Access to Music: The Music Library Association Thesaurus Project
http://velcome.iupui.edu/~lcarter/music_t/musictop.html

Gaylord Music Library Necrology File
Washington University in St. Louis, Missouri
http://library.wustl.edu/~music/#necro
    Updated monthly. Includes birth, death dates, and where the information was found. All conflicting information is included. While at this site, check out the Sheet Music Collection or the Manuscript Collection for a colorful treat (even holographs are included).

Indiana University William and Gayle Cook Music Library
http://www.music.indiana.edu/muslib.html
    Premier academic music library. Participate in the Music OCLC Users Group's NACO-Music Project. Check out the Core Music Reference Guide.

ISMN (International Standard Music Number)
http://www.nlc-bnc.ca/services/e-ismn.htm
    "A unique code for the identification of printed music publications."

MLA (Music Libraries Association) Obituary Index
http://www-sul.stanford.edu/depts/music/mla/necrology
    Colorful, information-filled site. Search by name or nationality.

Music Catalogers' Folder
http://www.library.cornell.edu/cts/music.htm
    Access Composer's Cutter Numbers and Instruments and Voices Codes.

Music Cataloging

Princeton University Libraries

http://infoshare1.princeton.edu/katmandu/music/mustoc.html

Detailed information concerning scores cataloging, sound recordings, and computer data files. See the Countries List for Folk and Non-Western Art Music Recordings at *http://infoshare1.princeton.edu:/katmandu/music/receth.html* ML410: Musician's Shelflist contains cutter numbers for frequently used, well-known authors. Types of Compositions and Cataloging Music Theses are also available.

Music Core Record Task Group Final Report

gopher://marvel.loc.gov/00/services/cataloging/coop/coop_cncl/tgmusic.1

Find here a Core Record for Printed and Manuscript Music and a Core Record for Music and Non-Music Sound Recordings.

Music Library Association Clearinghouse

http://www.music.indiana.edu/tech_s/mla/index.htm

Music Survey Results: Canadiana Cataloging

http://www.nlc-bnc.ca/services/catalog/emussurv.htm

Includes responses to a survey distributed over the Canadian Association of Music Libraries discussion list CANMUS-L and by mail to public libraries.

Music Thesaurus: A Faceted Approach to LCSH

Library of Congress Subject Headings

http://www.oclc.org/oclc/man/authconf/hemmasi.htm

By Harriette Hemmasi, Rutgers University.

Necrology

http://mahogany.lib.utexas.edu:1000/Libs/FAL/Necrology.html

Searchable by letter. Also lists place of death (all very helpful for creating name authority records and differentiating between musicians of the same name).

OCLC Scores Format

http://www.oclc.org/oclc/bib/1-2.htm

Online Music and Education Resources

http://www.ed.uiuc.edu/music-ed/on-line.html

Penn State Music/AV (Audio Visual) Cataloging Team Home Page
http://www.libraries.psu.edu/IASWEB/CatsWeb/musav/musicav.htm

Program for Cooperative Cataloging Core Record for Music and Non-Music Sound Recordings
http://lcweb.loc.gov/catdir/pcc/coremusic.html
> See also the Core Bibliographic Record for Printed Music and Manuscript Music.

Reference Works Used for Music Cataloging as Listed in the Music Cataloging Bulletins
http://www.music.indiana.edu/tech–s/mla/reflist.96
> Lois Kuyper-Rushing prepared this substantial bibliography.

Scores Cataloging (Non-Recon), Southern Illinois University at Carbondale
http://www.lib.siu.edu/swen/scorecat.htm
> Extensive document.

Selected Bibliography of Material About Sheet Music and Cataloging
http://www.lib.duke.edu/music/sheetmusic/wgbiblio.html

Sheet Music Cataloging Guidelines
http://www.lib.duke.edu/music/sheetmusic
> Very impressive piece of work provided by the Working Group, which reports to the Bibliographic Control Committee of the Music Library Association (MLA). These long-awaited guidelines are now on the Web— and in great detail. Sheet music has always been a complex genre to categorize—it's wonderful that someone has finally completed guidelines. It appears that everything related to sheet music cataloging has been covered. Check out the Glossary with terms unique to sheet music and the lovely illustrations (see chord diagrams).

Sibley Music Library Cataloging Page
http://rodent.lib.rochester.edu/sib/catalogi.html
> Information on catalogs, the Octavo Index, and the Rare Books File of the Eastman School of Music (Rochester, New York).

Sound Librarian: The Music Cataloging Tool for Windows
http://ourworld.compuserve.com/homepages/fivepoints/page2.htm
> Program consists of 3.5 floppy disks which promise to catalog all recording medias and formats.

Stanford Archive of Recorded Sound

http://www-sul.stanford.edu/depts/ars/ars.html

"Archive houses more than 200,000 recordings and over 4000 print and manuscript items." See Sound Bytes from the Archive for a description of the use of the AU format for sound and sound samples.

Thematic Indexes Used by the Library of Congress for Formulating Uniform Titles for Music as Listed in the *Music Cataloging Bulletin*

http://www.music.indiana.edu/tech_s/manuals/thematic/themind.ind

Totally Unofficial Rap Dictionary

http://www.sci.kun.nl/thalia/rapdict

An incredible work by Patrick Atoon and Niels Janssen.

Training Materials for Cataloging Music

http://www.music.indiana.edu/tech_s/mla/fair.txt

Types of Compositions

http://infoshare1.princeton.edu/katmandu/music/mustypin.html

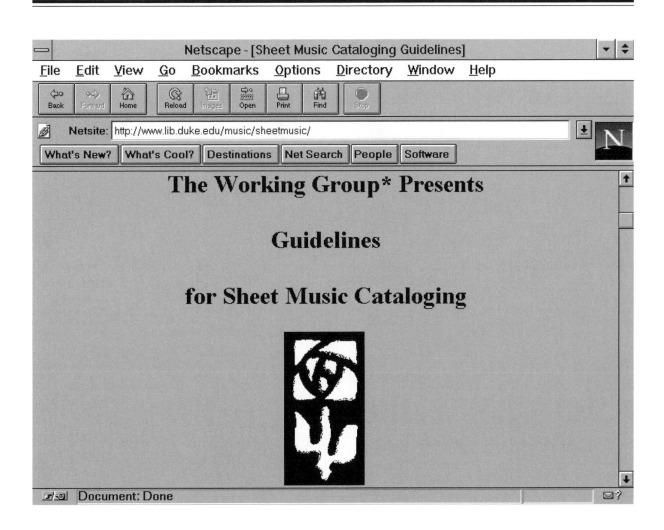

Figure 2.13
Guidelines for Sheet Music Cataloging

2.5.7 NONPRINT MATERIALS

Nonprint Material used to be the most problematic catalogers had to handle (before e-journals and the World Wide Web). There are still plenty of problems, though. Many sites now provide very informative documentation on how they catalog CDs, CD-ROMs, sound discs, laser discs, audiocassettes, multimedia, microforms, and floppy disks that accompany printed matter. Each format requires specific cataloging and processing instructions. Some items may be bar coded and others not. Some items may contain magnetic strips for theft detection and others not. Some items may circulate and others not. How are other libraries shelving them, storing them, preserving them? Find out in this section.

Artificat—Archaeological Cataloguing and Analysis Software
http://www.powersrvcs.com/Artificat.html
> Uses Macintosh chart/graphics packages to record classification for each artifact as it is determined.

AV (Audio Visual) Cataloging and Tagging
http://darkwing.uoregon.edu/~tsmith/workshop.html
> Workshop developed and presented by Terry Smith.

Cartonet Map Library Automation System
http://www.geo.ed.ac.uk/home/research/gisa/Cartonet.html
> "Powerful, yet ergonomic solution to the problem of cataloguing maps."

Catalogacion de Audiovisuales: un Repaso a la Situacion Internacional
http://www.nlc-bnc.ca/ifla/IV/ifla62/62–gallm.htm
> By Maria Pilar Gallego Cuadrado, Biblioteca Nacional, Madrid, Spain.

Cataloging Interactive Multi-Media (SUNY Cortland Memorial Library, New York)
http://www.cortland.edu/www/libwww/tech/interactive_multi.htmlx
> Covers the chief source of information, prescribed sources of information, and key fixed field and variable field elements.

Cataloging Photographs in Archival Repositories
http://www.sils.umich.edu/impact/Fall95/Papers-projects/Papers/james.html
> By Amy L. James.
>
> Discusses how photographs are not cataloged as individual items, but as part of a collection, and how many repositories are now using the 545 and 600 MARC fields to describe their collections.

Cataloging Unpublished Nonprint Materials: A Manual of Suggestions, Comments and Examples

http://ublib.buffalo.edu/libraries/units/cts/olac/reviews/urbanski.html

By Verna Urbanski, with Bao Chu Chang and Bernard L. Karon.

A collation of AACR2 rules pertaining to the cataloging of unpublished nonprint materials.

Gaining Access to Visual Information: Theory, Analysis, and Practice of Determining Subjects: A Review of the Literature with Descriptive Abstracts

http://www.uky.edu/Artsource/bibliographies/bellbib.txt

By Lesley Anne Bell.

Bibliography of works that discuss the cataloging and indexing of visual information.

Hypersonic Taming of the Wild Beast: The Impact of the Genesis of a Media Center

http://wings.buffalo.edu/publications/mcjrnl/v2n2/beast

By Lorre Smith and Lynne (Lyn) Martin, *Journal of Academic Media Librarianship*, v2n2, Fall 1994.

LCTGM—LC Thesaurus for Graphic Material: Topical Terms for Subject Access

http://palimpsest.stanford.edu/lex/lctgm/lctgm.html

Thesaurus compiled by Elizabeth Betz Parker (Library of Congress Prints and Photographs Division) to provide subject indexing of historical images, including original prints, drawings, photos, photomechanical prints, and pictorial ephemera.

MC Journal: The Journal of Academic Media Librarianship

http://wings.buffalo.edu/publications/mcjrnl

Free online journal.

Microforms and Documents Department Policies and Procedures Handbook

Auburn University Libraries, Auburn, Alabama

http://www.lib.auburn.edu/madd/docs/manual.html

Shelving, filing, and processing of documents using the SuDoc classification number for microforms.

Microforms and Photocopies: Cataloging Instructions

http://infoshare1.princeton.edu/katmandu/micro/inphocop.html

OLAC (Online AudioVisual Catalogers Web Page)
http://wings.buffalo.edu/libraries/units/cts/olac

"OLAC provides a means for exchange of information, continuing education, and communication among catalogers of AV materials and with the Library of Congress." Comments are requested on the Guidelines for Bibliographic Description of Interactive Multimedia. The OLAC site contains lengthy book reviews of such titles as *Cataloging Computer Files* by Nancy B. Olson and *Cataloging Nonbook Resources: A How-To-Do-It Manual for Librarians* by Mary Beth Fecko.

Preservation Microfilm Cataloging
Northwestern University Library
http://www.library.nwu.edu/sas/scp/scp87.html

Program for Cooperative Cataloging Core Bibliographic Record for Audiovisual Materials
http://lcweb.loc.gov/catdir/pcc/avcore.html

Reproductions and Original Microform Publications
http://www.oclc.org/oclc/bib/3_2.htm

Contains Library of Congress, National Library of Canada, OCLC, and Government Printing Office policies.

Video Processing: CTS Procedure #33
Cornell University Libraries
http://cts.library.cornell.edu/33video.htm

Chart demonstrates location, call number, how to apply bar codes, how many shelflist cards to produce, and any other physical processing instructions.

2.5.8 SERIALS

Serials are usually defined as publications issued in successive parts, usually employing a chronological or numerical designation, and intended to be continued indefinitely. Serials are also famous for dramatically rising subscription costs, for "hogging" the budget and resources, and also for containing a lot of "publish-or-perish" articles that only a small percentage of readers will ever read. Serials have always been at the forefront of getting the information out in a timely manner. E-journals are only an extenuation of this theme, with several advantages to printed serials. World Wide Web access to serials allows hypertext searching of full-text journals; e-journals are available much earlier than their printed version; and patrons now have the ability to print out individual articles on demand. Advantages of paper serials are: paper can be kept indefinitely and gathered together after a specific number of issues to create a bound volume; the threat of technology changing and limiting access is mitigated; and most users are familiar with print versions and assume that the longer, peer-reviewed aspect of scholarly journal publishing means a higher quality of information contained within. But hold on, folks! E-journals offer the possibility of combining audio, video, and other formats into their pages. E-journals can be individually custom-made to accommodate the needs of the patron. Some sources even include the savings of acquiring e-journals over paper as approximating 70–80 percent. Whichever side you're on, the section on Serials has some wonderful sites for you to explore!

American Library Association 1996 Midwinter Meeting: Minutes of the ALCTS/Serials Section Committee to Study Serials Cataloging
http://www.library.vanderbilt.edu/ercelawn/cssc96wn.html

Citations for Serial Literature
http://www.readmore.com/info/csl.html
   "Electronic index which publishes the table of contents and abstracts for articles related to the serials information chain." Back issues from 1992 on.

Completing Copysets and Linking Pieces
MIT Libraries
http://macfadden.mit.edu:9500/colserv/cat/sercat/newcop.htm

CONSER (Cooperative Program for Serials Cataloging)
http://lcweb.loc.gov/acq/conser/homepage.html
   CONSER began in the early 1970s as "a project to convert manual serial cataloging into machine-readable records, and has evolved into an ongoing program to create and maintain high-quality bibliographic records

for serials." This site includes documentation, a listing of products and publications, a membership list, annual reports, and more. Check out *CONSERline*, their semi-annual newsletter. Back issues are available from 1994.

Creating Serial Summary Holdings Statements in the UMCP Libraries
University of Maryland at College Park
http://www.itd.umd.edu/UMS/UMCP/TSD/tsd_serial_summaries.html
> Extensive document, containing the CARL Serials Summary Management Screen, NISO Standards, and much more.

CUL (Cornell University Libraries) Technical Services Manual
http://www.library.cornell.edu/tsmanual/serials/holdingsOUT.html
> Good section on electronic serials.

Description and Evaluation of the "Mr. Serials" Process: Automatically Collecting, Organizing, Archiving, Indexing, and Disseminating Electronic Serials
http://www.lib.ncsu.edu/staff/morgan/report-on-mr-serials.html
> By Eric Lease Morgan, *Serials Review* 21 no.4 (Winter 1995): 1–12.

Earliest, Latest, and Successive Entry Cataloging
University of Chicago Library
http://www.lib.uchicago.edu/~rdl3/latentry.html
> Policies and procedures also available for Serials Recon, including Uses of the 246 Field (Variant Titles) for Serials, Short Cat Serials, Critical MARC Elements for Serials Recon, and much more.

Electronic Journals and Libraries: A Resource Page
http://www.ub2.lu.se/NNC/workshop/ejournal.html
> An exhaustive series of links prepared for the Nordic Net Center Workshop, Lund University Library, October 10, 1996.

Format Integration and Its Impact on Serials
http://www.library.vanderbilt.edu/ercelawn/hirons.html
> Speech given at the ALCTS Institute on Serials in the Age of Format Integration, San Francisco, California, October 7, 1995 by Jean Hirons, Acting CONSER Coordinator, Library of Congress.

Format Integration: Major Changes for Printed Serials
http://tpot.ucsd.edu/Cataloging/Current/serialschanges.html
> By Crystal Graham, University of California at San Diego.

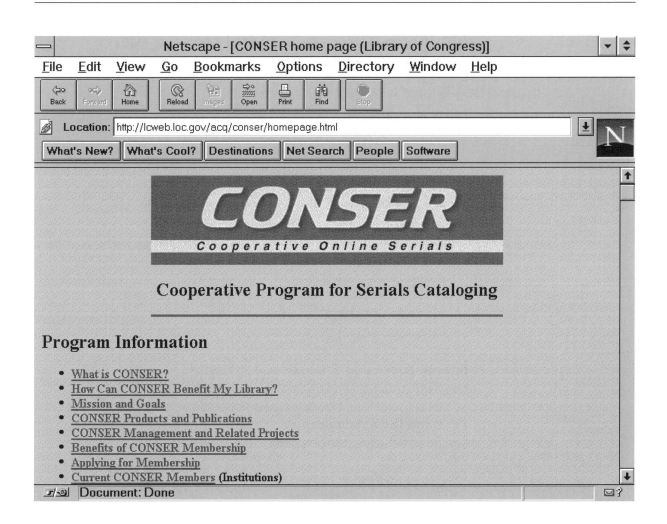

Figure 2.14
CONSER (Cooperative Program for Serials Cataloging)

ICEDIS: International Committee on Electronic Data Interchange for Serials
http://www.faxon.com/standards/ICEDIS.html

Index Morganagus
http://sunsite.berkeley.edu/~emorgan/morganagus
> This is a searchable index of library-related electronic serials created by Eric Lease Morgan. Currently 36 journals are available for searching.

Interactive Electronic Serials Cataloging Aid (IESCA)
http://www.library.nwu.edu:80/iesca
> Searchable page for serials catalogers. Contains examples of bibliographic records and object modules. See how the Nordic Linguistic Bulletin is cataloged with a serials format, computer format, or as an Internet object. Access MARBI Proposals, Internet and Cataloging Terminology, and FOLDOC, The Free On-Line Dictionary of Computing—*http://wombat.doc.ic.ac.uk*.

Interim Policies on E-Serials and CONSER
http://www.library.vanderbilt.edu/ercelawn/interim.html

ISSN and ISBN Numbers
http://www.ana.org.ulc/nsissn.htm

ISSN: International Standard Serial Numbers
http://www.issn.org/index.html

LibraryLand: Serials
http://www.rcls.org/libland/llserial.htm
> A wealth of information here. See Serials Librarianship, Electronic Serials, and more.

Memos on Serials Cataloging—Title Index
Harvard, Widener Library Cataloging Services Department
http://www-hcl.harvard.edu/wid-cat/cdsrti.html
> Memos on Classed-Together Series to Harvard Depository and the Policy for Use of the 752 Field.

MIT Serials Cataloging
http://wonder.mit.edu/sercat/info.html/
> Policies for Standard Abbreviations, New ISSN's, Notification to NSDP, and more.

NASIGWeb (North American Serials Interest Group, Inc.)

http://nasig.ils.unc.edu

Membership, job listings, and conference information, plus links to other sites of interest to serialists. Full text of NASIG publications available to NASIG members only.

Not Just E-Journals: Providing and Maintaining Access to Serials and Serial Information Through the World Wide Web

http://fas.sfu.ca/pub/cs/techreports/1996/CMPT96–01.html

By Robert D. Cameron, School of Computing Science, Simon Fraser University.

Paper version appeared in the *Serials Librarian*, vol. 29, nos. 3/4.

Remote Access Computer File Serials

CONSER Cataloging Manual: Module 31

http://lcweb.loc.gov/acq/conser/module31.html

Requests for New Serials Cataloging

Library Web Serials Manual, University of California, Berkeley

http://www.lib.berkeley.edu/AboutLibrary/Staff/BPM/8atoc.html

Instructions for both Innopac and non-Innopac branch libraries.

Sample Serials Decision Form

University of California, Berkeley

http://library.berkeley.edu/AboutLibrary/Staff/BPM/8a3.html

Scholarly Electronic Publishing Bibliography

http://info.lib.uh.edu/sepb/sepb.html

Compiled by Charles W. Bailey, Jr., University of Houston Libraries.

Serials

University of South Australia Library

http:www.unisa.edu.au/library/techser/serials/serials/htm

Discusses duplicates, CD-ROM titles, binding, e-journals, cancellations, and more.

Serials Cataloging Procedures, Northwestern University Library

Evanston, Illinois

http://www.library.nwu.edu/sas/scp/index.html

Quite extensive site. Details a serials retrospective conversion project.

Serials Cataloging Tools

University of California. Davis, General Library

http://neuheim.ucdavis.edu/staff/serweb/cattools.html

Nice selection of links.

Serials Department Annual Report 1994/1995
University of Indiana Library, Bloomington
http://www.indiana.edu/~libadmin/seriarep.html

Serials Department, Hamilton College Library
Clinton, New York
http://nemo.hamilton.edu/html/library/serdept.htm
    Discusses functions, services, policies, and procedures.

Serials Department Home Page
California State University, Chico
http://www.csuchico.edu/lbib/serials/serials.html

Serials Department, William F. Ekstrom Library, University of Louisville (Kentucky), Division of Technical Services
http://www.louisville.edu/groups/library-www/techserv/serials

Serials in Cyberspace: Collections, Resources and Services
http://www.uvm.edu/~bmaclenn
    Outstanding collection of serials-related links. Extensive list of sites with U.S. electronic journal collections and services, as well as Australian, Canadian, Scottish, and English sites.

Serials Manual, Smathers Libraries, University of Florida
http://nervm.nerdc.ufl.edu/~catwww/ser_man.html
    A wonderful site for serials catalogers. Check out the Serials Glossary, Guidelines for Treatment as Serial/Periodical, and Check-in by Branch Staff of Title Changes. Also discusses Serial CD-ROM Products, Print Serials Accompanied by Machine-Readable Formats, Computer Tapes, and Controlling Uncataloged Serials Not Held by Cataloging.

Serialst Archive Search
gopher://moose.uvm.edu:70/77/.index/wais-indexes/serialst

Taming the Serials Jungle with the ISSN
http://www.issn.org/index.html
    English-French site containing a multitude of ISSN information. Products like the List of Serial Title Word Abbreviations are for sale here. Also contains statistics by ISSN National Centres and the ISSN Register by Language.

Tools for Serials Catalogers: A Collection of Useful Sites and Sources
http://www.library.vanderbilt.edu/ercelawn/serials.html
    Ann Ercelawn's excellent page is updated frequently. Access the latest cataloging documentation from LC and OCLC, e-journals, newsletters,

discussion lists, and national and international serials programs and organizations. Also lists e-mail addresses for cataloging questions and/or problems.

United Kingdom Serial Group
http://epip.lboro.ac.uk/UKSG/hi/text.htm
> Links to the journal *Serials*, with complete table of contents and selected full-text articles online. See "Journal Consolidation: The Agent's Perspective" by Colin Harrison and "A Case Study in E-Journal Developments: The Scandinavian Position" by Harald Joa.

Unraveling the Mysteries of Serials
ALCTS Serials Section Education Committee
gopher://ala1.ala.org/00/alagophxiii/alagophxiiialcts/alagophxiiialctseduc/ serials.mystery

What's in a Name? Presentation Guidelines for Serials Publications
http://lcweb.loc.gov/issn/whats.html

2.6

Three Timely Topics of Importance to Catalogers

Here you'll find Web sources of information on three topics of current interest to catalogers: workstations, automation vendors, and the "O" word: outsourcing.

2.6.1 CATALOGING WORKSTATIONS

Many catalogers today are in the situation of moving from one terminal to the next, to a paper copy of the Library of Congress Classification Schedules, to the OCLC or RLIN terminal, to the local online catalog to check authority work, call numbers, and the like. Lugging materials from terminal to terminal is tiring at best, and downright unergonomic. The Cataloging Workstations section will describe the experiences of some major libraries developing and utilizing a one-stop workstation, one in which all needed cataloging tools and online services are combined into one location. Split screens or toggling from one database to the other are employed. All sites discussed here represent a significant improvement on previous work routines. Combining cataloging tools increases productivity. And now, with the advent of long URLs, without the benefit of cutting and pasting, it's a rare cataloger who can physically write and transfer a URL without transposing a letter, forgetting a tilde, or perhaps not capitalizing a letter or word.

Cataloger's Desktop
Library of Congress
http://lcweb.loc.gov/cds/cdroms1.html#desktop
> Quarterly CD-ROM product to be incorporated into a workstation. Includes *USMARC Codes and Formats*, *LC Rule Interpretations*, *Subject Cataloging Manual*, *CONSER Cataloging Manual*, *Music Cataloging Decisions*, and a host of other publications. It also includes a shadow file, or "overlay of an infobase in which personal editing, changes, style changes, notes, and highlighters may be stored."

Cataloger's Workstation and the Continuing Transformation of Cataloging
http://tpot.ucsd.edu/Cataloging/Current/catwork.html
> By Roger Brisson, Social Sciences Cataloger, Pattee Library, Penn State University, State College, Pennsylvania.

Cataloger's Workstation Hints: How to Write a Macro for NOTIS Using the McGill Software
http://infoshare1.princeton.edu/katmandu/work/macros.html
> Hints also available for RLIN.

Cataloger's Workstation Taskforce
Central Technical Services, University at Buffalo Libraries, New York
http://ublib.buffalo.edu/libraries/units/cts/cat/catws.html
> See what software they loaded on their Pentiums, what electronically available dictionaries they loaded, and much more.

CDS (Cataloging Distribution Service, Library of Congress)
Complete Catalog of Bibliographic Products and Services
http://lcweb.loc.gov/cds/cdsintro.html

> LC Classification Schedules B-BJ, C, E-F, H, J, L, N, Q, R, S, T, U-V, and Z are now ready. Classification Plus, a "full-text, Windows-based CD-ROM product which contains the Library of Congress Classification Schedules and Library of Congress Subject Headings" is also available as an annual subscription with quarterly updates. Copy and paste LC classification numbers or subject headings, and insert them into your own cataloging records. See *http://lcweb.loc.gov/cds/cdroms1.html#classplus* for details. The Cataloger's Desktop has some new additions—the AC (Annotated Card) Children's Subject Headings, the CONSER Cataloging Manual, the LC Cutter Table as a separate infobase, the LC Filing Rules, Standard Citation Forms for Published Bibliographies Used in Rare Book Cataloging, and the Thesaurus for Graphical Materials.

CLARR, the Cataloger's Toolkit
http://www.library.nwu.edu/clarr

> This program takes its name from the NOTIS command "clar" (claim authority record). CLARR can check all headings in a record in a few seconds, gather information rapidly, create authority records, and manipulate variable fields. This helpful user's guide was written by Gary L. Strawn, Authorities Librarian at Northwestern University (Evanston, Illinois).

Human Side of the Technical Services Workstation: The
Management of Computing in Library Technical Services
http://www.libraries.psu.edu/iasweb/personal/rob/tswhum.htm

> Fascinating and extensive article by Roger Brisson.

Implementing New Cataloging Workstation Software: The Joys
and Sorrows of Being a Beta Site
http://www.fiu.edu/~library/staff/catalog/poster/posttop.html

> An excellent presentation by catalogers from Florida International University/Florida Atlantic University, complete with technical services workstations graphics showing an ideal cataloging workstation.

McGill TCP3270
http://dsg.cac.psu.edu/tcp3270/TIPS.HTML

> TCP/IP terminal emulator which changes your workstation into a real 3270 and VT52–420 terminal.

OCLC Passport for Windows
http://www.oclc.org/oclc/passport/passport.htm

> Create logon and logoff macros using the OCLC characters, select ALA

macro language, open up multiple sessions with the OCLC, ALA True Type Font, and more. Export bibliographic records, view the latest Passport Internet archive messages at *http://purl.oclc.org/net/pfw*.

Retooling Technical Services: The Development of Technical Services Workstations

http://www.libraries.psu.edu/iasweb/personal/rob/tswdoc.htm
By Roger Brisson and Janet McCue.
"Pre-publication electronic version of an article entry appearing in a future supplement to the Encyclopedia of Library and Information Science."

Software Configuration for the Technical Services Workstation

Widener Library Cataloging Services Department, Harvard University, Cambridge, Massachusetts

http://www-hcl.harvard.edu/wid-cat/n960227.html
Discusses the change from a DOS-based system to a Windows-based system with Windows applications.

Technical Services Desktop: Desktop Tools and Their Organization in a Windows Environment

http://www.libraries.psu.edu/iasweb/personal/rob/tswinnj.htm

Technical Services Workstations

http://nervm.nerdc.ufl.edu/~catwww/robocat.html
Report of a workshop conducted in Atlanta, Georgia, March 17, 1995. Reviews experiences of Harvard, Yale, LC, and OCLC with Cataloger's Desktop and Classification Plus.

2.6.2 LIBRARY AUTOMATION VENDORS

The Library Automation Vendors covered here run the gamut from smaller vendors like the BlissLib Automated Library System, intended for smaller personal libraries, to mega services such as OCLC, Ameritech Library Services, and ISM Library Information Services. There's a vast assortment of options to choose from—all types of Web-accessible OPACs, authority control modules, bibliographic records, communication software, and many provide demos that can be downloaded. Have fun exploring!

Ameritech Library Services

http://www.amlibs.com

> World's leading library automation provider, established in 1994 by combining DYNIX (the "number one selling library automation system in the world") and NOTISLMS systems. NOTISLMS (Library Management System) offers as add-ons PacLink (a Z39.50 interface), QuikReports (which tracks acquisitions, cataloging, and circulation activities), and a WebPAC Link to NOTISLMS (gateway software that uses any Web browser). Ameritech Europe *http://www.amlibs.nl* provides a Web tutorial and information pertinent to the UK, Netherlands, France, Germany, and Sweden.

Auto-Graphics Inc.

http://www.autographics.com

> Offers retrospective conversion of library data to MARC records, data input and conversion (using AGILE III), and access to the complete LC files—supplemented by over 2,500,000 unique titles (primarily pre-1968 imprints).

Baratz Servicios Catalogacion Retrospectiva

Madrid, Spain

http://194.224.212.2/granada.html

> Experts in retrospective conversion of Spanish card catalogs, as well as data anlaysis, Outsourced Cataloging, changing ISBD to Marc format, and other services "to order."

BiblioFile Cataloging

http://www.tlcdelivers.com/tlc/ctlg.htm

> "The world's first commercial application of CD-ROM technology." The ITS for Windows Technical Services Workstation contains the Cataloger's Reference Shelf, an "in-line" (that is, locally available) collection of cataloging reference works, hyperlinked to your local and national standard bibliographic and authority files. BiblioFile proposes that data stored directly onto a local PC can be accessed more rapidly than online data or data stored on a CD-ROM or LAN file. Cataloging Reference Desk con-

tains most USMARC formats and code lists, LC Rule Interpretations, the Subject Cataloging Manual, the NACO Participant's Manual, the CONSER Cataloging Manual, and more. BiblioFile also offers NetPAC (http://www.bibfile.com/main/netpac.htm), which combines a MARC-based public access catalog with NLightN, the "largest pool of copyrighted information ever amassed." NetPAC offers keyword searching of any field, using Boolean operators and defining your own search features. Click on hypertext links, find additional information, access Web sites or NlightN, request ILL material—truly remarkable. Check out ROARing CAT (the Rochester Regional Library Council) at *http://206.102.94.216* or MAINECAT at *http://206.102.94.213*, the statewide catalog for libraries in the state of Maine. Finally, BiblioFile offers MARC Review: Database Inspector (*http://www.bibfile.com/main/marcrevw.htm*), a DOS-based software used to examine USMARC records to detect errors and inconsistencies. MARC Review checks format integration violations, misspellings, CIP records that haven't been updated, rule changes, missing data, and cataloging errors. MARC databases are also available for British, Canadian, Spanish, and French MARC records.

BLCMP Library Services LTD
http://www.blcmp.org.uk

"Leading supplier of computer systems to public and academic libraries in the British Isles."

Talis, a Unix library management system, combined with the BLCMP database of over 14 million MARC records, covers 90 percent of titles searched. TalisWeb is the Windows-based interface to the Talis OPAC.

BlissLib Automated Library System
http://www.newcomm.net/greatauk

is "intended to provide an alternative for those who do not require some of the advanced functionality present in other library systems currently on the market." They don't fully support AACR2 and do not import/export in MARC format. BlissLib is more suited for small personal, school, or corporate collections. Download a free demo version.

Carl Corporation Home Page
http://www.carl.org/carl.html

The CARL system provides a turnkey library management system to over 450 libraries. "Uncover" is their "online article delivery service, a table of contents database, and a keyword index to nearly 17,000 periodicals." With free access to their databases, CARL Corporation processes over 45,000 connections daily. Try them out at Uncover Web (*http://uncweb.carl.org/*). NoveList is an electronic reader's advisory. Available through Carl's Everybody's Catalog, NoveList assists readers to "find new books based on books they've read or topics in which they are interested.

By matching subject headings, NoveList provides access to approximately 34,000 adult fiction titles." Another great product is Everybody's Catalog Photo Imaging Module, which allows the display of high-quality images through your OPAC's graphical interface.

CASPR Library Systems Inc.
http://www.caspr.com
A library automation and information management company offering Library Works. Originally a Mac product, there is now an IBM Windows version. An unlimited site license is available, and prices are quite reasonable.

CatSkill InfoTrain
http://www.learning-curve.com.au/cat/info.html
"An interactive multimedia course on descriptive cataloguing using Anglo-American Cataloguing Rules, 2nd edition."

Cuadra Associates
http://www.cuadra.com
Producer of the STAR information management and retrieval system. Check out the section on STAR/Libraries.

Dataware Technologies
http://www.dataware.com
Provides software for over 2000 institutions utilizing the BRS/SEARCH system.

Del Mar Data Digital Document Conversions
http://www.wp.com/delmardata
"Paper-to-digital, paper-to-microfiche, paper-to-microfilm, text and images to CD-ROM, text to Acrobat, text to indexing software, and more!"

Diogenes, A New Concept in Cataloging, Becomes Marcadia
http://www.rlg.org/marcadia.html
Created by the Research Libraries Group and RetroLink, a division of Ameritech Library Services.

Marcadia uses RLIN and RetroLinks Z39.50, search-and-match and report writing software, to find appropriate cataloging records, modify them according to client's profile, and produce complete full cataloging records ready for the client's local system. They promise two to five day turnaround on records with copy, cost cutting, reduced backlog, and record delivery by Internet FTP. Here's a quote for you worried catalogers out there: "It frees you from more than minimal involvement in a straightforward, regularly repeated process."

DRA (Data Research Associates)

http://www.dra.com

> DRA, the only library automation vendor that is a member of the World Wide Web Consortium (W3C), offers a wide variety of products to assist catalogers. DRA Web offers simultaneous searching of multiple resources and the merging of search results into a single display. Use DRA Net to "enjoy a low-cost source of cataloging and authority records—from the LC MARC and LC authority databases, as well as through other libraries with whom you choose to share resources." Check out Data Research Associates Library of Congress Cataloging Records at *http://galaxy.einet.net/hytelnet/FUL012.html* DRA has made freely available the more than 3 million Library of Congress catalog records for searching. Search by classification number. Telnet *dra.com* to log in. Patience— only two guest users at a time between 8:00 a.m. and 5:00 p.m. The catalog is keyword searchable, and easier to use than LOCIS. Enter "M" for MARC to see fully tagged bibliographic records.

Electronic Online Systems International (a Dawson Company)

http://www.datatrek.com

> Newly combined Data Trek Inc. and IME Ltd. Specializing in library automation since 1981, they have automated more than 6,500 libraries in over 85 countries. They offer software subscriptions and backfile conversion services.

ESI—Educational Solutions Inc.

http://esinet.com

> Creators of the turn-key library automation program entitled "Surpass/ 2." They promise a 95 percent or higher hit rate on retrospective conversion, and users can import or export MicroLIF and MARC records to and from a floppy disk.

Follett Software Company

http://www.fsc.follett.com

> "Leading developer and publisher of microcomputer library automation and curriculum-related products and services with 27,000 customers in over 60 countries." This company provides a MARC Tag of the Month Page to help educate customers about MARC bibliographic formatting. The Tag of the Month archives appear to be quite useful. Other pages of interest include Audio-Visual Cataloging Hints and Are All MARC Records the Same?

GEAC Systems USA Home Page

http://library.geac.com/index.htm

> GeoPac is GEAC's personal-computer-based graphical user-friendly OPAC. Two Z39.50–compatible systems are available—ADVANCE and PLUS. ADVANCE is "the most functionally complete library system available."

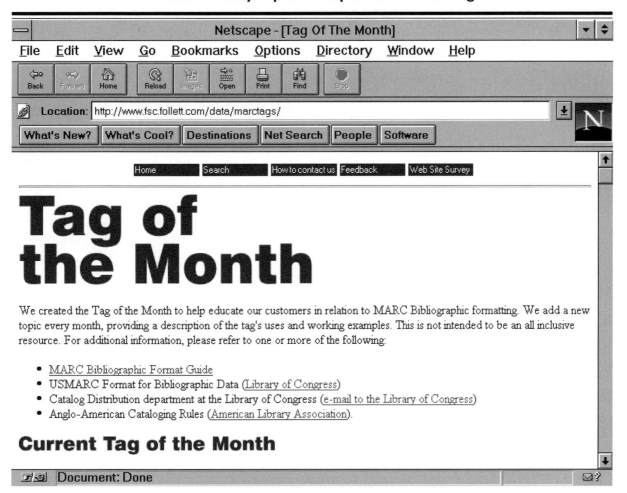

Figure 2.15
Follett Software Company's Tag of the Month Page

Information Dimensions
http://www.idi.oclc.org
> "System marketed exclusively to special libraries by OCLC."

InfoTrac Search Bank Information Center
http://www.iacnet.com/library/searchbank/search.html
> "Brings together a range of popular databases from leading information providers, full-service document delivery, a common user interface, Z39.50 compatability, and 24-hour, seven-day-a-week remote self-service."

Innovative Interfaces Inc. Innopac Cataloging Module
http://demo.iii.com/screens/iiiinfo.html
> Describes their OPAC, WindowPAC Graphical User Interface, and contains a short bibliography of published articles/books/reports about III. WindowPac (Innopac Web Server Software) offers a WWW library catalog interface. Tables of contents of books can be placed into MARC records to "utilize URLs placed on bibliographic records in the 856 field." Innopac handles the full ALA character set. Keep up with Innovative by reading Inn Touch. Innovative and RoweCom have entered into a partnership to "provide INNOPAC libraries with the ability to use the Internet to purchase and pay for journals and claim missing issues."

ISM Library Information Services
http://www.ism.ca/lis/lishpj.htm
> Formerly UTLAS International Canada, this computer-based service organization for libraries and the information industry currently counts more than 2,500 member libraries in North America, Australia, Asia, the Middle East, and Europe, making it the world's second largest bibliographic utility. ISM is the creator of CATSS (Catalogue Support System) (*http://www.ism.ca/lis/catssdes.htm*). This shared bibliographic utility was first offered online in 1973 and currently provides access to more than 60 million MARC records (of which 20 million are unique). CATSS contains significant collections in Swedish and Turkish, in addition to English and Western European languages. Also available are Japanese and Chinese CATSS. A unique feature of CATSS is their authority control module, which allows customers to link bibliographic records to authority records, allowing automatic global updating in all records linked to the heading. REMARC is a 4.3 million record file of Library of Congress records which are pre-1968. Outsourcing services are provided by MARCADVANTAGE. Because of an agreement with OCLC, ISM CATSS is not able to advertise in the U.S. (and vice-versa). However, membership is open to anyone that finds out about their services.

Knight-Ridder Information

http://www.dialog.com

"The acknowledged world leader in electronic information access and delivery . . . offering the DIALOG and DataStar services, which provide access to more than 600 online databases." Dow Jones, Financial Times Information, and Knight-Ridder are involved with the co-development of the "most authoritative global news resource for corporate, research, government, and academic customers."

Lex Systems

http://www.link.ca/~lex

Maker of LEXI File, the library automation software. Download a sample program to make MARC records.

Library Automation Vendor Home Pages

http://www.library.nwu.edu/lms/autovend.html

Librarian's Online Warehouse

http://www.libsonline.com

One thousand companies listed. Check out Automation—Cataloging and Database Management, and Cataloging and Processing Equipment and Supplies.

LIBRIS (Library Information System, Royal Library of Sweden)

http://www.libris.kb.se/index_eng.html

"Computer-based library system for the Swedish research and specialty libraries. The main functions of the system are cataloguing of literature, acquisitions, retrieval of bibliographic records, and interlibrary lending."

MicroCAT Manual

Total Knowledge Management, Manitoba, Canada

http://www.tkm.mb.ca/microcat-manual

MicroCAT is "the ideal library automation package for libraries of all sizes." Extensive instructions here which might be useful to those using other library systems. Especially clear are instructions on how to use the MARC Editor. Also covered are Cataloguing with MARC Records, How to Create a Shelflist, Bar coding and much more.

MITINET/MARC Software

http://www.mitinet.com

"Create MARC records without learning MARC rules." Compatible with over 70 library systems.

OCLC (Online Computer Library Center, Inc.)

http://www.oclc.org

OCLC is a "not-for-profit membership organization, where more than 24,000 libraries in 63 countries are working together to further access to the world's information." It would be impossible for me to describe everything offered on this site. However, I will attempt to mention the most important options offered here. OCLC offers many no-charge cataloging publications. *Technical Bulletins*, starting with no. 201 are available at *http://www.oclc.org/oclc/menu/tb.htm*. These bulletins can also be obtained via FTP for quicker downloading. Reference Cards are available for searching authority records in PRISM and for editing, cutting and pasting, creating new records, transferring, using workforms, and more. Documentation is available for First Search, EPIC, and CatME Plus (Cataloging MicroEnhancer Plus). OCLC MARC Code Lists (Country, Geographic Area, Language, Relator, and Source) are available at *http://www.oclc.org/oclc/man/code/codetoc.htm*. Some services that OCLC is now offering could have a major impact on Cataloging Departments as we know them. OCLC CatCD for Windows (*http://www.oclc.org/oclc/promo/5882ccdw/5882cdwn.htm*) offers offline cataloging in a stand-alone environment. PromptCat "provides copy cataloging for materials supplied by participating book vendors." PromptCat is currently working with Academic Book Center, Ambassador Book Service, Blackwell N.A., and Yankee Book Peddler, and is in the process of being implemented by Baker & Taylor. OCLC Selection (previously PromptSelect) "provides access to expanded selection and ordering information that enables you to identify material to be ordered and allows selectors to electronically communicate order requests to acquisitions staff in your library. Acquisitions staff can review these requests and export bibliographic and order information to your local ordering system to complete the order process." Both of these products, available from the world's largest bibliographic utility, could seriously compete with local staff and encourage outsourcing. Finally, OCLC is involved with another innovative program. OCLC is now permitting vendors to upgrade CIP records to full level (Encoding Level "blank") as newly published material arrives. They are loaded weekly to replace non-upgraded records.

OCLC Europe

http://www.oclc.org/oclc/europe/home.htm

Located in Birmingham, England, this new site serves more than 300 libraries in 27 countries. View OCLC from a slightly different perspective.

Onion Patch: New Age Public Access Systems

http://www.public.iastate.edu/~CYBERSTACKS/Onion.htm

Links to Joy Finnbar's Extending the Third Generation OPAC, the Experimental Library of Congress Catalog (utilizing INQUERY), the Cheshire II System, Okapi, and many more.

OVID Technologies Homepage
http://www.ovid.com
> Free trial of the OVID Web Gateway and much more from this developer of "platform and media independent database search software."

Pica II: Cataloguing Via Pica
http://www.pica.nl/docs/en/products/ggc.html
> Shared automated cataloging system of more than 200 libraries in the Netherlands and Germany, contributing to the Netherlands Central Catalogue.

ProCite for Windows
http://www.risinc.com/procite/procite.html
> "The software solution for managing bibliographic references." Available for Windows, DOS, and Macintosh systems. Biblio-Link II "transfers records retrieved from various electronic information services into a ProCite database." They also offer the Internet Enabler, which allows simultaneous searching of multiple on-line databases and ProCite Netpack, which allows multiple users.

RLIN (Research Libraries Information Network)
http://www-palni.edu/~cosmithb/rlin.html
> RLIN is "an information management and retrieval system used by hundreds of comprehensive research libraries, archival repositories, museums, and academic, public, law, technical, and corporate libraries for cataloging," making it the second largest national level database. Their OLUC has more than 63 million items, all created by members of the Research Libraries Group, Inc. (RLG). The catalog may be searched by Eureka (*http://www.library.cornell.edu/ha/eureka.html*) by using Zephyr, RLG's Z39.50 Service (*http://kweb.loc.gov/z3950/rlin.html*). Zephyr accesses complete MARC records as well as data in CJK and other non-roman scripts. LC is now using Zephyr to transfer their RLIN catalog records into the MUMS system. This is an example of shared cooperative cataloging at its best.

SinoCat
http://www.zeta.org.au/~grove/tvapleew.html
> First cumulated edition of the Chinese National Bibliography available on CD-ROM. Includes 200,000 Chinese records from the National Central Library, Taiwan. The application supports original cataloging, retrospective conversion, and has context-sensitive help on Chinese MARC.

SIRSI
http://www.sirsi.com/welcome.html

> SIRSI's Unicorn Web Cat System is a marvelous example of an interactive, online public access catalog. Pages are dynamically created from the library servers' database. They also offer free downloading of VIZION Pro with Z39.50 for Windows, an "icon-based capture system for your favorite Internet resources."

SLS (Information Systems) LTD
http://www.sls.se

> "Committed exclusively to the development and support of library systems" utilizing the LIBERTAS system. LIBERTAS users access OCLC as well as the SLS central database of over 11 million records. Online authority control, word processor-style editing, and an optional full MARC structure provided.

Voyager: Cataloging and Authority Control
Endeavor Information Systems, Inc.
http://www.4.okstate.edu/amtskfrc/2116.html

> Use multiple windows and cut and paste to create and edit records. Blind cross references are automatically suppressed in the OPAC. Catalogers will be "dynamically prompted" if a heading in a bibliographic record is in conflict with an established heading or if no authority record exists for the heading. For a spectacular graphic, check out *http://www.endinfosys.com/voyagent.html*

VTLS Cataloging
http://www.vtls.com/cat.html

> The VTLS Cataloging Client is "a DOS-based interface that allows full-screen entry and editing of MARC bibliographic and authority records." EasyCAT is "a Windows-based client" which uses VTLS EasyPAC Connectivity.

WLN (Western Library Network)
http://www.wln.com

> Nonprofit corporation, based in the U.S. Pacific Northwest, which provides many information products, including an online bibliographic database and authority control services. LaserCat is a CD-ROM database containing 4 million cataloging records. Connect to the WLN Online System with LINC TCP/IP communications software. MARS, the WLN MARC record service, offers authority control, bibliographic records, and updating. Serials cataloging outsourcing available.

2.6.3 OUTSOURCING CATALOGING (AND MORE)

"Outsourcing" is a topic uppermost in our thoughts recently. Many of us have been affected by a new "trend" of vendors offering all types of cataloging services—from OCLC's PromptCat and TECHPRO services, to vendors offering speeded-up upgrading of CIP copy (Cataloging in Publication) in the OCLC database. Since vendors receive most material first, this allows a certain unfair advantage over libraries with sizable staffs of LC and copy catalogers, trained and ready to do the same work. OCLC, Baker and Taylor, Yankee Book Peddler and many other vendors are now offering fully updated MARC records to accompany each title purchased. Unfortunately, when vendors talk about reducing the costs of cataloging and technical services, what it means is that they are removing those particular job functions from libraries. A major concern is that cost-cutting administrators, faced with skyrocketing journal prices, a steadily shrinking budget, and the maintenance cost of new equipment, will be attracted to these new cost-cutting programs. Witness the recent signing of Hawaii Public Libraries with Baker and Taylor, and complete cataloging departments outsourced at Kent State and at Central Michigan University to OCLC TECHPRO. And who could ever forget Wright State University, whose decision to outsource all of its cataloging department functions in late 1993 caused an uproar in cataloging departments worldwide?

At this stage of the game, catalogers must make their voices heard. If LC and copy cataloging must be outsourced to vendors, then stress must be placed on the unique original cataloging each library does. A case must be made for updating and maintaining the database. New services to patrons must be considered—local indexing and abstracting services never before offered, increased catalog access through additional subject headings, and even increasing access retrospectively to materials currently owned by libraries and now receiving minimal use. Other "preservationally challenged" materials can be scanned and transferred to digital format. Some, or all of these ideas, should be considered to maintain the technical services aspects of libraries. We were not all cut out for public services jobs at the reference desk. After all, another new trend to consider is the downloading of huge vendor databases to increase the OCLC database with minimal-level records, frequently with little or no authority control, thereby necessitating extensive local editing and denying original record creation credits to libraries. Recent examples of this are Puvill Libros, from Spain, and Casalini Libri, from Italy, inputting their records into OCLC. These types of records may be adequate for languages without language specialists, but academic language specialists may cringe at the prospect of such a plethora of "bad records." Enhanced job security? Perhaps. Increased major editing of records? Most certainly. I believe that this section will present interesting arguments, both pro and con, on this provocative issue.

Auslang Supply Cataloguing Services
http://www.auslang.com.au/company/services.html

Confidentiality, Outsourcing, and the Library
http://library.ljextra.com/out.html
> By Richard Sloane. Special to the *New York Law Journal* (p.5, col. 1), October 17, 1995.

ISAcomplete: Accessioning/Consolidation Service
http://www.isa.com.au/consol.htm
> Outsourcers of Australian journal check-in and claiming.

Library Associates—We Catalog the World!
http://www.primenet.com/~fastcat
> FastCat's mission statement is "to provide services and support to librarians who have neither the staff nor the resources for some or all of their technical services needs. We don't aim to replace staff, but to supplement catalogers, reference librarians, and the solo librarian with too much to do and no time to do it."

Maruzen Online Network
http://www.maruzen.co.jp/marunet.html
> Read about Super Choice-kun, an "excellent outsourcing system which uses the international environment for the management of book selection, ordering, and acquisitions in libraries."

Microsoft and Readmore: Partners in Outsourcing Serials Activity
http://www.readmore.com/about/reporter/rr9505/microsof.html
> By Nancy Gershenfeld. *Readmore Reporter*, v.2, issue 2, Spring 1995.

The O Word
http://www.infotoday.com/searcher/jul/oword.htm

OCLC TECHPRO Service
http://www.oclc.org/oclc/promo/6171tech/6171tech.htm
> "Your personalized cataloging service offering off-site, short- and long-term cataloging and physical processing, tailored to meet your specific needs." Case studies of TECHPRO clients also on this page. Currently provides cataloging in 48 languages.

Outsourced Law Library Serves as a Wake-Up Call
http://library.ljextra.com/onge.html
> By Michael Sainte-Onge (Law Librarian, Coudert Brothers, San Francisco and San Jose, California). Special to the *National Law Journal* (p. 3, col. 1) July 17, 1995.

Discover what happened to the entire library staff of the Chicago office of Baker and McKenzie.

Outsourcing and Libraries: A Threat or Promise?
http://www.nla.gov.au/flin/outsourc/asl.html

Outsourcing Library Technical Services: A How-to-Do-It Manual for Librarians
http://www.lehigh.edu/~arh5/bookad.htm. By Arnold Hirshon and Barbara Winters.
Overview and summary of each chapter. Chapters include "Outsourcing the Acquisition of Serials," "Books, RFP Specifications," and "Re-engineering."

Outsourcing (Quick Strear Software)
http://www.quickstream.com/html/outsourcing.html

Re-engineering and Outsourcing: The Hawaii Experience
http://www.hcc.hawaii.edu/hspls/reos.html
Collection of hundreds of full-text articles concerning the outsourcing agreement between Baker and Taylor and the Hawaii State Public Library System.

Resolution on Hawaii State Public Library Systems Oursourcing
http://www.punawelewele.com/halepai/release/resoluti.htm

Selected References on Contracting Out and Outsourcing Library Services
http://www.sla.org/membership/irc/contract.html

Special Libraries Cataloguing (SLC) Inc.
Victoria, British Columbia, Canada
http://www.slc.bc.ca
Quality outsourcing cataloging, based on "mailed or couriered photocopies of the front and back of title pages with collation," written on 24 hours to one-week turnaround. Check out the page on Cuttering. Must reading is The Cataloguer's Role in Catalogue Construction: A Modest Proposal by J. McRee Elrod. Also, don't miss their SLC Librarian's Launchpad.

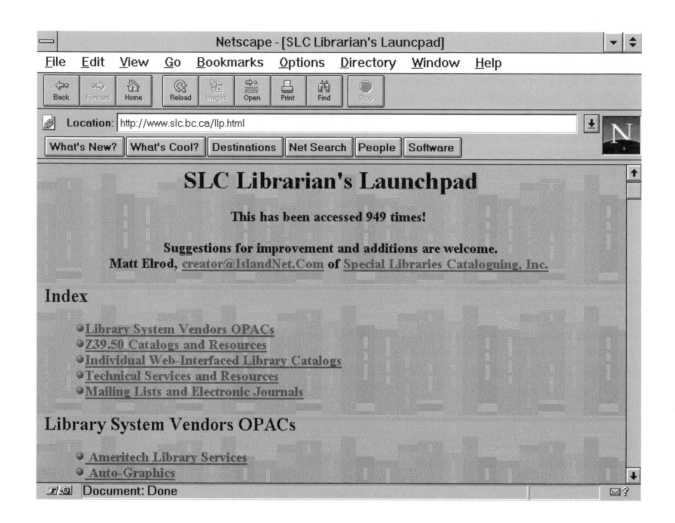

Figure 2.16
Special Libraries Cataloguing Inc.

2.7

Other Useful Internet Sources of Information for Catalogers

This potpourri of assorted—but important—sources and services contains many items of interest for every cataloger. Your challenge will be to stop surfing the Web and get back to your backlog.

2.7.1 CATALOGING ORGANIZATIONS

This section lists Web sites related to professional organizations relevant to catalogers.

Abbreviations for International Organizations and Groups
http://pwa.acusd.edu/~jcrossen/appendb.html

ALIA (Australian Library and Information Association) Cataloguers' Section, Queensland Group
http://www.alia.org.au/~catalog/qld-section.html

Association for Library Collections and Technical Services (ALCTS)
http://www.ala.org/alcts.html
> American Library Association Cataloging Form and Function Committee primarily discusses online catalogs. CFFC Minutes are available for 1995 and 1996. The Cataloging and Classification section provides annual reports, a listing of Resources for Catalogers, and more.

Australian Committee on Cataloguing
http://www.nla.gov.au/lis/stndrds/grps/acoc/acoc.html
> Goals are to monitor national and international cataloging and classify developments. Meeting minutes from 1994–present are available.

Cataloguing and Indexing Group in Scotland
http://www.almac.co.uk/business_park/slainte/slainte2/slainteg/2catani0/generali.html
> This group represents the interests of the Library Association, based in London. Check out the CIGS Archive, containing annual reports from 1983 to the present, as well as a goodly collection of papers, articles, and press releases.

Cataloguing and Indexing Group of the Library Association in London
http://www.fdgroup.co.uk/pubslist.htm
> Annual reports available as well as issues of *Catalogue and Index* (archives from Spring 1994 to the present). Read the famous article "How Microwaved Is Your Poodle?" by Derek Law at *http://www.fdgroup.co.uk/article.htm*.

2.7.2 CATALOGING RELATED PAPERS

This section on Cataloging Related Papers is particularly interesting. Here are listed articles that take a broader view of cataloging, including some from an historical context and others with a decidedly European flavor. Now you can find out what the state of the art in cataloguing in Turkey is.

Catalog Librarian in the Age of the Smart Machine
http://www.library.yale.edu/~mbeacom/newbreed.htm
    By Matthew Beacom, Yale University Library.

Commencement and Advancement of China's Cataloging-in-Publication
http://www.nlc-bnc.ca/ifla/IV/ifla62/62–zhih.htm
    By Hao Zhiping, Archives, Library of China.

Concepto de Autoria Corporativa de Panizzi a Cutter
http://cuib.laborales.unam.mx/publicaciones/revista/r4a4rs.html
    By Ofelia Solis Valdespino, (CUIBUNAM).
        Discusses the concept of corporate authorship, Antonio Panizzi and Charles Ammi Cutter.

Corruption of Cataloging by Michael Boman
http://duchess.lib.csufresno.edu/Publications/GormanArticle.html
    Everyone involved with cataloging must read this article, if only to acquaint themselves with terms like "modernizing, restructuring, and outsourcing."

Desperately Searching LISA: Talking About Libraries in the Semiotic Era
http://epip.lut.ac.uk/bailer/09–hoi.htm
    By Tord Hoivik, Department of Journalism, Library and Information Science, College of Oslo, Norway.

Es Necesario un Nuevo Paradigma en Catalogacion? (Is a New Paradigm Necessary in Cataloging?)
http://cuib.laborales.unam.mx/publicaciones/revista/r5a1p1rs.html
    By Ramiro Lafuente, CUIB Investigador.
        One of many articles available from the Centro Universitario de Investigaciones Bibliotecologicas.

How Catalogers Really Edit OCLC Records
http://fringe.lib.ecu.edu/Periodicals/nclibs/fall.91/high.fall.91.html
    By Walter M. High, University of North Carolina at Chapel Hill.

Legacy to Heritage: Subject Access to Manuscript Collections in the Electronic Age

http://www.uidaho.edu/special-collections/legacy.html

> By Terry Abraham, Head, Special Collections and Archives, University of Idaho Library, Moscow, Idaho.
>
> Discusses the inadequacies of the Library of Congress Subject Headings.

Libraries and Their Relevance to Digital Media: Notes for 4 April 1996

http://longwood.cs.ucf.edu/~moshell/DigitalMedia/Lecnotes.misc.html

> By J. Michael Moshell.
>
> A delightful overview of cataloging.

Mainstreaming our Library Catalogs

http://dmcpl.dayton.lib.oh.us./~kambitsch/niso/lotf.html

> By Tim Kambitsch (Butler University Libraries, Ohio).
>
> Discusses the similarities and differences between searching in traditional OPACs and the retrieval of Internet accessible resources.

Manifestations of Fiction Work

http://www.oclc.org/oclc/research/publications/review94/part1/ficworks.htm

> By Edward T. O'Neill.
>
> This study was devised to develop software which has the capability of clustering all manifestations of a work of English language fiction. A successive clustering algorithm was devised, with high recall and precision. A Table of Common Works of Fiction is included.

Manuel ou Informatise, le Catalogage est une Affaire Serieuse

http://www.france.diplomatie.fr/frmonde/coope/crfbib/bullB04a.html

> By Marie-Claude de Crignis, Discotheque des Halles.
>
> A wonderful overview of cataloging, MARC format, UNIMARC, and more.

National Bibliographic Access to Asian Materials

http://www.nla.gov.au/dnc/asiart/TRAINOR.html

> By Julia Trainor, National Library of Australia.
>
> Discusses the construction of a national CJK database.

Prototype Catalogue of Super Records: An Experiment

http://wilma.silas.unsw.edu.au/students/rfattahi/super.htm

> By Rahmat Fattahi.
>
> Manages to tie all manifestations and editions of a work into a super record. Very interesting concept.

Recordando la Conferencia Internacional sobre los Principios de Catalogacion
http://cuib.laborales.unam.mx/publicaciones/revista/r1a3p1rs.html
   By Ofelia Solis Valdespino, Investigadora de CUIB.
      Discusses the history of the International Conference Concerning the Twelve Principles of Cataloging.

State of the Art in Cataloguing in Turkey
http://www.nlc-bnc.ca/ifla/IV/ifla61/61–atld.htm
   By Dogan Atilgan, School of Library Science, Faculty of Letters, University of Ankara, Ankara, Turkey.

Status of Catalogers in Academic Libraries and Implications for Chinese American Librarians
http://www.lib.siu.edu/swen/iclc/clpprtan.htm
   By Wendy Tan, Head Cataloger, Hunter College, The City University of New York, submitted to *Chinese Librarianship: an International Electronic Journal*.

Der Uberregionale Verbundkatalog als Instrument fur die Retrospektive Katalogisierung
http://sunsv01.swbv.uni-konstanz.de:7000/wwwroot/text/nu94_v01.html
   By Regina Marzline, SWB-Verbundzentrale.

2.7.3 E-JOURNALS, NEWSLETTERS, ETC.

Get your news on these fantastic sites.

ALCTS Network News Archives
http://ala1.ala.org:70/1/alagophxiii/alagophxiiialcts/alagophxiiialctspubs/an2
    March 17, 1994 to the present.

BackLOG (Napier University Library Cataloguer's Desktop)
http://www.napier.ac.uk/depts/library/backlog.html
    "Collection of Internet resources aimed primarily at the Scottish cataloguing and technical services community."

Bits and Pieces (OCLC Newsletter)
http://www.oclc.org/oclc/bit/202/toc.htm
    Started in January 1996, it has primarily been concerned with OCLC cataloging changes, format integration issues, and resource sharing.

Cataloging and Classification Quarterly
http://www.bubl.ac.uk/journals/lis/ae/cacq/index.html
    Provides abstracts of articles in upcoming issues, editorials, and announcements, as well as the full text of cataloging news and book reviews. Tables of contents and abstracts from v. 19 no. 1, 1994 to present. Posted articles may be obtained through Haworth Document Delivery Service.

Citations for Serial Literature
http://www.readmore.com/info/csl
    Also known as SERCITES. Full-text issues from v.1, February 1996 to the present.

CONSERLINE (Newsletter of the CONSER Program)
http://lcweb.loc.gov/acq/conser/consrlin.html
    Published at least semi-annually by LC's Serial Record Division. Current issue available here. Back issues for 1994 and 1995 are accessible by gopher.

D-Lib Magazine, The Magazine of Digital Library Research
http://www.dlib.org
    Full-text archives from July 1995 to the present.

Journal of Internet Cataloging: The International Quarterly of Digital Organization, Classification, and Access
http://jic.libraries.psu.edu

Library of Congress Cataloging Newsline (LCCN)
http://www.lib.ncsu.edu/stacks/l/lccn

Compiled at least quarterly. Archives are available for 1993 to the present. Reports on cataloging activities at LC and includes policy decisions, technological developments, meeting reports, employment opportunities, and more.

LITA (Library and Information Technology Association—A Division of the American Library Association) Newsletter
http://www.lib.utk.edu/litanews/LITA.html

This electronic version of their quarterly newsletter is available free from LITA.

MARCIVE Newsletter
http://www.marcive.com/contents.htm

Complete text of newsletters from June 1995 to the present. Issues covered include Record Conversion to Full MARC, Outsourcing Cataloging, Purchasing Cataloging for Government Documents, and Medical Titles.

Newsletter on Serials Pricing Issues
http://www.lib.unc.edu/prices

(Marcia Tuttle, editor). Biweekly; published continuously since February 1989. Besides serials pricing, also covers library cancellation projects, electronic publishing that may impact paper pricing, journal publisher and subscription agent efforts to reduce costs, conference announcements, and more. All issues including the most recent are archived here.

OCLC Newsletters List
http://www.oclc.org/oclc/new/t-list.htm

All the latest cataloging information here. Full text from September/October 1994, no. 211 to the present. Also available in Spanish.

OCLC Technical Bulletins
http://www.oclc.org/oclc/menu/t-tb.htm

Clearly organized site that contains all valid bulletins from no. 201, "Documentation Distribution Policies," to the present. This is an excellent resource for format integration documents, PRISM service changes, Harvard database access news, and more.

Public-Access Computer Systems Review (PACS Review)
http://info.lib.uh.edu/pacsrev.html

Started in 1992. Published by the University of Houston Libraries. Fully searchable keyword index. An interesting section contains the Topic Articles requested in the previous month.

2.7.4 LISTS, DISCUSSION LISTS, AND ARCHIVES

ASIS-L Listserv
http://www.njit.edu/njIT/Library/asis/asis-l.html
> Subscription information for the American Society for Information Science Listserv.

Autocat—Library Catalog and Authorities Discussion Group and Mailing List
news:bit.listserv.autocat
> Access to current messages through newsgroup. Autocat FAQ is available at *http://www.mun.ca/library/cat/autocat.htm.*

COOPCAT (Cooperative Cataloging Arrangements Between Libraries Discussion Group)
http://www.hbz-nrw.de/hbz/tools/scholar/section2_5_49.html
> Information clearinghouse to aid in the formation of cooperative cataloging arrangements between libraries. Only subscription information is available on the Web at this time.

DigLib—Digital Libraries Research Discussion List
http://www.nlc-bnc.ca/cgi-bin/ifla-lwgate/DIGLIB/archives
> Provided by Iflanet to assist librarians interested in the creation of digital libraries. "Lightly moderated." Hypertext Archive available for August 1995 to the present.

Dynix-L Archive
http://library.adelaide.edu.au/m/dynix_l
> Many cataloging/authority/library OPAC issues discussed here. March 1995 to the present is archived by thread (which means that messages concerning the same topic are grouped together and presented in date order).

EMEDIA (Electronic Media Issues in Libraries)
http://info.lib.uh.edu/liblists/emedia.htm
> Subscription information.

GSAFD
http://www.cfcsc.dnd.ca/links/lib/litn.html
> Concerned with literary subject access to fiction. Discussion on assigning topical, character, setting, and genre headings to individual works of fiction.

Index-L: Indexer's Discussion Group Archives
gopher://eagle1.cc.GaSoU.edu:70/77/GeorgiaSouthernUniversity/
HendersonLibrary/assistance/Index-L/ListservArchives/.index/index
Eight hundred twenty-nine subscribers. Search archives from 1992 to the present. An Index for Indexers is available at *http://www.well.com/ user/asi/backndx.htm* (see Alphabetization, History of) for a start.

Innopac Listserv Archives
http://corso.ccsu.ctstate.u.edu/innopac
Keyword searchable from 1991 to the present.

Intercat Listserv Archive
http://ftplaw.wuacc.edu/listproc/intercat/archive.html
February 1995 to present.

LAW-TECH
http://lawlib.wuacc.edu/scall/liblists/liblists/3.htm
Discussion group for technical services law librarians. Subscription information here.

Library-Oriented Lists and Electronic Serials
http://info.lib.uh.edu/liblists.htm
Now keyword searchable.

lis-serials
http://www.mailbase.ac.uk/lists-k-o/lis-serials
Informal U.K. list.

Medlib-L
http://listserv.acsu.buffalo.edu/archives/medlib-1/.html
August, 1993 to present.

MLA-L—Music Library Association List
Archives available at *http://www.netspace.org/cgi-bin/lwgate/MLA-L/ database.html*
Request a Web search online and receive an e-mail reply.

Notis-L
news:bit.listserv.notis-l

OCLC Lists
http://www.oclc.org/oclc/forms/listserv.htm
Subscribe to the following lists at this site: EPIC-L, FIRSTSEARCH-L, INTERCAT, OCLC-CJK, TAPECHANGE-L, TECHBUL-L, and WEBSCRIPT-L.

PACS-L
http://info.lib.uh.edu/pacsl.html
> Premier moderated list dealing with all library computer systems, digital libraries, CD-ROM databases, etc. Current messages available here. For two years of archived material, see the PACS-L Usenet site at *news:bit.listserv.pacs*-1.

purl.archive by Thread
http://www.oclc.org:5046/archive/purl
> OCLC Purl Resolver software is discussed here.

SERIALST Scope and Purpose (Including Fileserver Information and Selected Command Options)
http://www.uvm.edu/~bmaclenn/serialst.html
> Moderated Listserv established in 1990 to discuss most aspects of serials processing in libraries. Currently, there are more than 2,530 subscribers in 35 countries. The Fileserver contains the CONSER Core Record Guidelines for Printed Serials and the Format Integration Guide for Printed Serials by Crystal Graham, among others. To search the archives, go to *http://list.uvm.edu/archives/senslst.html*

TINLIB Cataloguing and Authority Control Electronic Discussion Group Archives
http://dec59.ruk.cuni.cz/~brt/tinkat/tinkat.html/

USMARC Forum
gopher://marvel.loc.gov/00/.listarch/usmarc/usmarc.inf
> Archives available from December 1994 to the present. Maintained by the Library of Congress Network Development and MARC Standards Office.

WebCat-L
http://library.wustl.edu/~listmgr/webcat-l
> This list discusses "webcats" or "webpacs" such as the Ameritech Library Services WebPAC at *http://webpac.als.ameritech.com* or SIRSI's WebCat at *http://www.sirsi.com/webcattoc.html*. Also check out the Innopac WebServer Software at *http://www.iii.com/screens/opacintro.html*

Web4Lib
http://sunsite.Berkeley.EDU/Web4Lib
> Described as "An electronic discussion for library-based World Wide Web managers," this list is of special interest to catalogers as well. Archives are searchable by date, author, or subject from April 1995 to the present.

PART III

WEB PAGES OF
SPECIAL INTEREST FOR ALL
TECHNICAL SERVICES
LIBRARIANS

OVERVIEW

Here everything comes together—just like it does in your own library. From small departmental home pages to big associations, there's a vast amount of information out there that will appeal to all technical services people.

3.1

Technical Services Departmental Home Pages

Now that you're thoroughly familiar with acquisitions and cataloging home pages, I would like to introduce what I consider to be the best of both worlds—the technical services home page. Combining links for acquisitions, cataloging, and preservation makes the most sense for small and medium-sized libraries, especially those without great amounts of documentation. The options of what to put into a technical services home page are extensive. For example, the acquisitions section might contain links to lists of new materials, or link to a materials request form, as well as contain favorite links to other acquisitions sites. Whether to annotate the links or not is up to you. Some libraries find it more convenient to list the links as simply as possible. Other libraries find that adding special notes to particular links adds to their usefulness.

The cataloging section may not differentiate between monographs and serials, for example, but it might contain annual reports, local memos, and documents, and those inevitable favorite links. The emphasis might be public services oriented (listing only what might be of interest to the library patron), technically oriented (discussing OPAC news, fixes, computer documentation, etc.), or geared specifically to the needs of the Technical Services department staff. Many sites utilize this page to link to local newsletters, gift and exchange information, bindery instructions, and conservation and preservation details. Whatever particular needs your library has, I'm certain that the sites chosen here will be both interesting and useful.

About Technical Services in the Oakland Public Library
Oakland, California
http://acorn.ci.oakland.ca.us/Oakweb/library/about/techserv.htm

Acquisitions and Cataloging, Jessie Ball DuPont Library
University of the South, Nashville, Tennessee
http://smith2.sewanee.edu/moneill/libdptacqcat.html

Acquisitions, Cataloging, and Periodicals
Luther Seminary Library, St. Paul, Minnesota
http://www.luthersem.edu/library/homeacqu.htm
> Contains extensive bimonthly acquisitions lists, and links to bookstores, publishers, and presses.

Bibliographic Services
Old Dominion University Library, Norfolk, Virginia
http://www.lib.odu.edu/bibserv/index.html
> Contains ordering information, publisher's addresses, gifts policy, serials and cataloging issues.

Blackwell North America Technical Services for Public Libraries
http://www.blackwell.com/services/techserv/publib.htm
> The Pseudonym Plus File offers a "file of pseudonym authority records which can optionally override the LC authority control processing."

Bob Warwick's Technical and Automated Services Home Page
Rutgers University, New Brunswick, New Jersey
http://warwick.rutgers.edu/homepage.htm
> Many technical and cataloging-related documents here. Locally written reviews of Cataloging Service Bulletins can be found, as well as profiles, RLIN information, a subject Cutter Number list compiled to supplement the LC Classification schedules, and more. The Adaptive Cataloging Section Memos List includes memos on cataloging Acta Horticultura and barcoding books.

Bodleian Library Report for the Years 1985–1993 : Department of Oriental Books and Manuscripts
Oxford University, Oxford, England
http://www.rsl.ox.ac.uk/mh/rpt/rpt93orb.html
> Very interesting report on acquisitions, cataloging, and manuscript cataloging over an eight year period. The department of Printed Books, Acquisitions, and Collection Development Report is also quite interesting.

Cabrillo College Library Technical Services Department
Santa Cruz, California
http://libwww.cabrillo.cc.ca.us/html/techserv/tshomepage.html
   Mission statements and links to special cataloging policies and procedures (for example, Cabrillo College faculty authors are listed in a 710 21
   field in their local catalog records). The background colors of these pages
   are truly incredible.

Cataloging, Acquisitions, and Publishing Resources on the Web
Ruben Salazar Library, Sonoma State University, Rohnert Park, California
http://libweb.sonoma.edu/resources/cataloging.html
   Wonderfully organized selection of quality links.

Cataloging and Order Department
Library Affairs, Southern Illinois University at Carbondale
http://www.lib.siu.edu/swen/index.html
   Choose from Catalog or Order memos, Resources, or Statistics.

Cataloging Manual (University of South Carolina Libraries)
http://www.sc.edu/library/catalog.catman.html
   Although listed as a cataloging manual, this page links to various acquisitions sites, such as information on Flags, and Minimal-Level NOTIS
   records. Cataloging sections cover Modifying LC Authority Records,
   Monographic Copy Cataloging Workflow, and much more.

CCS Technical Services Page
Cooperative Computer Services, Chicago, Illinois
http://ccs.nslsilus.org/tech.html
   Useful links to LC MARVEL, Technical Services Home Pages, and other
   sites.

Colby College Libraries Technical Services Department
Waterville, Maine
http://www.colby.edu/librarybase/tech.serv/tsd.html
   This home page has a different format. It contains a block of searchable
   Favorite Web Search Tools and links to a Technical Services Staff Schedule and a variety of interesting Department Working Papers. See
   Cheatsheets on Ordering Workflow for a great example. The Cataloging
   "Mega" Chart describes specific MARC fields, bibliographic material type,
   item record, policy notes for "paper, film and magnetic media, and sound
   and video recordings." The Job Descriptions are phenomenal and probably quite useful for other library technical services departments. Finally,
   check out the APSOP Work Team Home Page (acquisitiions/periodicals/
   standing orders/preservation).

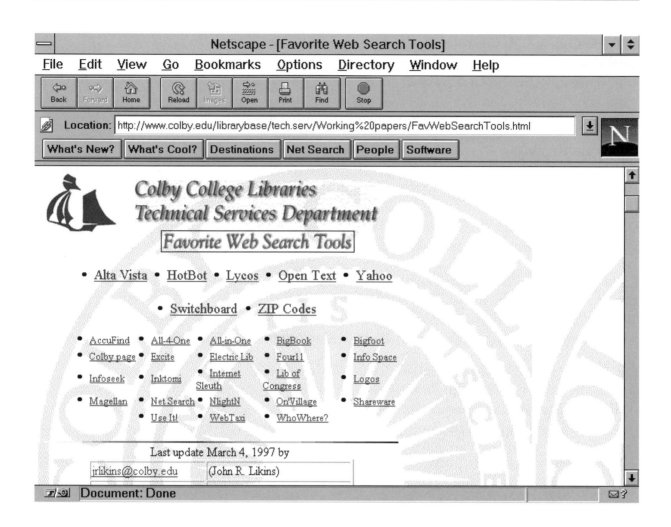

Figure 3.1
Favorite Web Search Tools

Cornell University Library Central Technical Services Procedures Page

Ithaca, New York

http://cts.library.cornell.edu/ctsproc.htm

Many of these procedures involve cataloging, but procedures are also available for Recording Technical Services Statistics, and a guide to Computer Disk Processing. Also see the Technical Services Manual at *http://www.library.cornell.edu/tsmanual*.

CQU Library Technical Services

Central Queensland University Library, Australia

http://ruby.cqu.edu.au/techserv/tserv02.htm

Describes the functions of the Technical Services department and provides forms to make an order recommendation or to reserve a newly received item.

CWRU University Library Technical Services Division

Case Western Reserve, Cleveland, Ohio

http://www.cwru.edu/CWRU/UL/ts.html

Although the dark grey background makes this page a tad somber, it does provide links to cataloging, information a2cquisitions, preservation, and administration.

Dokumenten lieferung: Akquisition, Katalogisie rung

http://www.unisg.ch/~biblio/internet/Dokulief.html

ELEC-TECH: ELECtronic Documentation of Central TECHnical Services

University of New York at Buffalo

http://wings.buffalo.edu/libraries/units/cts

Click on a file cabinet drawer to enter the realm of acquisitions, cataloging, government documents, policies, and procedures, etc. There is an excellent page on library mail and delivery service, as well as a preservation program page. This site is particularly attractive for a variety of reasons; first, their print typeface is large and very clear; second, clicking on an item provides succinct, numbered procedures.

Fort Collins Public Library Online Cataloging/Acquisitions Resources

Colorado

http://www.ci.fort-collins.co.us/C_LIBRARY/tech6.htm

Gail Borden Public Library Technical Services Department

Elgin, Illinois

http://nsn.nslsilus.org/elghome/GailB/nsntsser.html

Activities listed are primarily computer-oriented, i.e., "The Technical Services Department is responsible for the computer records which indicate what is in the library and where it is located."

GCI Library Support Services/Library Technical Services
http://www.garcia.com/otherpag/i1–libra.htm
> Who provides serials support, cataloging, and centralized acquisitions services to the Pentagon, NASA headquarters, the Patent and Trademark Patents Law Library, and the EPA? Garcia Consulting Inc, of McLean, Virginia, that's who.

Georgia College and State University Library Information Acquisition and Organization
http://Peacock.GAC.Peachnet.EDU/~techserv
> It's not large, but I wanted to include an example of a very small, attractive technical services home page. This page links to Information Acquisitions, Thesis Binding, and a listing of technical services staff.

Ithaca College Library Technical Services
Ithaca, New York
http://www.ithaca.edu/library/htmls/techserv.html

James White Library Technical Services Department
Andrews University, Berrian Springs, Michigan
http://www.andrews.edu/library/collections/departments/tech.html
> Mission, location, hours and staff of the acquisitions, cataloging, and periodicals units.

Kommission fur Erwerbung
Universitatsbibliothek Augsburg, Germany
http://www.bibliothek.uni-augsburg.de

Library Collections and Acquisition and Processing
National Assembly Library, Korea
http://www.nanet.go.kr/nal/1/libe1–45.htm

Library Technical Service Homepages Provided by Commercial, Academic, and Special Institutions
Memorial University Library, Newfoundland, Canada
http://www.mun.ca/library/cat/techwebs.htm

Library Technical Services Resources
http://www.vnet.net/users/fingram/fi-libts.html
> Good selection of documentation—rich sites compiled by Floyd Ingram, Alabama State University, Montgomery, Alabama.

Library Technicians Technical Services Links
Australian Library and Information Association,
Library Technician's Section
http://www.ntu.edu.au/library/techserv.html
> Links to commercial sites (publishers, vendors) and other library's technical services departments.

Lillian Goldman Library at Yale Law School Technical Services Homepage
New Haven, Connecticut
http://elsinore.cis.yale.edu/lawweb/tech.htm
> Many links to top quality sites.

Linfield College Libraries Technical Services
McMinnville and Portland, Oregon
http://www.linfield.edu/library/techsrv.html
> Sections on book ordering, thesis binding, and gifts.

Listing of Internet Resources for Technical Services
http://www.msoe.edu/library/ts_list.html
> One of the first technical services lists, compiled by Debbie Cardinal, Virginia Scheschy, and Mary Rieder.

LSU Libraries Technical and Financial Services Technical Services Manual
Louisiana State University, Baton Rouge, Louisiana
http://indigo.lib.lsu.edu/tecsrv/techman/techman.html
> Links to a local manual with documentation, vendors, acquisitions and cataloging links, NOTIS, and software documentation.

Malcolm A. Love Library Technical Services Division
San Diego State University, California
http://libweb.sdsu.edu/tech/tshome1.html
> List of personnel in acquisitions and cataloging.

Mansfield University Library and Information Science Page
Mansfield, Pennsylvania
http://www.clark.net/pub/lschank/web/library.html
> The library's Organizations site is extensive and gives major attention to sites like the ALA Gopher. The Books, Catalogs, and OPACs section combines access to publishers, vendors, and online catalogs in a pleasing, but somewhat confusing mixture. The annotations provided for each link are useful. Larry Schankman, the creator of this page, is one of the forerunners of librarians involved with establishing lists of subject-oriented resources on the Web. The Web outgrew Larry's ambitions, of course, but

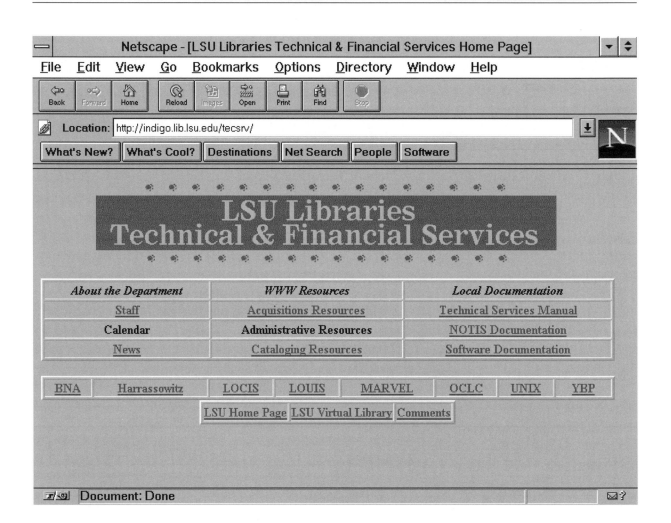

Figure 3.2
LSU Libraries Technical and Financial Services

take a look at the Mansfield Cybrarian Page at *http://www.mnsfld.edu/ depts/lib* and browse through the Virtual Subject Library to see the results of Larry's efforts.

MIT Libraries Collection Services
Massachusetts Institute of Technology, Cambridge, Massachusetts
http://macfadden.mit.edu:9500/colserv

MIT's page is divided into People, Folklore, Procedures and Workflow, and Organization. The People section personalizes a large division, with names, e-mail addresses, job responsibilities, and personal home pages listed. Folklore contains the Collection Services Division Archive. This is a wonderful way to collect those memos, e-mailed decisions, etc. Searchable by subject, author, date of e-mail sent, or by thread, this archive contains messages such as Subscription Review Date for Serial Orders, Music Shelflist Cards, and Format Changes and Advance Procedures. The Procedures and Workflow Section contains links to monographic and serials acquisitions, MIT's famous Cataloging Oasis, the Advance Training Web (explaining their Advance Training Database System), a Book Search Request form, and the ACME Bindery list (what's out, when it's expected back). This site is developmental and well worth a visit.

Murphy Library Projects
University of Wisconsin, La Crosse
http://www.uwlax.edu/MurphyLibrary/projects.html

Music Library Technical Services Division: Manuals, Documentation, Reference Sources, Etc.
Indiana University, Bloomington, Indiana
http://www.music.indiana.edu/tech_s/manuals.ts.htm

A multitude of cataloging and processing text files can be found here. Check out the list of the 1996 NACO Music Project Participants and a host of other worthwhile links.

National Agricultural Library Technical Services Division
Beltsville, Maryland
http://www.nalusda.gov:80/tsd

Explore the Acquisitions and Serials Branch, the Cataloging Branch, and the Indexing Branch. The Indexing Branch selects, indexes, and inputs approximately 70,000 MARC-based records annually into ISIS, NAL's integrated library system. "Indexers are responsible for subject analysis and library technicians are responsible for descriptive indexing and data entry (both manual and optical scanning)."

Network-Accessible Resources and the Redefinition of Technical Services
http://dspace.dial.pipex.com/jose/neilthesis.html. By Neil Jones, Liverpool John Moores University, England.

NMSU Library Technical Services Department
New Mexico State University Library, Las Cruces, New Mexico
http://lib.nmsu.edu/aboutlib/detinfo/depts/techsvs.html
> It's always nice to see some statistics from technical services departments, and this one is very well done. Of special interest is the Technical Services Department Fact Sheet and ZIA Documents—State of New Mexico Documents.

Northern Illinois University Libraries Collections and Technical Services
http://www.niu.edu/depts/library/cats.html

Northwestern University Library Technical Services Departments
Evanston, Illinois
http://www.library.nwu.edu/tech
> Links to a rather simplified Cataloging page and a Serials and Acquisitions Services (SAS) page. The Collection Management Division page links to the Music Library page, the Preservation Department, Approval Plans, and Selectors' Names.

Penn Library Information Processing Center
University of Pennsylvania, Philadelphia, Pennsylvania
http://www.library.upenn.edu/ipc/ipct.html
> Discusses East Asia Technical Processing, Middle East Technical Processing, Policies and Procedures, Cataloging for Special Collections, Post Cataloging Monographs and Serials Acquisitions.

Penrose Library: Library and Information Science Resources Web Sites
University of Denver, Denver, Colorado
http://www.du.edu/~penrosel/subject/libsci.html
> Interesting selection of links to acquisitions and collection development, cataloging, serials and archival tools, and more.

Peru State College Library Technical Services
Peru, Nebraska
http://www.peru.edu/departments/libtech.html
> Includes the Peru State College Cataloging Policy, Processing Procedures, and a Student Assistants Manual, in addition to links to vendors, LC, serials sites, and more.

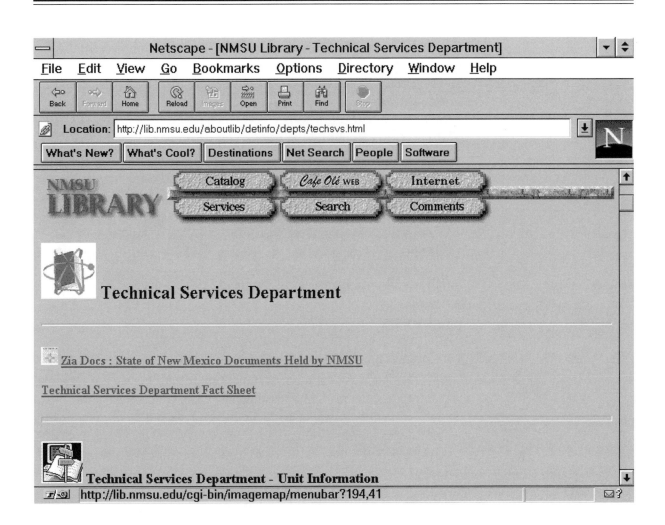

Figure 3.3
NMSU Library Technical Services Department

Princeton University Library Technical Services Department
Princeton, New Jersey
http://infoshare1.princeton.edu/tech/hptsd.html
 There's so much information available here that it doesn't fit on the page. Links to organizational and departmental information, and to *News and Notes*, an informative weekly technical services documentation news journal. No. 7 (May 15, 1996) thoroughly discusses subject heading contributions procedures. Archives are available for the previous two issues. Beside the catalog section, find out about the circulation division, database management (they even have a SWAT team), Near East Technical Services (NETS) (Arabic, Persian, Hebrew, Turkish, and Ottoman NACO cataloging and classification procedures), and the order division (links to the periodicals receipt unit, approvals and continuations unit, invoice unit, and the monographic receipts and holds unit).

QTECHWeb
Queen's University Libraries, Kingston, Ontario, Canada
http://stauffer.queensu.ca/techserv/qtechweb.html
 This premier technical services site offers a carefully selected yet extensive listing of acquisitions and cataloging links. Highlights include one of the best sections available on Technical Services and Related Discussion Lists and to Library Utilities and System Vendors. One very nice feature of this site is the use of the "new" icon to point out recently added features.

RCLS (Ramapo Catskill Library System) LibraryLand Technical Services
http://www.rcls.org/libland/lltech.htm

Resource Sites for University of Calgary Technical Services
Calgary, Alberta, Canada
http://www.ucalgary.ca/~mhemming/index.html
 Here's a very informative site with a sense of humor—see Cataloging Funny Formats if you don't believe me. Many cataloging, acquisitions, and general reference sites are listed here, along with a "cool tools" section and some library humor thrown in for good measure.

Resources for Librarians and other Information Specialists
http://www.unbsj.ca/library/libriries1.htm#tech
 UNB Saint John Ward Chipman Library, New Brunswick, Canada

Resources for Researchers and Professional Librarians
University of Hong Kong Libraries
http://www.hku.hk/lib/Internet/intlibr.html
 Annotated set of links.

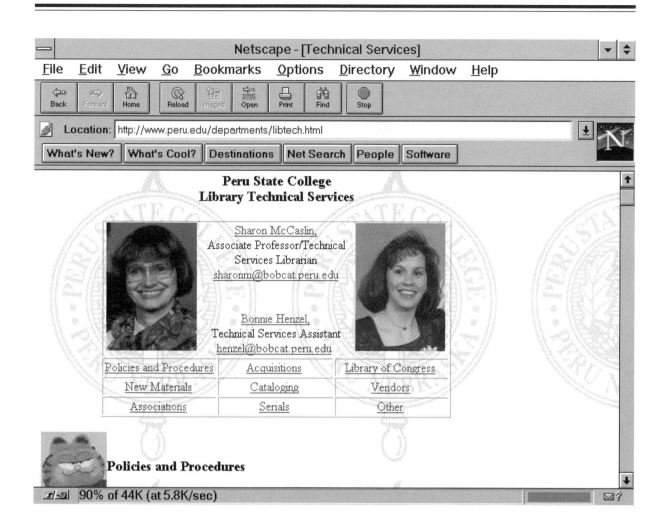

Figure 3.4
Peru State College Library Technical Services

**Sabinet Compiler: the Electronic Solution for Libraries'
Cataloguing and Acquisition Needs**
http://www.sabinet.co.za/prod10.htm
   "Largest and most established supplier of online bibliographic information in southern Africa."

SBU University Library Services
Southwest Baptist University Library, Bolivar, Missouri
http://www.sbuniv.edu/library/libserv.html

Southern Oregon University Library Technical Services Resources
Ashland, Oregon
http://www.sosc.osshe.edu/library/techserv.htm
   Cataloging, acquisitions, serials, and collection development resources
   linked here, as well as some interesting help sheets. Take a look at Frequently Used MARC Tags, MARC Tags Divided by Hundreds, and Par-
   allelism in MARC Tags for Entry Headings.

Spencer E. Eccles Health Sciences Library Technical Services
University of Utah, Salt Lake City, Utah
http://www-medlib.med.utah.edu/waxtab/TECHSVC.HTM
   Lists faculty, staff, and services of the department.

**Stanford University Libraries Request for Information Vendor
Services for Technical Services Redesign**
http://www-sul.stanford.edu/depts/diroff/ts/redesign/rfi.html
   This site is absolutely essential reading for anyone involved with revamp-
   ing or reconfiguring their technical services departments.

Swarthmore College Library Technical Services Resources
Swarthmore, Pennsylvania
http://www.swarthmore.edu/Library/About/tsres.html
   Acquisitions and cataloging teamed up to provide a nice list of relevant
   links. The cataloging section has some local documents, like Cataloging
   United Nations Documents, Working with BNA Lists, and Local Call
   Numbers for Literary Authors. This locally assigned call number list is
   checked periodically to see if LC has assigned a number, and if so, the
   local number is then changed to conform with the Library of Congress.

Tarlton Law Library Technical Services Home Page
University of Texas at Austin School of Law
http://www.law.utexas.edu/tech/tech.htm
   They offer contents pages from law reviews and scholarly journals received in the last week.

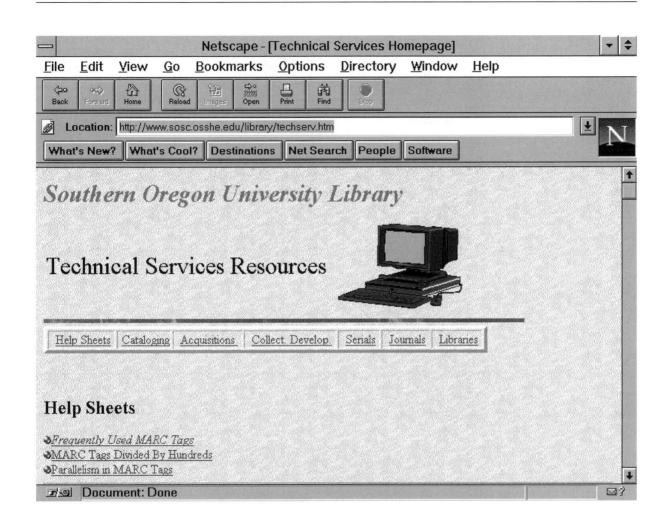

Figure 3.5
Southern Oregon University Library Technical Services Resources

Technical Processing Online Tools (TPOT)
University of California at San Diego
http://tpot.ucsd.edu
> Choose the frames version of TPOT if your browser permits. Although much of TPOT's documents have not been converted from their previous gopher format, the bulleted links and interfaces are state of the art. Links are provided to acquisitions, cataloging, Innopac, special collections, OCLC, the Library of Congress, Melvyl, and the Internet. The What's New? and For Your Information pages are very comprehensive, and include dates added, particular sections, and all other appropriate information. Also recommended is the TPOT Technical Services Advisory Committee page (*http://tpot.ucsd.edu/tsac/charge.html*).

Technical Services @ Bowdoin College Library
Maine
http://www.bowdoin.edu/dept/library/staff/ts
> Extensive page, with the promise of many good links to come.

Technical Services, Albertsons Library
Boise State University, Boise, Idaho
http://library.idbsu.edu/users/gostrand/tshp.htm
> Nicely structured page which provides the purpose, staff, and lists of funds, liaisons, and representatives for the acquisitions, cataloging, serials, and collection development staff.

Technical Services (Brodart)
http://www.brodart.com/books/b_tech.html
> Choose from primary Technical Services, which allows Brodart to "complete the tedious details of cataloging and processing" or Contract Technical Services, which offers the "Compleat Bookserv," circulation-ready material-in-hand customized cataloging and materials processing. Currently staffed by 65 catalogers who process over 500,000 items annually.

Technical Services
Cleveland-Marshall College of Law, Cleveland State University, Ohio
http://www.law.csuohio.edu/lawlibrary/info_services/tech_serv.html

Technical Services
Monash University Library, Clayton, Victoria, Australia
http://www.lib.monash.edu.au/library/1994.html#tec

Technical Services
Nova Scotia Provincial Library, Canada
http://rs6000.nshpl.library.ns.ca/services/techserv

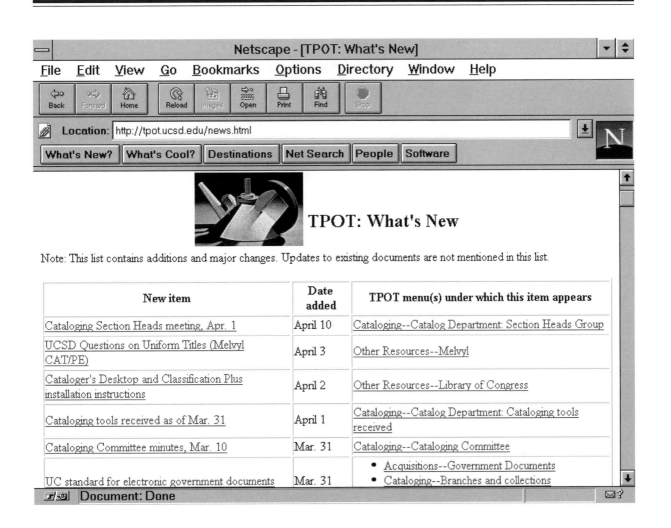

New item	Date added	TPOT menu(s) under which this item appears
Cataloging Section Heads meeting, Apr. 1	April 10	Cataloging--Catalog Department: Section Heads Group
UCSD Questions on Uniform Titles (Melvyl CAT/PE)	April 3	Other Resources--Melvyl
Cataloger's Desktop and Classification Plus installation instructions	April 2	Other Resources--Library of Congress
Cataloging tools received as of Mar. 31	April 1	Cataloging--Catalog Department: Cataloging tools received
Cataloging Committee minutes, Mar. 10	Mar. 31	Cataloging--Cataloging Committee
UC standard for electronic government documents	Mar. 31	• Acquisitions--Government Documents • Cataloging--Branches and collections

Figure 3.6
Technical Processing Online Tools (TPOT) What's New? Page

Technical Services
University of South Australia Library
http://136.169.62.185/library/techser/techser.htm

Technical Services Branch
State Library of North Carolina
http://hal.dcr.state.nc.us/tss/tsshome.htm
    Simple and effective links.

Technical Services Department
Dewitt Wallace Library, Macalester College, St. Paul, Minnesota
http://www.macalester.edu/~library/about/techser.html
    A witty, informal page discussing who does what and what services are
    available from technical services.

Technical Services Department
Leonard H. Axe Library, Pittsburg State University, Pittsburg, Kansas
http://library.pittstate.edu/techsrv

Technical Services Department
Levi Watkins Learning Resource Center, Alabama State University
http://asu.alasu.edu/library/manual.txt
    Gopher-based manual.

Technical Services Division
Elizabeth Huth Coates Library, Trinity University, San Antonio, Texas
http://www.trinity.edu/departments/maddux_library/tsintro.html
    Exceptional annual report and vision statement.

Technical Services Division
Hamilton College, New York
http://nemo.hamilton.edu/html/library/TECHSERV.HTM
Excellent collection of dictionaries and thesauri.

Technical Services Division of the George A. Smathers Libraries
University of Florida, Gainesville
http://www.uflib.ufl.edu/ts/tsp.html
    Links to a very colorful Preservation Department page. Check out the
    Newspaper Microfilming Queue or the Security and Disaster Plans page.
    Some tantalizing resource services links may be found here, including
    the Handbook for Easy-Scanner and Decoder Web Page, as well as a
    fabulous Gifts and Exchange page and very creditable Cataloging and
    Serials Manuals.

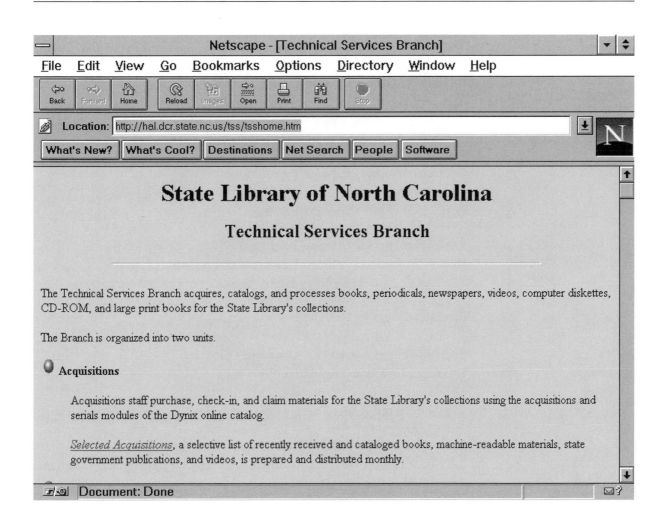

Figure 3.7
Technical Services Branch (State Library of North Carolina)

Technical Services Help Page
University of Texas at Austin, Graduate School of Library and Information Science
http://volvo.gslis.utexas.edu/~catalog/tshp.html
   "Customized bookmark for researchers, professionals, and students interested in cataloging and related topics."

Technical Services Home Page
University of Nevada, Reno
http://www.library.unr.edu/~catalog

Technical Services Home Page
William F. Ekstrom Library, University of Louisville, Kentucky
http://www.louisville.edu/groups/library-www/techserv/index.html
   Links to OCLC/Solinet Documentation, LC Resources, and a Serials Department page.

Technical Services in the Lawrence Library
Lawrence University, Appleton, Wisconsin
http://cwis.lawrence.edu/www/lib/techserv.html
   Still-developing set of links with good potential.

Technical Services Missions and Functions
John Vaughan Library, Northeastern State University, Tahlequah, Oklahoma
http://www.nsuok.edu/jvl/jvl/jvlts.html
   This mission statement links to various library teams—the coordination team, acquisitions, data initiation, and quality control. See their extensive Collection Development page.

Technical Services Steering Committee Minutes
University of Florida Libraries
http://www.uflib.ufl.edu/ts/min507.html

Technical Services U.W.S. Hawkesbury Library
University of Westtern Sydney, Australia
http://sybil.hawkesbury.uws.edu.au/techserv.htm
   Discusses order requests and subject liaison librarians.

Texas Women's University Library Technical Services Department
http://twu.edu/www/twu/library/teks.html

Thomas Cooper Library Technical Services Home Page
University of South Carolina, Columbia, South Carolina
http://www.sc.edu/library/catalog/catalog.html
   Links to acquisitions, bindery and preparations unit, cataloging, and col-

lection management. A cataloging manual with authorities and workflow documents is available.

TSLAC (Technical Services Directory of the Texas State Library) Technical Services
http://www.tsl.state.tx.us/TECHNICAL/tech_homepage.html

UNE Technical Services Department
University of New England, Armidale, NSW, Australia
http://www.une.edu.au/~library/techserv.htm
Simple, yet elegant—this might be all some libraries need.

University at Albany Libraries Technical Services Division
State University of New York, Albany, New York
http://www.albany.edu/library/oldlib/services/technical.html
Discusses the libraries' online information system, ADVANCE.

University of California, Berkeley, Library Web Technical Services Organization Chart
http://www.lib.berkeley.edu/AboutLibrary/Staff/techorg.html
This is a very large site, so starting with the Organization Chart makes sense. Meeting minutes and a staff directory are available for the Branch Technical Services Discussion Group (*http://library.berkeley.edu/AboutLibrary/Staff/BTECH*). Biweekly copies of the *CU News* contains technical services information. "Tech Services Notes," an electronic attachment to *CU News*, contains much data—documents like Periodical Binding, the Beginning of PromptCat Services of Yankee Book Peddler, and the Academic Book Center for Berkeley, and links to the Serials Manual Home Page and the Branch Processing Manual Page.

University of Chicago Library Technical Services Division
Chicago, Illinois
http://www.lib.uchicago.edu/LibInfo/Directory/techservices.html
Basically a staff directory of the acquisitions, cataloging, and serials departments.

University of Connecticut Libraries Technical Services Links to Internet Resources for Use by Staff
http://www.ucc.uconn.edu/~hbladm11/tssd.html
Large collection of links, especially for preservation and imaging sites.

University of Houston—Downtown Technical Services
W.I. Dykes Library, Houston, Texas
http://www.dt.uh.edu/library/tech.htm

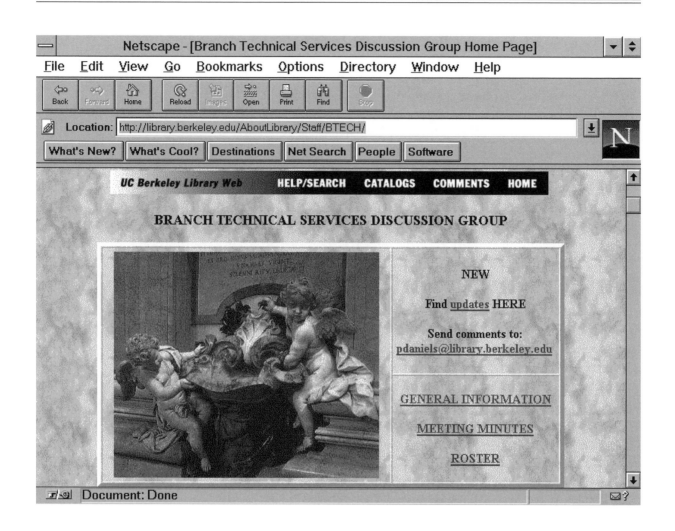

Figure 3.8
Branch Technical Services Discussion Group (University of California, Berkeley)

University of Maryland at College Park Libraries Technical Services Division
http://www.lib.umd.edu/UMCP/TSD/tsd.html
> TSD News provides interesting vignettes about technical services activities. Check out the Potomac Technical Processing Librarians Meeting Report. A good selection of statistics is provided, including Accomplishments and Highlights of Fiscal Year 95 and Goals for FY 96 as well as Disaster Plan Salvage Procedures for UMCP Libraries.

University of Minnesota Libraries Technical Services Units
Twin Cities Campus, Minneapolis, Minnesota
http://www.lib.umn.edu/ts
> A very interesting document found here is the Materials Acquisitions and Control (MAC) Functions List, which discusses vendor relations; gifts, exchanges, and depository programs; bibliographic organization; control bindery operations; and strategic planning.

University of Oregon Library Technical Services Division
Eugene, Oregon
http://libweb.uoregon.edu/techsrvc/techserv.html
> This page includes a mission statement, as well as links to acquisitions, cataloging, ILL, and preservation and binding. The Preservation page is wonderfully laid out, and even contains a song—Before All the Books Disappear—sung to the tune of Swing Low, Sweet Chariot.

University of San Francisco Law Library, Technical Services Department
http://www.usfca.edu/law_library/ts/tshome.html
> Like its counterpart cataloging page, a truly exceptional site. See Aiding and Abetting the Acquisitions Process.

University of South Australia Library Technical Services
http://136.169.62.185/library/techser/techser.htm
> Mission statement, goals, and links.

University of Toledo Libraries Technical Services Assistance Tools
Toledo, Ohio
http://www.cl.utoledo.edu/userhomes/ahogan/tspage.html
> A substantial collection of links.

University of Wisconsin—La Crosse
http://www.uwlax.edu/MurphyLibrary/ar945pt3.html#acq
> Annual reports of the Acquisitions/Collection Development Department.

University of Wyoming Libraries Technical Services
Laramie, Wyoming
http://www.uwyo.edu/lib/techserv.htm

UTA Libraries Acquisitions and Cataloging Services
University of Texas at Arlington Library
http://library.uta.edu/staff/~acs/welcome.htm
    Includes policies, procedures, and government documents.

Van Pelt Library Middle East Technical Services Home Page
University of Pennsylvania, Philadelphia, Pennsylvania
http://pobox.upenn.edu/~rld
    Offers archived lists of new Arabic and Persian books added to their da-
    tabase, HTML Primers, and links to other Middle Eastern sites.

Vancouver Public Library Central Branch Technical Services
http://www.vpl.vancouver.bc.ca/branches/LibrarySquare/misc/techserv.html
    One of the best public library pages I've seen. Large acquisitions, cata-
    logue, serials, and continuations sections. Everything is clearly set out.

Vassar College Library Departments
Poughkeepsie, New York
http://iberia.vassar.edu/ucl/acquisitions.html

Vermont Department of Libraries Technical Services Home Page
http://dol.state.vt.us/WWW_ROOT/000000/HTML/LLHOME.HTML
    Learn about the Vermont Centralized Card/MARC Service, Vermont
    Library Guidelines for MARC Record Input Level K, and Cataloging for
    Original Input of Monographic Records.

Wayne State University Library Technical Services Home Page
Detroit, Michigan
http://gopher.libraries.wayne.edu/techserv
    Browse acquisitions, cataloging, database management and authority con-
    trol, and binding and preservation.

William G. Squires Library Technical Processes Department
Pentecostal Resource Center and Lee College, Cleveland, Tennessee
http://www.leecollege.edu/library/technical.html
    Meet the department staff, check In-house Binding Information, or
    browse through a booklist of monthly acquisitions.

**WINSLO—World Wide Web Information Network State Library
of Ohio Technical Services**
http://winslo.ohio.gov

World Wide Web for Technical Services Workshop (University of Wisconsin)

http://milky.wils.wisc.edu/events/wwwtech/wwwtech.html

> This fabulous site has organized technical services components into a logical course offering, and taught a six–week course on the subject. The demo sites are the best; the outline is intriguing, the concept scintillating. Highly recommended.

Yale Medical Library Technical Services FAQ

Harvey Cushing/John Hay Whitney Medical Library

http://info.med.yale.edu/library/techservices/faq.html

> This FAQ explains the meaning of "in process" and "on order", and discusses binding and location of journal issues.

Yankee Book Peddler Bibliographic, Cataloging, and Processing Services Prospectus

http://www.ybp.com/tsprospectus.htm

It's very important to keep up with new developments concerning this state-of-the-art outsourcer.

3.2

Associations, Discussion Lists, E-Journals, and Newsletters

A necessarily selective sampling of the best of the broad interest sites, lists, and electronic periodicals.

ALCTS (Association for Library Collections and Techncial Services) Network News
http://www.coalliance.org/unitrec/ej000268.html
   Subscription information available.

American Association of Law Librarians Technical Services Special Interest Section
http://www.aallnet.org/sis/tssis/tssis.htm
   Excellent selection of technical services legal links.

Investigacion Bibliotecológica
http://cuib.laborales.unam.mx/publicaciones/revista/ca_rev.html
   Index and extensive abstracts of this journal published by the Centro Universitario de Investigaciones Bibliotecologicas (Universidad Nacional Autonoma de Mexico). Contains many technical services-related articles.

LITA Newsletter
Library and Information Technology Association
http://www.harvard.edu/litanews
   Quarterly ALA division publication. Demo WWW version of the *Newsletter* is available from Spring 1995 v. 16, no.2, to the present.

Medical Library Association Technical Services Section
http://www-mlatss.stanford.edu
   Don't miss the Future of Technical Services section.

Nebraska Library Association Technical Services Round Table
http://www.peru.edu/~nlatsrt
   Read back issues of *Technically Speaking*, a technical services newsletter for Nebraska libraries, or link to board meeting minutes or other technical services-related conference information.

OCLC Collections and Technical Services News Releases
http://www.oclc.org/oclc/press/cattoc.htm

PACS-L
http://info.lib.uk.edu/pacs/html

Technical Trends
http://www-mlatss.Stanford.edu/TT
   Medical Library Association, Technical Servcices Section.

Web4Lib Electronic Discussion List
http://sunsite.berkeley.edu/Web4lib

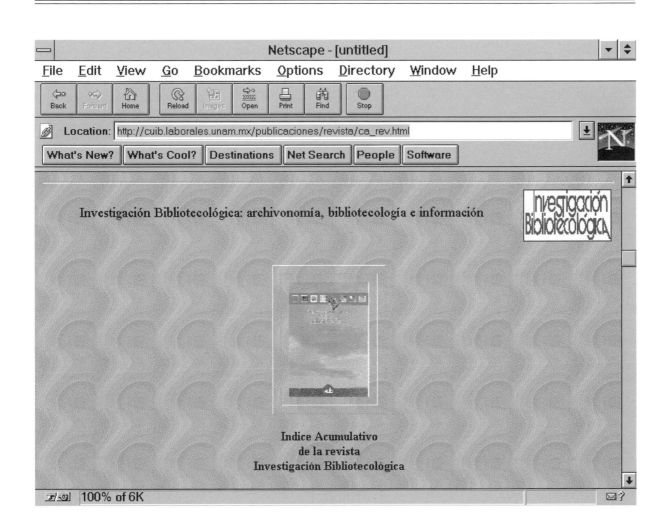

Figure 3.9
Investigacion Bibliotecologica

INDEX

About the Author

Barbara Stewart is a Latin American Cataloger, currently employed at the University of Massachusetts, Amherst. Barbara has been a librarian for 17 years, and has worked in all types of libraries: from being a director of a one-room small public library, to Head of Reference at a multi-type library (junior college, graduate school, and public library) on the Texas-Mexico Border, to supervisor of the automotive and welding libraries at Houston Community college. (And yes, those books did get greasy!) She also worked as Serials Librarian at a two year vocational-technical school in Texas.

Her entry into Technical Services came about 10 years ago, with the position of Head of Technical Processes at Cambria County Library in Johnstown, Pennsylvania. There she began to discover the intricacies both of computers and of acquisitions, cataloging, book-binding and repair, etc. Her next jump was to the University of Pittsburgh, becoming a Latin American Cataloger because of her language skills (fluency in both Spanish and Portuguese). There she managed to upgrade her skills, and became acquainted with the Internet and the World Wide Web.

In her current position at UMass, Barbara has been able to create an extremely popular home page, entitled the "Top 200 Technical Services Benefits of Library Home Page Development"—http://tpot.uscd.edu/Cataloging/Misc/top200.html. This home page proved so popular that Barbara has now given 15 presentations, including ones at SLA in Montreal, ALA in New York City, and also in Bethesda, Maryland, Ithaca, New York, San Jose and Santa Clara, California, as well as many local presentations. She has had an article published in the DES IDOC *Bulletin of Information Technology*, (v. 16, no, 3, May 1996 entitled "Internet Advantages for the Technical Services Librarians"), and will soon appear in the SALALM papers for 1996 with a paper entitled "Latin American Web Pages of Interest for the Technical Services Librarian." She is a strong advocate of technical services librarians, and has a great interest in utilizing the new technologies provided by the World Wide Web.

4284